T0247788

FROM BARBYCU TO BARBECUE

FROM BARBYCU TO BARBECUE

The Untold History of an American Tradition

Joseph R. Haynes

THE UNIVERSITY OF SOUTH CAROLINA PRESS

Published by the University of South Carolina Press
Columbia, South Carolina 29208

uscpress.com

Manufactured in the United States of America

32 31 30 29 28 27 26 25 24 23
10 9 8 7 6 5 4 3 2 1

Library of Congress Cataloging-in-Publication Data can be found at
http://catalog.loc.gov/.

ISBN: 978-1-64336-391-2 (hardcover)
ISBN: 978-1-64336-392-9 (ebook)

Some sources quoted herein include racial language and slurs that were in common use during the times in which they were written. Today, we understand such language and slurs to be tools of dehumanization and oppression, and we do not condone them in our publications.

Knife and Fork image credit: Lnhi/The Noun Project

CONTENTS

INTRODUCTION *7*

ONE **HERNANDO'S BARBACOA**
Spanish Explorers and Outdoor Cooking in Latin America *25*

TWO **HERBERT'S PATTA**
The Birth of Jamaican Jerk *49*

THREE **JEAN-BAPTISTE'S BOUCAN**
A Seventeen-Century "Buccaneer" Picnic *70*

FOUR **BEAUCHAMP'S BARBECADO**
Native American Food Preservation *94*

FIVE **RICHARD'S BARBYCU**
The English Word Barbecue *112*

SIX **GEORGE'S BARBICUE**
The Beginnings of Southern Barbecue *130*

SEVEN **JUBA'S 'CUE**
The Original Southern Barbecue *166*

EIGHT **NED'S BARBACUE**
Transatlantic Misunderstandings *204*

NINE **SAM'S BARBECUE**
Uncle Sam's Barbecue Tradition *227*

Acknowledgments *247* *Notes* *249*
Selected Bibliography *285* *Index* *293*

INTRODUCTION

If any people in the world could be described as "barbecue people," it's the people of the United States. As much as "80% of all homeowners and 70% of all households in the United States own at least one grill or smoker," and most use them year-round to cook breakfast and brunch in addition to dinner.[1] Many towns in the United States have their own celebrated barbecue guru no matter if they are self-proclaimed as such or anointed so by adoring fans. Just about every weekend in the year, barbecue events, contests, and festivals are conducted somewhere in the country.[2] A quick look through the weekly television listings reveals a plethora of barbecue-themed shows. There is a deluge of magazines, websites, and blogs devoted to barbecuing and grilling as well as numerous barbecue clubs, societies, and associations. Many products referred to as "barbecue" or "barbecued" nowadays are being mass-produced and sold on grocery store shelves, through mail order, and barbecued meats are even sold out of vending machines.[3] To this day, many Americans still share the sentiment expressed by a barbecue enthusiast long ago in 1844, "[Barbecue is a witness] to the open-heartedness and hospitality of our people."[4]

The mass media is full of claims that barbecuing was born in the Caribbean after the islands were first visited by Spanish explorers led by Christopher Columbus (1451–1506). After that event, it is claimed, eventually what became the southern way of barbecuing made its way from the Caribbean to the British North American colonies. That theory, referred to herein as the Caribbean Origins Theory (COT), has existed in one form or another since at least the eighteenth century. According to the COT, indigenous people in North America had little to nothing to do with the development

Simmering barbecue hash at a barbecue in Augusta, Georgia. By Davis, *Harper's Weekly*.

of southern barbecuing. Instead, barbecuing left the islands and made its way to North America either with Spanish conquistadors, with enslaved people, or with other immigrants from the islands. Most versions of the COT start with Spanish explorers, the Taíno people of sixteenth-century Haiti (one of the several groups of Indigenous people who inhabited the Caribbean), and the mistaken belief that the Spanish word *barbacoa* referred to a cooking technique. The following is a compilation of the various versions of the COT that can be found in mass media today:

In 1492, Christopher Columbus sailed with a band of explorers across the Atlantic and "discovered" the Americas. After they arrived on an island that's today known as the Dominican Republic and Haiti, they discovered barbecue after witnessing the Taíno people there practicing a way of cooking, they called "barbacoa." The Spanish explorers were so impressed, they enthusiastically embraced that way of cooking. As explorers moved west, they took that new way of cooking pigs with them everywhere they went in the Americas. During the early 1540s, the barbecue-loving Spanish conquistador Hernando de Soto introduced "the original southern barbecue" in what is today the southern United States along with a spicy, vinegar-tomato based barbecue sauce. Soon after the colonization of the Carolinas, people who immigrated from the Caribbean brought their West Indies way of cooking pigs using a spicy citrus-based barbecue sauce with them that didn't have tomatoes in the recipe. Because lemon and lime trees are scarce in North Carolina, Carolinians replaced the citrus juice with vinegar, and North Carolina barbecue was born! Eventually, barbecuing spread from eastern North Carolina to Memphis, Kansas City, and, of course, central Texas.[5]

Thanks to mass media and social media, there is more information about barbecuing available today than ever before. Regrettably, that has also resulted in the repeated parroting of the COT in a way that has unjustifiably exalted it to a de facto status of barbecue dogma. That outcome is not due to anyone's ill intent. It's because the details regarding barbecuing in the Americas over the previous 500 years are sometimes confusing, convoluted, and difficult to interpret. Perhaps that explains why the COT enjoys such a remarkable lack of scrutiny. Unfortunately, that has led some to the mistaken assumption that there is nothing left to tell on the subject of the origins of southern barbecuing. Nevertheless barbecuing, as it was originally practiced in the southern United States, is a uniquely American tradition. It was born after enslaved Africans were brought to Virginia in 1619 from West Africa. Eventually, enslaved people of African descent, along with people of European descent, and others of American Indian descent combined their cooking traditions and created what we today call southern barbecue.

Several excellent books and articles about barbecuing have been published over the last decade or so and I am indebted to those authors for the knowledge they have shared. A few authors have elevated the study of the history of barbecuing beyond oral legends and folklore. For example, in *The Slaw and the Slow Cooked*, James R. Veteto and Edward M. Maclin reveal how southern barbecue traditions are "often aspects of a localized and particular Southern culture that is deeply infused with history, identity, ritual, memory, gender, and sense of place and belonging."[6] Robert F. Moss discusses the history of American barbecue from the early years of the colonial United States to modern times and describes it as a driver that helped shape American culture.[7]

There is a broad spectrum of opinions of what *real* barbecuing is or is not. On one end of the spectrum is Jim Auchmutey's assertion that barbecue is food that's been "doused with barbecue sauce, as long as it's fun and informal and tastes good."[8] At the other end are those who argue that barbecuing has existed all over the world since ancient times, and today it includes any kind of cooking outdoors with fire and smoke.[9]

There are also differing claims regarding the origins of barbecuing, in general, and southern barbecuing, in particular. For example authors such as Steven Raichlen, Natasha Geiling, and John Shelton Reed argue in favor of the COT in their respective titles.[10] Andrew Warnes, on the other hand, contends that the word *barbecue* is related to *barbaric* and, as a result, the American barbecue tradition was invented much like the American Thanksgiving tradition.[11] A growing group of authors have embraced the notion that barbecuing in the United States was born in the eastern seaboard during colonial times after it was adopted from Native Americans. However, few details are provided for how or why it emerged.[12] Adrian Miller chronicles the significant contributions African Americans have made to American barbecue including the labor, ingenuity, hard work, and passion to help create, perfect, and exalt southern barbecuing.[13] The book *Virginia Barbecue: A History* is a deep-dive into the history of barbecuing in Virginia that explores the roles of the three main contributors to the development of southern barbecuing—Native Americans, people of African descent, and people of European descent—and the cultural exchanges that took place in seventeenth-century Virginia that made it possible.[14] Still, there are gaps in our knowledge of southern barbecuing's history that haven't been adequately addressed. This book is intended to fill some of those gaps while inspiring scholarly research on the subject.

FIVE CS OF HISTORICAL ANALYSIS

All people who study the history of barbecuing work from the same body of knowledge, referred to herein as the Barbecue History Body of Knowledge (BHBoK). The BHBoK is information about barbecuing in the Americas that has been recorded since CE 1492. It exists in artifacts such as oral and written accounts, photographs, videos, illustrations, paintings, and archeological findings. This book provides an alternative to the COT by analyzing and interpreting the BHBoK in accordance with principles that some historians call the five Cs of historical analysis, which are change over time, causality, context, complexity, and contingency.[15] The five Cs help answer the critical questions of barbecuing history, which are who, what, when, where, why, and how.

Recognizing change over time assists with understanding how people's notions of what is and what isn't barbecuing has changed over the centuries. It also assists with avoiding the error of Presentism, which occurs when present-day notions and perspectives are introduced into interpretations of the past.

Causality refers to the intersection of people and events and how those events impacted the emergence of barbecuing among European colonies in the Americas. It helps to identify answers to questions, such as: How did people who were forcibly brought to the Americas adapt? What influence did enslavers have on the people they enslaved? What influence did enslaved people have on their enslavers? How did the Spanish influence other Europeans? How did Europeans influence Native Americans and vice versa? How did people of African descent interact with and influence people of Native American descent and vice versa?

Context is important because no work of literature can be properly analyzed or understood without a clear understanding of its historical context. This is particularly true when studying the history of barbecuing.

Understanding the complex issues surrounding the history of barbecuing is important because, as is demonstrated by the COT, an uncomplicated myth is often more attractive than a complicated fact. Nevertheless barbecuing's history is complex as is the world in which it developed, and understanding it requires contributions from many disciplines including history, anthropology, archeology, sociology, linguistics (including etymology), and the culinary arts to name a few.

The birth of southern barbecuing wasn't inevitable. Identifying contingencies in the history of barbecuing uncovers key events that prompted the development of barbecuing and the changes in people's understanding of it. What are the essential factors that brought about southern barbecuing's birth? If any of those factors were missing would southern barbecuing have emerged? What might have been different if enslaved Africans weren't brought to Virginia in 1619? Why did backyard barbecues become popular? The answers to questions like these help us identify contingencies that assist with more clearly understanding barbecuing history.

BARBECUING PERIODS

Some historians divide the past into periods or eras to facilitate the study and analysis of history. That practice is called *periodization*. When periodization is applied to barbecue history it assists with understanding when and how what people have considered to be barbecuing changed over time. Recognizing those changes and when they occurred helps to organize the history of barbecuing into a more easily understandable narrative. Changes in what people considered to be barbecuing (or what they no longer consider to be barbecuing), didn't always bring older ways of barbecuing to an end. Indeed, understanding what changed is as important as understanding what stayed the same. Just as the advent of the Iron Age didn't cause people to stop using bronze, the change in what people considered to be barbecuing introduced something new but didn't always entirely eliminate the old.

The earliest period of barbecuing in the Americas after the arrival of Europeans occurred roughly between CE 1492–1625. During this time period (pre-Southern Barbecuing period), "barbecuing" was confined to being a way to preserve foods practiced by Europeans in the Americas, enslaved Africans and their descendants born in the Americas (both enslaved and free), and Native Americans. It also included a way of cooking food by wrapping it in leaves and burying it with hot rocks in earth ovens. The noun *barbacoa* was adopted by Spanish speakers presumably from Native Americans in what is today Haiti. The noun was used to refer to wooden structures used for beds, bridges, porticos, grills for smoking and drying foods, and as storage bins for valuables and food. Flat slabs used for drying foods were also called barbacoas. Some accounts from this early barbecuing period describe cannibalistic societies in the Americas who used to *boucaner* (French for making jerky) flesh from bodies of their enemies. Albeit the truthfulness of those assertions is disputed. It's also important to point out that the English word barbecue didn't exist during this period.

The next period of barbecuing history is the Original Southern Barbecuing Period (OSBP), which occurred roughly between CE 1625 and the end of the Reconstruction period in 1877. One of the significant changes during this period is the emergence of the English word barbecue. Another significant change was the development of a new way of barbecuing referred to herein as the Original Southern Barbecuing Technique, or OSBT. The third significant change from this period occurred when people in the American colonies started to refer to outdoor social events where barbecued meats are served as barbecues. The OSBT was ubiquitous in the southern American colonies during the OSBP and, after 1776, the southern United States. It was characterized by whole animal carcasses cooked on grills set above open pits. The meat wasn't seasoned with salt or other seasonings before going on the pit. The seasoning was applied while the carcass cooked by being basted with a mixture of ingredients that almost always included hot salted water or a mixture of vinegar, butter, salt, and red pepper pods. The cooking temperature was highest at the beginning. As the cook progressed, the temperature was lowered either by using fewer hot coals or simply because the coals were being depleted. Those characteristics of the OSBT differentiate it from the modern way of barbecuing whole hogs. Today, a common approach to barbecuing a whole hog carcass is to apply salt or a barbecue rub before placing it meat-side down on a grill with the coals beneath placed around the perimeter of the carcass or off to the side if using an indirect-heat cooker. The lid of the cooker is then closed, and the carcass cooks undisturbed *low and slow*. When the pitmaster is satisfied that the meat side is properly browned, the carcass is flipped over so the skin side is facing the heat source to crisp the skin while the meat continues to cook until the desired tenderness is reached. Some baste the meat while it cooks, some don't, but almost all apply a sauce after the meat is finished cooking.

An illustration of a barbecue hosted in Tennessee by Virginian John Sevier in 1780. Gordy, *Stories of American History*.

At around the turn of the eighteenth century, people in Britain had a short-lived fascination with their own version of barbecuing—most often for family meals rather than large gatherings. As is usually the case the old ideas of what barbecuing is, such as making jerky and cooking in earth ovens, continued to be practiced and referred to by English speakers as barbecuing. People in the United States also considered the act of smoking venison hams in smokehouses to be barbecuing during the OSBP.[16]

During the Reconstruction period, the OSBP was coming to a close, and the post-Original Southern Barbecuing period began as American notions of barbecuing were beginning to change. By 1871 the first commercially bottled barbecue sauces were emerging on the market, such as the one sold by Dr. J. H. Larwill of Georgia with the tagline, "For fresh meats of all kinds it cannot be excelled."[17] In 1872, *Mrs. Hill's Southern Practical Cookery and Receipt Book* became one of the first to include a "Sauce for Barbecues" recipe.[18] Not only did the practice of serving sauce on the side begin to become widespread, the practice of cooking in covered barbecue pits was also born. In the 1890s, events in California where Mexican barbacoa was served began to be known as barbecues. Fireless, electric, and gas-powered barbecue cookers emerged at the end of the nineteenth century. At around the turn of the twentieth century, most Americans stopped referring to meats that had been dried and smoked as being barbecued and started almost exclusively referring to them as *jerky*. By the 1920s, Americans had started referring to the act of smoke-roasting meats as barbecuing. By the 1930s, backyard barbecuing was becoming popular in California. Fewer and fewer people were barbecuing whole carcasses over open pits using the OSBT. By 1942 Americans all around the country started to embrace backyard barbecues, understood as outdoor social events that feature foods cooked on grills or in pots and pans sitting over coals. By the 1950s, many barbecue restaurants and vendors were barbecuing roasts and large cuts of meat in covered pits or *smokers* instead of whole carcasses. By the 1980s, the mass media had greatly increased its coverage of barbecuing and central Texas–style barbecued brisket was becoming popular all over the country.

The internet barbecuing period was born after the World Wide Web debuted in 1989, and it only took a few years for changes to emerge that were inspired by information shared online. Today, many people across the globe have been introduced to American barbecue through the internet. As a result, the practice of using the word barbecue to refer to grilled foods and outdoor parties that feature them is popular in many countries.

COOKING WITH FIRE AND SMOKE

Cooking outdoors with fire and smoke is the oldest way of cooking. However, when the murky origins of the word barbecue are considered in light of its many and changing definitions, and the differences in its meanings in different cultures, it's clear that the styles of barbecuing that Europeans witnessed in the Americas during the sixteenth to eighteenth centuries were far more than merely cooking outdoors with fire. Moreover if all ancient ways of cooking with fire and smoke are barbecuing, Spanish explorers and the Taíno people in sixteenth-century Haiti were a few thousand years late to the party.

Many people in the southern United States still recognize the differences between barbecuing and other outdoor cooking techniques, such as grilling, spit roasting, and baking. To them, barbecuing hasn't changed. The change is in how some people now use the word barbecuing to refer to just about any kind of outdoor cooking. That explains why many southerners scoff at the notion of barbecued hamburgers, hotdogs, steaks, sausages, and tofu.

In times before cookstoves became ubiquitous, open-hearth cooking was the norm. That made it easy to recognize clear distinctions between barbecuing, roasting, baking, and grilling meats. Roasting in those times was a way of cooking a large cut of meat while it turned on a spit that sat beside—not over—a flaming fire, and generally with temperatures in the 350°F–400°F range.

Baking is a cooking technique where roasts are placed inside an enclosed chamber and usually in the same temperature range as roasting. For centuries, Europeans

Roasting before the fire with a dripping pan. Bailey, *Dictionarium Domesticum*.

have been grilling foods on gridirons that sat directly over hot coals. What we today call grilling was often referred to by early modern [1500–1800] cookbook authors as broiling. Grilling is best suited for cooking small cuts of meat, such as chops and steaks, directly over a heat source at temperatures as high as 800°F.

Since ancient times, people all over the world have used smoke to preserve meats and fish. There are two ways to smoke meats: One is cold smoking where meats, such as Virginia-smoked hams, are smoked in a smokehouse or other enclosed compartment at low temperatures (usually under 100°F) without cooking them. Hot smoking is done

European-style Gridiron used in open-hearth cooking. Photo by the author.

by cooking foods in an enclosed chamber filled with smoke such as how restaurants in central Texas cook briskets. This can be done at temperatures as high as 600°F.[19]

Barbecuing as it was originally done in the South, on the other hand, was not merely cooking outdoors with fire and smoke nor was it a roasting, baking, grilling, or smoking technique. Cookbooks written in the eighteenth and nineteenth centuries contain recipes for roasting pigs outside on spits beside *quick fires* alongside recipes for barbecuing pigs outside directly over *clear fires* comprised of hot coals with no flames. Those old cookbooks also contain recipes for grilling food on gridirons. The clear distinctions convincingly testify to the fact that roasting, baking, smoking, and grilling were not considered to be barbecuing.

During the twentieth century, people in the United States started to conflate barbecuing with other ways of cooking outdoors with fire. That has resulted in fanciful stories about sixteenth-century Taínos "barbecuing" pigs with indirect heat in Haiti, people in ancient Greece "barbecuing" pigs during the turn of the first millennium, ancient Israelites "barbecuing" lambs on the temple altar in Jerusalem, and the fatted calf that was "barbecued" in the bible story about the prodigal son. Such claims make entertaining stories, but they are not supported by the BHBoK.

AVOIDING COMMON PITFALLS

Much has been written about barbecue since Europeans arrived in the Americas. That has created many opportunities for mistakes to emerge, such as typographical errors, embellishments, translation errors, and misinterpretations. For those reasons, when studying the history of barbecuing, it's important to avoid common pitfalls by applying the Five Cs, scrutinizing sources and, whenever possible, consulting primary sources.

Charles Loftus Grant Anderson was born in Maryland in 1863, and he lived to the venerable age of 89.[20] Although he was a medical doctor, his personal interest in archeology and anthropology led him to write several books about sixteenth-century Spanish expeditions in the Americas. He identified several mistakes made by historians that he believed explain how "errors creep into history."[21] His observations provide essential lessons for those who study the history of barbecuing.

SHORTCOMINGS OF DICTIONARIES

Dictionaries are helpful tools that provide definitions, synonyms, and the etymology of words. However, they aren't meant to be history books. The English lexicographer Samuel Johnson (1709–84) was the compiler of the *Dictionary of the English Language* published in London in 1755. He once wrote to a friend, "Dictionaries are like watches; the worst is better than none, and the best cannot be expected to go quite true."[22] One example of how dictionaries can introduce problems when studying the history of barbecuing is found in the English scholar Richard Hopwood Thornton's (1855–1932) *An American Glossary* published in Philadelphia in 1912. He described barbecue by citing the phrase "an elephant of four years old, barbecued at a fire of sanders and aloes wood."[23] That short quote makes it appear that someone barbecued an elephant. However, it turns out Thornton was quoting a satirical column published in the March 11, 1799, edition of the *Aurora General Advertiser*.[24] That's certainly not an authoritative source for barbecuing knowledge. It provides another reminder that quotations found in dictionaries and glossaries that demonstrate the usage of the word barbecue should not be taken at face value.

TRANSLATION ERRORS

Anderson identified a mistranslation in historian Paul Gaffarel's (1843–1920) French translation of a letter a Spanish conquistador wrote in 1513. Pointing out that this "is another example of how errors get into history," Anderson took issue with how the

Spanish word barbacoa was translated as the French word *sac* ("sack" or "bag" in English).[25] Obviously sacks and barbacoas are very different things.

The English author Sir Arthur Helps (1813–75) made a similar error in *The Spanish Conquest in America* (1856).[26] It includes Help's English translation of a passage from Bernal Díaz del Castillo's (1496–1584) eyewitness account of the conquistador Hernán Cortés's (1485–1547) campaign to conquer the Aztec empire in 1519–1521 where the Spanish word barbacoas was rendered in English as *barbacans* (archaic spelling of barbicans).[27]

Translating barbacoa as barbecue can result in "another example of how errors get into history." One instance is found in British explorer James Burney's (1750–1821) *History of the Buccaneers of America* published in London in 1816. In reference to buccaneers, French hunters in Tortuga and Hispaniola who made their living trading hides and smoked-dried meat, boucan, and "Caribbe Indians" (see chapter 3 "Jean-Baptiste's Boucan"), Burney wrote, "The meat was laid to be dried upon a wooden grate or hurdle [*grille de bois*] which the Indians called *barbecu*, placed at a good distance over a slow fire. The meat when cured was *boucan*, and the same name was given to the place of their cookery."[28] That passage leaves the impression that sixteenth-century "Caribbe Indians" referred to a wooden grill as a *barbecu*, an archaic spelling of the word barbecue. However, they didn't have barbecue in their vocabularies. Burney sourced his description from a French-language account of privateers that was published in Paris in 1686.[29] He inserted his personal understanding of barbecuing when he translated the Spanish word barbacoa in the passage as the English word barbecue. That underscores the importance of examining primary sources when studying the history of barbecuing.

TYPOGRAPHICAL ERRORS

When Anderson discussed the history of buccaneers and how they received their name from the French word *boucan*, he associated it with the Spanish barbacoa and added, "Also written *barbacra*."[30] An editor of *Histoire de la Révolution de France* (*History of the French Revolution*), published in Paris in 1797, also described how the word boucan was learned from what he believed to be cannibalistic Aboriginals in South America. He wrote, "These racks were called *barbacra*; the place where they were, *bucan*; and the act of roasting human flesh, *boucaner*" (author's translation).[31] The October 1881 edition of the French magazine *L'Intermédiaire des Chercheurs et Curieux* (*The Intermediate of the Researchers and Curious*) includes an article about the origin of the word boucan, "the racks used by [sixteenth-century] natives in the Caribbean to smoke meat were called by the word *barbacra* instead of *barbacoas*" (author's translation).[32]

The first appearance of *barbacra* is found in a French dictionary titled *Dictionnaire Universel François et Latin* (English speakers refer to it as *The Trévoux Dictionary*), that was published in several editions in Paris during the eighteenth century. Under the definition of *boucanier* is found, "The Caribbean Indians of the West Indies have been accustomed to cut their prisoners of war into pieces that they put on racks under which they start a fire. They named these racks *Barbacra* and the place where they are *boucan* which is where they *boucaner*, or roast & smoke, [the flesh] all together" (author's translation). Every edition of *The Trévoux Dictionary* from 1721 to at least 1771 includes *barbacra* in that passage.[33] Relying on editions of that one dictionary printed in the eighteenth century as the authoritative source, the mistaken belief that the word barbacra came from a Native American language gained a lot of traction in the nineteenth and early twentieth centuries. That fact provides an important lesson.

The compilers of *The Trévoux Dictionary* copied their entire account of the supposed origin of barbacra from spurious passages found in the aforementioned 1686 French language account of buccaneers. However, instead of containing barbacra the original source on which the French account is based contains the word barbacoa. Therefore a typographical error in *The Trévoux Dictionary* resulted in the letter *r* in place of the rightful *o*. Anderson was careful to check sources in the case of barbacoa being mistranslated as the French word sac. However, he and others failed to check sources in the case of the mythological word barbacra.

A similar typographical error is found in *The Universal Dictionary of Trade and Commerce* published in London in 1766. In the passages about buccaneers, we find, "Large forked stakes, two feet high, support that kind of gridiron, from distance to distance, and raise it above the ground, that wood, or other combustible matters, may be kindled under it, which produce more smoke than heat. Over this machine, which the Indians call barbucoa, they put the fish, or flesh, which they would buccaneer."[34] Clearly barbucoa is a typographical error.

In *The History of Signboards: from the Earliest Times to the Present*, published in London in 1867, is an advertisement that was placed in the February 9, 1726, edition of *Mist's Journal* that reads, "On Tuesday next, being Shrove Tuesday, will be a fine hog barbygu'd whole at the house of Peter Brett, at the Rising Sun, in Islington Road, with other diversions. It is the house where the ox was roasted whole at Christmas last."[35] When the advertisement was mentioned again in John Timbs's (1801–75) *English Eccentrics and Eccentricities*, published in London in 1877, *barbygu'd* was spelled as *barbyqu'd*.[36] Until someone locates a copy of the original advertisement, it's up to the reader to determine which spelling was originally printed.

CULTURAL DIFFERENCES

According to linguists, cultural differences often create more significant communication difficulties between people who speak different languages than language differences. That results in the occasional distortion introduced by translators. Additionally, the various strategies translators use to overcome cultural differences can also result in unintentional misinterpretation. Problems compound when it comes to the subject of barbecuing simply because the American understanding of it, especially in the southern United States, is so different than the understanding of it in other parts of the world. Those differences are why it's important to be very precise when translating passages written about outdoor cooking in different languages, times, and cultures.

Enter the French word boucan into an online translation service, and it might provide several English alternatives such as racket, loud noise, smoke, wallop, and even hullabaloo. Enter the Spanish word *parrilla* into an online translation service and the response will sometimes be the correct word grill but is too often barbecue. Enter the Portuguese word *churrasco*, and barbecue is often offered in response. A similar situation arises when the Haitian word *boukannen* is translated as barbecue. Haitian boukannen is actually grilled meats, fish, or vegetables, but not barbecued meats as they are understood in the South. The point is that people in different parts of the world have different interpretations of words that refer to cooking outdoors. Therefore it is critical to observe cultural differences.[37]

Other sources of unintentional mistakes occur when the translator inadvertently injects their understanding of the word barbecue into the translation. In such cases, the meaning of the translated passage takes on the translator's understanding rather than the meaning of the person who wrote the original passage. Therefore caution must be exercised when accepting stories passed off as "barbecue history" at face value. If the translator of non-English sources doesn't consider how the definition of the English word barbecue has changed over the centuries and how it's defined in different cultures, it's possible to inject presentism or other errors into the translation. In order to avoid issues that may arise because of cultural differences, words like barbacoa, boucan, parrilla, *asado*, *asada*, and churrasco should not be translated into English as barbecue simply because those words, and others, have diverse cultural meanings that often rely upon context, geography, culture, and time.

Depiction of an antebellum barbecue. Goodrich, *The Universal Traveller*.

ILLUSTRATION ERRORS

When studying barbecuing and southern barbecuing in particular, illustrations shouldn't be taken at face value. Reverend Charles Augustus Goodrich (1790–1862) is best known as the person who popularized the phrase, "A place for everything and everything in its place." His book with an excessively long title *The Universal Traveller: Designed to Introduce Readers at Home to an Acquaintance with the Arts, Customs, and Manners, of the Principal Modern Nations on the Globe* was published in 1837.[38] In it, Goodrich wrote a reasonably accurate description of a southern barbecue during the OSBP. Unfortunately, the illustration provided depicts a pig being roasted on a spit rather than being barbecued over an open pit.

The sixteenth-century French explorer Jean de Léry (1536–1613) commented on the errors artists made in images of Native Americans in Brazil roasting flesh on spits. He pointed out that Native Americans in sixteenth-century Brazil were ignorant of the ways of cooking that were depicted in those illustrations. In fact, on one occasion, Native Americans laughed at him when they witnessed him roasting a bird on a spit. They didn't believe that meat could be cooked that way until he demonstrated it to their satisfaction.[39]

"How Native Americans Cook Fish." By Theodor de Bry, ca. 1590. Based upon John White's artwork.

English artist John White's (1539–93) illustrations of eastern Algonquians in North America cooking on wooden hurdles can also be misleading. The flaming fire underneath the wooden grill leaves the impression that the people depicted in the woodcuts were roasting foods on wooden hurdles. However, eyewitness accounts of Native Americans preparing foods on wooden hurdles during the sixteenth and seventeenth centuries make it clear that the process was far more complex, as explained in Chapter 4, "Beauchamp's Barbecado."

EMBELLISHMENTS

Much of the "proof" used to support the COT exists in the form of tall tales. An example of one is the story of the eighteenth-century Scots-Irish immigrant Neill "Red" McNeill. The story tells how McNeill named a creek in Harnett County, North Carolina, "Barbacue Creek" sometime around 1750. In 1757, a church was established in the area that took its name from the creek. The reason McNeill named the creek Barbacue, we are told, is because the morning mist above it reminded him of barbecue pits he witnessed in the West Indies. That also appears to be the source of the claim that McNeill was the one who introduced barbecuing in North Carolina after, ostensibly, learning it while he was in the Caribbean around those misty pits. Versions of that story are repeated without question in some North Carolina barbecue histories.[40] Nevertheless the assertion that the creek was named after barbecue pits in the Caribbean is not based upon fact. Instead, it comes from an editor's speculation recorded in the *Official History of Barbecue Church* published in 1965. Rather than an authoritative source for the claim, it's offered as what the editor called a "logical explanation."[41] The speculation and the logic behind it seems to be rooted in the COT. Moreover the editor's assumption that McNeill's experience with barbecuing was limited to the Caribbean is unfounded. By the 1730s, there were numerous barbecue pits in Virginia, Maryland, and North Carolina. Myths like McNeill's supposed Caribbean barbecue experience is another reminder of the importance of checking primary sources.

Another unfortunate embellishment was made by Timbs in his version of the *Rising Sun*'s advertisement for "a fine hog barbyqu'd." He added "roasted whole, with spice, and basted with Madeira wine."[42] That embellishment wasn't in the original advertisement. It's a paraphrase of a passage found in an eighteenth-century British travelogue that was written after the *Rising Sun*'s advertisement was printed (discussed further in chapter 5, "Richard's Barbycu"). Such embellishments add to the sometimes-confusing nature of the history of barbecuing.

FULL DISCLOSURE

I grew up in central Virginia. My father tilled his own gardens and raised his own livestock. We butchered, salted, and smoked our own homegrown pork. Some of it was barbecued, some of it was used to make country sausage, souse, and scrapple. Some of it was used to make lard. Yes, we also ate the chitterlings, or *chitlins*, as we called them, and the trotters (pig's feet). We drew the line at the lights and goozles (lungs and windpipes). Albeit, my grandfather did eat those parts. He used to say of pigs he raised, "We eat everything but the squeal." While growing up, we had a barbecue pit, a charcoal grill, and as many as three smokehouses. I've never had a problem recognizing the differences between grilling pork, barbecuing pork, and smoking pork. Because of those experiences, I am firmly in the camp that believes authentic southern barbecuing can only be done by cooking whole or half carcasses or large cuts with direct heat over an open pit. No seasoning whatsoever should be applied to the meat before cooking it; not even salt. The seasoning should be applied with a vinegar/butter-based sauce that's used to baste the meat while it's cooking. All that said, this book isn't written to convince the reader that other opinions of what "real" barbecue is (or isn't) are wrong. This book isn't written to criticize barbecue that isn't cooked over open pits. What a person believes to be real barbecuing today isn't important. This book is an attempt to assist the reader with comparing and contrasting the different ways people in Europe and the Americas understood barbecuing during the time period in which southern barbecuing emerged during the seventeenth century in the colonial United States. That knowledge is critical for understanding the history of southern barbecue.

Neglecting to consider how notions of barbecuing have changed over time makes it more difficult to recognize the uniqueness of the OSBT and that, in turn, makes it more difficult to correctly interpret the history of barbecuing. Therefore it's critical to recognize and understand that before the twentieth century, people saw sharp differences between what they called barbecuing, roasting, grilling, baking, and smoking meats. That's the real key to being able to recognize how special, unique, and wholly American southern barbecuing and southern barbecue traditions are in the wide, ever-changing world of barbecue.

ONE

HERNANDO'S BARBACOA

Spanish Explorers and Outdoor Cooking in Latin America

The belief that the English word barbecue was derived from the Spanish word barbacoa has led some to assume that southern barbecuing was born in the Caribbean and imported into the South during colonial times. However, assumptions should only be made in the absence of credible information, and then with caution. A careful analysis of trustworthy historical and contemporary sources provides authoritative information that contradicts the prevailing assumptions made about the supposed Caribbean origins of southern barbecuing.

HERNANDO DE SOTO

The Spanish conquistador Hernando de Soto (1497–1542) arrived in the Americas in 1514. In only a few years, he had made a fortune trading enslaved Africans and Native Americans. In 1532, he joined Francisco Pizarro (1478–1541) on his expedition to subjugate the Indigenous people of Peru. In 1539, de Soto landed in Florida with an army of about 600 men, over 200 horses, 2,500 salted pork shoulders, and several hundred pigs, hoping to find great sources of gold like those encountered in Mexico. He and his men

Hernando de Soto at the Mississippi River. Quackenbos. *Elementary History of the United States.*

explored a portion of today's southern United States, traveling as far west as the Mississippi River before he died on its banks in present-day Arkansas from a fever in 1542. After de Soto's death, the decision was made to end the expedition. Only about 300 of de Soto's men were still alive when they reached a Spanish colony in Mexico in 1543.

There is no evidence to indicate that Spanish explorers embraced barbecuing and spread it around the Americas. If de Soto's cooks ever cooked a whole pig during his North American expedition, there can be little doubt that they used a traditional Spanish roasting method to do so. One of the most iconic dishes of Spain and Portugal is Lechón: roast suckling pig. It's been a part of the Iberian Peninsula's cuisine at least since the Roman invasion in the second century BCE. Lechón is not barbecued pork. It's traditional European roast pork that's still a popular dish served on holidays in Spain and parts of Latin America. On at least one occasion, de Soto shared pork dinners with Native Americans. Some also claim de Soto served barbecued pork on religious feast days such as the Feast of St. Lucy and Christmas Day.[1] Nevertheless there is no evidence that he or his cooks ever barbecued pigs, and he was very stingy with fresh pork because he wanted to reserve a sufficient number of hogs for the colony he hoped to establish. Consequently at one point in the expedition, de Soto limited each man's ration of pork to half a pound per day.[2]

The claim that de Soto served "the original southern barbecue" with a sauce made of tomatoes and vinegar is apparently based on passages such as this one from American historian Edward Gaylord Bourne's (1860–1908) *Narratives of the career of Hernando de Soto*, "The Governor invited the caciques and some chiefs to dine with him, giving them pork to eat, which they so relished." Nonetheless that passage doesn't provide any evidence for the claim that de Soto introduced barbecuing or barbecue sauce in North America.[3] Moreover there are several examples of de Soto's inhumane treatment of Native Americans that demonstrate he was probably more interested in subjugating them than living with them as equals and adopting their cuisine.[4] Like other Spaniards of his day, de Soto was convinced of the Spanish superiority over Native Americans and believed he was on a divine mission to convert "savages" to Christianity.[5] Therefore it's doubtful that he was open to adopting their customs. Unfortunately, embellishments and assumptions play a role in giving far more credit to de Soto and other Spaniards for the *birth of barbecue* and its imagined migration to North America from the Caribbean than is deserved.

A GENERAL LANGUAGE

Sixteenth-century conquistadors encountered many different languages and dialects in the Americas. Consequently they started incorporating words from those languages into their vocabulary almost immediately after their first contact with the Taíno Natives in the Caribbean. They continued to incorporate Native American words until the Spanish conquest of the Americas was complete. After that time, Spanish colonists took over the process of incorporating words into Spanish from Native American languages. Scholars refer to those Spanish words as *loan words*. Borrowing words was crucial for developing a general language that governors could use to establish laws, for priests who were evangelizing Native American populations, and for trade. They also played an essential role for communication among conquistadors who were seeking gold. All of that resulted in sixteenth-century Spanish speakers in the Americas regularly using a mishmash of loan words from different languages in official documents.[6]

The majority of Native American words loaned to Europeans, such as tomato, potato, tobacco, maize, barbacoa, and avocado, are nouns simply because there were so many things in the Americas that Europeans had never witnessed.[7] That reinforces a crucial point. Barbacoa is a loan word that had no suitable counterpart in the European languages. Therefore the Spanish word parrilla, the English word *gridiron*, and the French word *gril* don't adequately describe barbacoas as they were understood during the early modern period.

Following the route of conquest, conquistadors incorporated new loan words as they moved into the mainland Americas. Scholars tell us that out of the Native American words borrowed by the Spanish, 40 percent came from the Aztec (Nahuatl), 30 percent from the Taíno (Arawak), 10 percent from the Incas (Quechua), and 20 percent came from other languages.[8] The most geographically dispersed loan words in the Americas were borrowed from Arawak. Aztec loan words are the second most geographically dispersed, but few were used outside of their native territory during the sixteenth century. Spaniards took the words they borrowed from the Caribbean with them and imposed them on societies all around the Americas.[9] For example, in the early years of the Spanish colonization of Mexico, the Taíno word *aji* was used to refer to hot peppers instead of the local Aztec word *chile*. That's because words were only borrowed from the Aztecs for things that Spaniards hadn't previously witnessed for the first time. It wasn't until the late sixteenth century that Aztec words finally started to displace some Arawak words among Spanish speakers in Mexico, but not all. For example, the Taíno words *maize* and barbacoa are still used in Mexico to this day. Just because Spanish records tell of barbacoas everywhere Spaniards went in the Americas, that's not proof that all societies they encountered had the word barbacoa in their vocabularies. What it means is that structures Spaniards called barbacoas were ubiquitous and used by Native Americans all over the Americas and weren't devices only used by the Taíno.

SIXTEENTH-CENTURY CHRONICLERS

An entry in Christopher Columbus's log from his second voyage to the Americas in 1494 describes the "wooden spits" he saw in Cuba on which fish, small mammals, and iguanas were being preserved. On one occasion, when a member of Columbus's crew asked the Aboriginals why they "cooked" fish, "they replied that they did so to preserve it from corruption."[10] In 1509, a ship returning from the Americas docked at the city of Rouen in France. Among its passengers were seven kidnapped Native Americans who had been taken from the east coast of Brazil. Besides comments about their appearance, clothes, and the claim that they had no religion, very little else was recorded about them except the statement, "Their diet includes dried flesh and water. They are ignorant of bread, wine, and money" (author's translation).[11]

Native Americans preserving fish on a wooden hurdle (a.k.a. barbacoa). By Theodor de Bry, ca. 1550.

Just about all of the claims made today about de Soto's supposed love of barbecuing are found in the records left to us by four chroniclers, hereafter referred to as Oviedo et al. A careful review of those records and how the chroniclers used the noun barbacoa suggests that sixteenth-century Spaniards were fascinated by the devices, but that fascination had nothing to do with barbecuing.

Gonzalo Fernández de Oviedo y Valdés (1478–1557) was a Spanish historian who participated in the early sixteenth-century Spanish colonization of the Americas. Known as "the chronicler of the Indies," he is credited with being the first European to create a literary work in the Americas. In 1526, he wrote the following description of how a barbacoa was used for culinary purposes, "Because they have no knives, the Natives butcher animal carcasses with stones and flints before roasting [*asanlos*] the meat over a fire while it is suspended on grills or trivets made of sticks that they call barbacoas. They also roast fish in the same way. Because of the hot climate, if meat is not soon roasted in this way it will spoil" (author's translation).[12] That passage makes

Juan Ortiz being tortured on a barbacoa. By John William Orr. Wilmer, *The Life, Travels, Adventures of Ferdinand De Soto*.

it clear that the way the Taíno people cut carcasses into pieces and "roasted" meats on barbacoas was very different than how whole animal carcasses were barbecued using the OSBT.

Oviedo's work also includes portions of the now lost diary of de Soto's personal secretary Rodrigo Ranjel. After his death in 1557, publication of Oviedo's work stopped and was nearly forgotten until the entirety of extant portions of his *Historia general y natural de las Indias* was finally published in 1851–55 by the Spanish Academy of History.[13] In 1609, the English author Richard Hakluyt (1553–1616) translated portions of Oviedo's work, becoming the first to use the word barbacoa in English literature.[14]

In 1557 Fidalgo de Elvas, referred to hereafter as Elvas, published an account of de Soto's North American expedition titled *Relaçam Verdadeira* (*True Relation*) written in Portuguese. It was translated into English by Richard Hakluyt in 1609.[15]

Luys Hernández de Biedma, referred to hereafter as Biedma, was one of three royal representatives on de Soto's North American expedition. He wrote *Relación de la Isla Florida* from memory. It was published in 1557 in a report addressed to government officials. According to scholars, his work contains little commentary or embellishment.

Garcilaso de la Vega (1539–1616), referred to hereafter as Vega, was born in Peru. He had a Spanish father and an Incan mother. When he was 21 years old, he was sent to Spain to be educated and remained there for the rest of his life. His *La Florida del Inca* was first published in 1605. Vega's account of de Soto's expedition is based upon legend and stories told to him by at least one soldier that accompanied de Soto on his expedition. Therefore scholars do not consider his account to be fully reliable.[16]

The word barbacoa appears two times in Vega's work as part of an account of a Spanish soldier named Juan Ortiz. Ortiz was captured and enslaved by Native Americans in Florida in 1528 while searching for survivors from an unsuccessful expedition led by conquistador Panfilo de Narvaez (1478–1528). Although several accounts of de Soto's expedition mention Ortiz, only Elvas and Vega shared details about his captivity. According to Vega, a cacique named Uzita tortured Ortiz by tying him to a barbacoa set over live coals. Ortiz's life was saved by the cacique's daughter who couldn't bear the sound of his agony and pleas for mercy. After eleven years of ill-treatment and captivity, Ortiz was finally rescued by de Soto in 1539. He served as an interpreter and guide before dying of natural causes in the winter of 1541–42.[17]

The aforementioned Edward Gaylord Bourne's *Narratives of the career of Hernando de Soto* was published in 1904. Bourne never claimed that conquistadors were fond of barbecuing. He defined barbacoa not as a barbecue grill but as "a kind of scaffold or framework on posts, used for drying meat, for a burial place, or as a look-out. It is also used for our familiar corncrib."[18] That definition is consistent with the one found in *The Narrative of Castañeda*, a sixteenth-century record of the expedition of Francisco Vázquez de Coronado (1510–1554) through what is today Arizona, New Mexico, Texas, Oklahoma, and Kansas, during 1540–1542. The author, Pedro de Castañeda, penned *balbacoas* (a variation of barbacoas) to refer to lofts used for storage.[19]

There are few passages written by Oviedo et al. that mention barbacoas in the context of food. Of those few, some describe barbacoas as corncribs and fewer describe how meat and fish were being preserved by a process that was strange to Europeans. One of the European verbs they used to explain how foods were cured on barbacoas was *asa*, which refers to roasting—not drying, smoking, and preserving foods, which is what was actually being done in a single process. Because Oviedo clarified, "if meat is not soon roasted [*asa*] *in this way* it will spoil," it's clear that what was happening was more than merely roasting. Based on Oviedo's own words, meats being "roasted" on a barbacoa was a strange, Native American way of simultaneously cooking, smoking, and drying meats on a barbacoa.

Understanding how sixteenth-century Spaniards understood the word barbacoa is crucial for avoiding the error of presentism. The twentieth-century American definition of barbacoa and the mistaken notion that the Taíno in sixteenth-century Haiti barbecued whole carcasses in a way that's similar to the OSBT is reflected in the following statements:

- Barbacoa means to cook on green sticks directly over smoldering coals.[20]
- Barbacoa is a form of roasting meat over an open fire.[21]
- Barbacoa describes the Taíno Indian method of smoke roasting.[22]
- Barbacoa was derived from a word for the cooking practices of Native Americans in Haiti.[23]
- Barbacoa was a unique way of cooking over indirect heat that was developed by Native Americans in Haiti. It was discovered by the Spanish who brought it to North America.[24]
- Barbacoa is the "original southern barbecue."[25]

Claims such as those reflect the twentieth-century American usage of the word barbacoa as a noun and a verb rather than how it was used only as a noun to refer to wooden structures in passages written by Oviedo et al. Understanding that is important because context and an accurate understanding of terminology used in the historical sources is critical for understanding the history of barbecuing.

THE NOUN BARBACOA

The word barbacoa doesn't refer to a cooking technique. It was never a "new way of cooking," and it doesn't refer to the cooking practices of the Indigenous people of sixteenth-century Haiti. As previously discussed, the Taíno people in Haiti didn't invent barbacoas and the use of them wasn't confined to them. In 1891, Daniel Brinton (1837–99), an American archaeologist and ethnologist, stated that barbacoa is derived from the Arawakan noun *barrabakoa* that was spoken by sixteenth-century Aboriginals of Haiti. It means "a place for storing provisions."[26] In 1865, the English anthropologist Edward Tylor (1832–1917) defined barbacoa as "The Haitian name for a framework of sticks set upon posts."[27] In 1836, the French philologist Constantine S. Rafinesque (1783–1840) argued that barbacoa is the Haitian word for bed.[28] Over 100 years before Rafinesque, *A New Dictionary, Spanish and English, and English and Spanish* published in London in 1726, offered, "Barbacóa, a scaffold, or any such like place raised high above the ground; also a couch or bed made of canes in the West Indies."[29] None of those sources define barbacoa specifically as a cooking device or a food, which is in keeping with the sixteenth-century Spanish understanding of the word. It's also in keeping with the way

THE WORD BARBACOA IS NOT SYNONYMOUS WITH THE WORD BARBECUE

The following are paraphrases of passages in which Oviedo and the other chroniclers of the de Soto expedition recorded the word barbacoa. They reveal that a barbacoa was simply a device for support or storage built of sticks set upon posts. They also reveal clues as to why conquistadors were so interested in them.

A man is stricken down with a battle axe while defending the entrance to a barbacoa (maize crib); the tribute their people give caciques are stored in many barbacoas; a barbacoa was found full of parched meal and some maize; large quantities of clothing were found in barbacoas; a cacique gave de Soto maize from twenty barbacoas; Native Americans gave them corn and many fowls roasted on a barbacoa; some soldiers provisioned themselves from, or, rather, stole some barbacoas of corn; the soldiers, as usual, climbed on barbacoas prompting the cacique's warriors to defend them by taking up clubs and their bows and arrows; a band of de Soto's men breakfasted on some fowl of the country and some strips of venison they found on a barbacoa (framework of sticks); boys sat on barbacoas while guarding fields from birds; houses built in trees in South America were called barbacoas; people slept on barbacoas; a bridge was built using a barbacoa as its underlying structure; porches and large porticos were called barbacoas; rafts had barbacoas attached for hauling cargo; animal carcasses were butchered with flints and stone hatchets before being cured on barbacoas; Spaniards found a large quantity of fish that had been "roasted" on barbacoas; supposed Native American cannibals "roasted" human flesh on barbacoas like on grills; Juan Ortiz was tied to a barbacoa set over burning embers; de Soto and Ranjel entered a temple and found bodies of men fastened on barbacoas that were adorned with pearls.

(continued from page 32)

early modern Native Americans used barbacoas for many purposes such as bridges, porticos, corncribs, storage bins, beds, crypts, treehouses, shelters, food dehydrators/smokers, ovens, and cooking grills. Still today a barbacoa in Cuba is a loft inside a house used for storing food, tools, and other objects.[30] In Venezuela and Colombia, a barbacoa is a large box filled with soil, raised a few feet above the ground used to grow vegetables. In the Andes, it's a style of tap dancing. In Mexico, it's an earth oven, and the meats cooked in it.[31]

TREASURE-FILLED BARBACOAS

Conquistadors' interest in barbacoas wasn't rooted in their appetite for barbecued pigs. It was rooted in their desire for gold. Hernando Cortez (1485–1547) arrived in Hispaniola in 1504 at the age of 19. In 1519 he and his soldiers invaded Mexico. By 1521 they had defeated the Aztec Empire and set the stage for Spanish colonization. Cortez's motivation was the same as many other conquistadors. When offered a land grant in the Americas, he responded, "I came to get gold, not to till the soil like a peasant."[33] That statement provides an essential clue for understanding the sixteenth-century Spanish fascination with barbacoas.

Although Oviedo was the first to use barbacoa in a published book, contrary to claims in some versions of the COT, he wasn't the first to record it in a document.[34] An earlier appearance of the word was penned 13 years before Oviedo published his first book and it wasn't used in the context of cooking. It was used in the context of gold.

In 1513, the conquistador Vasco Núñez de Balboa (1475–1519), the first European to lead a quest across Panama's Isthmus and to march to the Pacific Ocean, wrote a confidential letter to King Ferdinand II (1452–1516) that contained a closely guarded secret. He informed the king that caciques secretly hid vast amounts of gold in barbacoas.[35] To King Ferdinand II and his conquistadors, the closely guarded secret message was clear. Find a barbacoa, and you will find treasure. That is one reason Indigenous people vehemently fought to defend the devices.

The gold hidden in barbacoas explains why sixteenth-century Spanish soldiers searched for them and their habit of climbing on them while seeking treasure.[36] An example of that can be seen in how Ranjel rifled through the garments on dead caciques that were resting on barbacoas while searching for the treasure that adorned their corpses.[37] In addition to gold, barbacoas were also used to store maize and other foods that could provide sustenance for the conquistador's men. Regardless of whether the conquistador found food or gold, the barbacoa's contents were critical to his mission. An example of how conquistadors covertly searched for barbacoas is illustrated when conquistador Francisco Pizzaro (1478–1541) sent Jorge Robledo (1500–1546) on a mission in 1539 through what is today Colombia and Peru. Robledo reported that he found many barbacoas in the mountains.[38] Pizzaro wasn't interested in taking a road trip through the scenic route

BARBACOA, NATIVE AMERICAN FOOD DEHYDRATOR

The following passage from Oviedo about de Soto's expedition through what is today Georgia demonstrates the sixteenth-century Spanish use of the word barbacoa, "[B]ut first they dined on some hens of the land they call guanaxas and venison loins that they found roasted on a barbacoa, which is similar to a grill" (author's translation).[32] Notice the author didn't record that they found "barbacoa" or "barbacoa'd hens" and "barbacoa'd venison." They found food sitting on a barbacoa that had been roasted (*assado*). As previously discussed, the adjective roasted was used because there was no other Spanish word to adequately describe the way foods were preserved on barbacoas. Bourne's translation of the passage also bears that out. His use of the phrase "some strips of venison they found on a framework of sticks" indicates that the venison Spaniards found on a barbacoa was being dried to preserve it.

(continued from page 34)

to enjoy a barbecue sandwich in the mountains. The barbacoas were important to Pizzaro and his men because they knew that caciques stored treasure in them.

CHARQUI

The common assumption that sixteenth-century Spaniards used barbacoa as a noun and a verb like Americans use the word barbecue is incorrect. The word Spaniards used during the early modern period as a noun and a verb like English speakers use barbecue is *charqui* (pronounced "shark-ē"). Charqui was borrowed from *ch'arki*, which was spoken by the Quechua people in South America. A Quichua-Spanish dictionary published in 1560 defines the noun charqui as *tasajo*, which is dried meat. That dictionary defines *charquini* (also spelled *charquear*) as a verb that refers to the act of making charqui.[39]

The cattle that sixteenth-century Iberian settlers released in the Americas thrived and it was only a matter of time before entrepreneurs took advantage of the opportunity presented by hunting the animals for their hides and meat.[40] By the mid-sixteenth century, settlers in the Caribbean and South America found a profitable vocation

Driving Wild Cattle in Haiti. Buel, *Heroes of Unknown Seas and Savage Lands.*

feeding soldiers, sailors, and enslaved people with charqui. Because European sailors were fed with salted and dried pork and beef during their voyages to the Americas, they embraced meat that was preserved with techniques inspired by Native American and African practices.[41] Sixteenth-century Spanish missionary José de Acosta (1540–1600) wrote of Peruvian charqui: "[From] the flesh of these sheepe they make charqui, or dried flesh, the which will last very long, whereof they make great accompt."[42] Ship captains, including Francis Drake (1540–1596), sought out charqui because it remained edible for a long time and was relatively inexpensive.[43]

In South America, charqui was made by cutting beef into long, thin strips that were salted and allowed to brine for several hours. The excess moisture was drained from the meat before it was salted again and allowed to rest overnight. The most experienced charqui makers could take a chunk of beef and cut it into a single, long, thin ribbon in a way that made the beef appear to "unwind" much as is done when peeling an apple. After the meat was thoroughly saturated with salt, it was hung on hurdles in the sun for several days until it had sufficiently dried. No smoke or fire was involved in the process.[44]

The charqui business eventually became a significant industry in South America and the Caribbean. By the mid-nineteenth century, charqui was being defined as "dried meat prepared with salt that is exported." It and cowhides became two of South America's most important exports.[45] After slavery was abolished in the Caribbean and South America, demand for charqui diminished.[46]

Although men who participated in de Soto's North American expedition didn't barbecue hogs, they did salt and dry pork and horse meat using a typical European method. For example, on one occasion, they salted pork and preserved horse meat by parboiling it before leaving it in the sun to dry.[47] There is no mention of barbacoas in the process. Even though some English translations of the accounts of de Soto's expedition use *jerked* to describe the process his men used, the underlying text simply refers to drying the meat and doesn't include the words charqui or charquini. Hakluyt's 1609 translation states, "they made dried flesh of," which is a literal translation of the original text.[48]

The geographic distribution of the word charqui demonstrates how Spanish colonists established their "general language" in the Americas. For example, some Native Americans in the Caribbean and South America called their wooden grills *aribelet*.[49] However, Spaniards still referred to them as barbacoas. The critical point in all of this is, while the words we use today to refer to such things as tobacco, maize, jerky, and wooden hurdles came to North America from the Caribbean, the objects to which they refer did not. When English colonists arrived in Virginia in 1607, Native Americans there had been cultivating corn and tobacco and using wooden scaffolds/hurdles/grills for centuries. That emphasizes the fact that although the words barbacoa and barbecue may have originated in the Caribbean, it isn't evidence that southern barbecuing was born there.

BARBECUING IN LATIN AMERICA

People in different Latin American countries have different outdoor cooking terminology. Instead of words born in the Americas, such as barbacoa, people in Latin America often prefer European words such as parrilla (grill), asada (used in Mexico), asado (used in Argentina), and churrasco (used in Brazil).[50] The preference for referring to outdoor cooking with European words reveals an important point. Proponents of the COT connect the use of the word barbecue among English speakers to the Spanish word barbacoa and the Taíno people in sixteenth-century Haiti. Nonetheless if barbecuing was passed directly from Spanish speakers to English speakers sometime during the sixteenth or seventeenth centuries, it isn't unreasonable to expect Spanish speakers to prefer the word barbacoa just as English speakers prefer the word barbecue. However, that's not the case. That stems in part from the fact that "barbecuing" in Latin America exhibits far more European traits than the OSBT exhibits. Although people in the southern United States have used the words roasting or broiling since colonial times when discussing barbecuing, the word barbecue was almost always in the conversation. That's not true of the word barbacoa and outdoor cooking in Latin America. For example, in Argentina, an outdoor social event that features grilled foods is called either a *parrillada* or an asado. The grill on which the meats are cooked is called a parrilla. The Grill Master of the United States is called al Asador or Parrillero in Argentina. If the Parrillero is roasting whole carcasses vertically on an iron cross, they are called Asador Criollo (Creole Grill Master).[51]

People in Spain and in Latin America today occasionally use barbacoa to refer to outdoor social events, grilled meats, and grills used for cooking in much the same way as some in the United States today use barbecue. That has fostered the incorrect assumption that the definitions of the word barbecue we have today were brought over from the Spanish language. The fact of the matter is it was the other way around. The use of barbacoa as a verb was learned from how Americans use barbecue as a verb. Furthermore, the word barbiquiu (a distortion of barbecue) is preferred over the word barbacoa in several Latin American countries. It entered the Spanish language from the word barbecue as used in the United States.[52] Indeed, English speakers have contributed far more to how Spanish speakers today use the word barbacoa than Spanish speakers have contributed to how English speakers use the word barbecue. Some people in the Dominican Republic use the English word barbecue as a verb and the Spanish word parrilla as a noun to refer to the grill.[53] It's notable that people who live in the place that proponents of the COT claim gave us the word barbacoa (Haiti) prefer the American way of using the word barbecue as a verb while practically neglecting the noun barbacoa.

Before the twentieth century, the word barbacoa wasn't defined or equated with barbecue in Spanish dictionaries. For example, a Spanish–English dictionary published in London in 1800 reflects the typical British definition of the word barbecue and the word barbacoa is conspicuously absent. It defines barbecue as "puerco asado entero" (whole roast pig) and the phrase to barbecue as "asar un cochino entero" (to roast a whole pig). However, the definition given for the Spanish word barbacoa is, "[A] scaffold of any such like place, raised above the ground."[54] *Anglicismos en El Idioma Español de Madrid* (*Anglicisms in the Spanish Language of Madrid*) published in 1968

LATIN AMERICAN BARBECUE ORIGIN MYTHS

According to one Latin American legend, the parrilla was invented centuries ago in a small European kingdom after a wealthy nobleman hired a blacksmith to build an iron fence around his castle. After the fence was constructed, the blacksmith realized that he overestimated the amount of iron needed. After he informed his customer of the oversight, the nobleman refused to pay for the surplus iron. In revenge, the blacksmith decided to construct metal grills with the leftover iron on which he grilled meat day and night in front of the nobleman's castle. The smoke from the fires, along with the noise from the crowds, annoyed the nobleman. Eventually, the nobleman grew weary of the smoke wafting into his castle and choking his family. He finally ended the ordeal by paying the blacksmith in full. Following the blacksmith's lead, people have been cooking on grills since that time.

In Uruguay, the claim is made that the first modern barbacoa (defined with the American notion of a metal grill explicitly made for cooking) was created when thousands of political prisoners were released from jail in 1832. The revelers were fed with beef cooked on grills made from their jail cells' doors. People in Argentina disagree with that story, however. They credit Gauchos with inventing modern barbacoas in the mid-eighteenth century on which they grilled los asados (the roasts).[60]

(continued from page 38)

defines the English word barbecue as an outdoor social event, and the editors specifically reference southern barbecues hosted in Virginia.[55] No such definition of barbacoa is given. Twentieth-century philologist Tomás Buesa Oliver (1923–2004; referred to hereafter as Buesa), who specialized in the study of Spanish etymology, lexicography, and lexicology, stated that the use of barbacoa to refer to a grill used for cooking is an Anglicism that was adopted into Spanish from the way Americans define barbacoa and use it interchangeably with barbecue.[56] According to other scholars, the process of borrowing the American definitions of the words barbecue and barbacoa spread around Europe after the end of World War II.[57] Additionally, it's not widely believed among people in Latin America that the origins of their style of barbecuing are found in the Taíno people of Haiti.

In Mexico City, the phrase *carne asada* simply refers to grilled beef. However, in Sonora in Northwest Mexico, carne asada can be a noun that refers to grilled beef, a verb that refers to grilling beef, and a noun that refers to social events where grilled beef is served—similar to how Americans use the word barbecue.[58] Because Sonora shares borders with New Mexico and Arizona, it's not surprising that Americans have influenced language and culinary traditions there. Other American influences in Sonoran cuisine include macaroni salad and the Sonoran hot dog.[59]

PITMASTER VERSUS ASADOR

During the Original Southern Barbecuing Period (OSBP), barbecue was cooked on a grill set over a pit filled with live embers using the OSBT. In Latin America, there is no requirement for a pit to hold coals. Everything from small cuts of meat, sausages, sweetmeats, offal, and vegetables are grilled at relatively high temperatures, and meats are often cooked to a medium-rare or medium state of doneness. Furthermore the Asador Criollo doesn't cook a form of barbecue that resembles the OSBT. The Asador Criollo roasts whole carcasses beside a fire.

In addition to significant differences between barbecuing in Latin America and the South (what is today the southern United States), there are also significant differences in the meanings of words used to refer to barbecuing and outdoor cooking. Traditionally, events Americans call *backyard barbecues* are referred to by people in Latin America as parrillada, asado, asada, *fiesta*, or *jerra*. In Brazil, grilled skirt steak and the event where it's cooked and served outdoors is called churrasco.[61] Unfortunately, those words are sometimes translated into English as barbecue. This is a case where the translator's understanding of barbecuing is expressed more than the Spanish speaker's understanding. The lack of clarity that stems from ignoring cultural differences goes both ways. When the phrase *southern barbecued pork* is translated into Spanish as *cerdo a la parrilla del sur* (southern grilled pork) or *carne de cerdo asada al sur* (southern roast pork), the meaning is distorted. Southern barbecued pork is not merely roasted, nor is it grilled. The phrase *barbecue pit* can be translated into Spanish as *hoyo de la barbacoa*. However, that translation can give people in Mexico the impression that southern barbecued pork is slowly cooked in an earth oven. The way interpreters, dictionaries, and online translation services routinely translate Spanish words—such as asada, parrilla, and barbacoa—and Portuguese words—such as churrasco and jerra—into English as the word barbecue is unfortunate because it can convey the false notion that barbecuing in Latin America is similar to southern barbecuing in the United States.[62] That mistake lends undeserved credibility to the COT. When more precise language is used,

Asado a la cruz de cordero (lamb roasted on a cross). Notice how the meat is being roasted beside flames and there is no pit.

it becomes clear that southern barbecuing differs significantly from "barbecuing" as it's known in Latin America. Those differences are evidence that the OSBT wasn't imported from the Caribbean or Latin America.

MEXICAN BARBACOA

Mexico's barbacoa tradition has nothing to do with cooking on a barbacoa set over hot embers. Instead, Mexicans use the word barbacoa to refer to an earth oven and foods cooked in it. It can also refer to meat marinated with chili sauce and other condiments.

Although the word barbacoa was imported into Mexico from the Caribbean, the Mexican way of preparing barbacoa was not.[63] That's similar to how American colonials imported the word barbecue from the Caribbean, but not the OSBT.

In 1856 Edward Tylor travelled through Mexico to study its antiquities and people. In the account of his journey published in 1861, he described "a kid that had been cooked in a hole in the ground, with embers upon it, after the Sandwich Island [Hawaiian] fashion. This is called barbacoa—a barbecue."[64] *A New Pronouncing Dictionary of the Spanish and English Languages* published in New York in 1901 defines barbacoa only as a noun that means "meat roasted in a pit in the earth" and "[a] framework suspended from forked sticks."[65]

People all around the world have been known to cook in earth ovens.[66] People in Hawaii have been cooking kalua pig in earth ovens since before the English explorer Captain James Cook (1728–79) arrived there in 1778.[67] People in Jamaica used to "barbecue" pigs in earth ovens. The carcasses were placed on a "*frame of wicker work.*" Britons called both the wicker fame and the pig "a barbecue."[68] The wicker work provided a convenient way to remove the tender, fall-apart meat from the earth oven. A seventeenth-century French missionary in the Caribbean recorded detailed instructions for cooking a tortoise in an earth oven, a dish he called *boucan de tortuë* (buccaned tortoise). He also described how to cook a whole sheep carcass in an earth oven. He didn't refer to it as boucan, although he noticed that the cooking method was similar to the one used to cook buccaned tortoise.[69] The Māori people arrived at what is today Stewart Island in New Zealand from Polynesia in the thirteenth century. They call their version of the earth oven *hāngī*.[70] In southern Chile, the earth oven is called *curanto*. In Peru, it's called *pachamanca* and, sometimes, barbacoa.[71]

Some claim that the use of the word barbacoa in Mexico came from the Mayan *Baalbak-kaab*, which means "meat covered with earth."[78] If true, that would be a strong witness against the COT. However, a more plausible explanation for why people in Mexico adapted the noun barbacoa to their way of cooking foods in earth ovens stems from the frame of wicker work made of leaves or reeds that were weaved together and wrapped around meat before being placed in the earth oven. In Jamaica, Britons called the "frame of wicker work" a barbecue.[79] A frame of wicker work was also referred to as a barbacoa in South America.[80] Much like the chicken wire Hawaiians wrap around kalua pig at luaus, the wicker work helped prevent the cooked carcass from completely falling apart, thus making it easier to remove from the earth oven.

It's important to point out that barbacoa in Mexico doesn't refer to a form of cooking. Just as you can't "oven" foods, you can't "barbacoa" them. You bake in an oven

(continued on page 44)

EARTH OVENS AROUND THE WORLD

FIJI. In the early 1850s, the English missionary Thomas Williams (1815–91) visited the island of Fiji in the South Pacific. He described how Fijians cooked in earth ovens:

> The ovens, which are large holes or pits sunk in the ground, are sometimes eight or ten feet deep, and fifty feet in circumference; and in one of these several pigs and turtles and a large quantity of vegetables can be cooked. English roasters of an entire ox or sheep might learn some useful philosophy from the Fijian cook, whose method insures the thorough and equal baking of the whole carcass. The oven is filled with firewood, on which large stones are placed, and the fire introduced. As soon as the fuel is burnt out, the food is placed on the hot stones, some of which are put inside the animals to be cooked whole. A thick coat of leaves is now rapidly spread over all, and on these a layer of earth about four inches thick. When the steam penetrates this covering, it is time to remove the food.[72]

AFRICA AND AUSTRALIA. People in Africa and Australia are known to make earth ovens out of abandoned termite mounds. Australian Aborigines also cook foods buried in pits with hot rocks.[73] French Explorer François Le Vaillant (1753–1824) visited the Cape of Good Hope in 1780. While there he witnessed people cooking elephant meat in an earth oven.[74]

MEXICO. The Mexican cookbook *Diccionario de cocina; o, El nuevo cocinero mexicano en forma de diccionario*, published in 1845, includes many barbacoa recipes. One of them is for African Barbacoa that was possibly inspired by Vaillant. Translated, the recipe is as follows:

> A hole is dug large enough to contain the piece that is to be cooked. A great fire is kindled in it with very dry wood and after it has heated up, all the fire is removed. The meat with the skin still on is placed in the hole and covered with the hot embers. Another fire made with dry wood is kindled on top of the embers and maintained until the

(continued next page)

next morning when the cooked meat is removed. In this way people in Africa cook the horns and feet of elephants which is a very tasty treat.[75]

ALASKA. In 1903, ethnographic photographer George Thornton Emmons (1852–1945) observed Native Americans in Alaska cooking meat wrapped in leaves by burying it in an earth oven lined with hot coals. Heat was maintained in the hole all night long by a fire kindled above it.[76]

VIRGINIA. After colonists arrived in Virginia in 1607, they observed how Native Americans there cooked tuckahoe, a tuber that grows in the marshes around the Chesapeake Bay, and used it to make bread. They buried the tubers in a pit over which they built a large fire and cooked it for twenty-four hours.[77]

(continued from page 42)

and, in Mexico, you can bake in a barbacoa and grill foods on parrillas.[81] Furthermore Mexicans don't hold events called barbacoas. In Mexico, an event that features barbacoa is referred to as a *barbacoa fiesta* or a *barbacoa dinner*, and sometimes as a jerra. A nineteenth-century Mexican–Spanish dictionary demonstrates that the noun barbacoa didn't refer to an outdoor event or a cooking technique. It defines barbacoa as, "[A] very hot hole dug into the ground used to cook a young goat or other kind of meat or fish" (author's translation). The dictionary states, "Roasting in a barbacoa is widely done in country grocery stores and on days when families take the time to go out to the countryside to enjoy the outdoors" (author's translation).[82]

Based upon the claim that Spanish explorers embraced barbecuing, one would think that if any people in the world would have a way of barbecuing similar to the OSBT it would be people in Mexico. However, they don't. In the aforementioned *Diccionario de Cocina*, the following description is given of Mexican barbacoa:

> Among the many ways to cook meat invented by humans, none can compare to the way barbacoa is cooked. It doesn't require liquid, that might dilute its flavor, nor does it require a fire, that might dry up the juices, as fire never contacts the meat as it cooks, only steam from the heated earth. The barbacoa oven preserves all the meat's nutritional qualities while it becomes so perfectly cooked and tasty

> it whets the appetite and even the weakest stomach can easily digest it. There are several recipes for cooking barbacoa, but the essential ingredient is steam without the need of liquids nor close contact with fire.[83] (author's translation)

Notice the differences between cooking barbacoa in Mexico and the OSBT during the OSBP. Had de Soto and other conquistadors introduced a way of barbecuing that was similar to the OSBT, logically it would have been in New Spain, which is what Spaniards named their Mexican colony. However, they didn't introduce it in Mexico—or the South.

By the time Mexico won its independence from Spain in 1821, Mexican culture had been forged through three hundred years of Spanish, African, and Native American influences. Spaniards brought European livestock, salt, and their general language, which included the word barbacoa. The Maya people and enslaved people from Africa contributed their ways of cooking in earth ovens. Together, they created what we know today as Mexican barbacoa. That process demonstrates how the word barbacoa was applied to new foods that were independently created by creole societies.

SOUTH CAROLINA ORIGINATION THEORY

The South Carolina origination theory argues that barbecue (meaning barbecued pigs) was introduced to mainland North America first during the last half of the sixteenth century through a collaboration between Native Americans and Spaniards who occupied the Santa Elena colony in what today is South Carolina.[84] That theory relies on the hogs that Spaniards brought to Santa Elena. Because you can't have barbecue without pork, according to some, barbecue must have first originated after pigs were available. However, barbecue in the southern United States has always referred to "an ox or perhaps any other animal dressed in like manner" and is not confined to pork.[85] Because pork is not a requirement for southern barbecue everywhere in the South, hogs are not vital to southern barbecue's existence. Spain abandoned the Santa Elena colony in 1587, and none of that colony's hogs survived after the Spanish left.[86] If Santa Elena–style pork barbecue existed at all, it ceased to exist when the Spanish abandoned the settlement and, therefore, can't be the ancestor of southern barbecuing.

In 1801, the South Carolina politician Ralph Izard (1741–1804) wrote home to his mother while he was visiting Virginia and mentioned the barbecues hosted by Virginians: "In Virginia they have once a fortnight what they call a fish feast or Barbicue [*sic*] at which all the Gentry within twenty miles round are present with all their families."[87] Izard implied that barbecuing and hosting barbecues wasn't well known in

South Carolina in 1801. If southern-style barbecuing had been born in South Carolina, it's doubtful that more Virginians would know about it in 1801 than South Carolinians.

There is no compelling evidence in Oviedo et al. to support the claim that the OSBT originated with conquistadors, in the West Indies, or South Carolina. Southern barbecuing was created independently, just as several other barbecue styles found in the Americas were created. The fingerprints of creolization are all over Jamaican jerked pork, Argentine *asado con cuero*, and Mexican barbacoa, just as they are all over the OSBT. All of those cooking styles exhibit signs of cultural negotiation and the independent invention of something new. The common denominators shared by those cooking methods is not the word barbacoa or a unique Taíno cooking method. The common denominators are the enslaved Africans, Native Americans, and poor Europeans who served an elite class in the Americas while combining their cooking traditions to create a unique way of cooking that didn't exist before.

Slow-Cooker Barbacoa

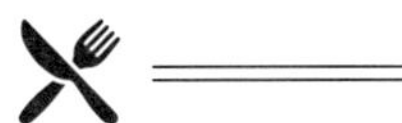

In Mexico, barbacoa is often cooked for special events such as celebrations and holidays. The best barbacoa is made with a labor-intensive process that includes slaughtering an animal, dressing its carcass, preparing the earth oven, and cooking the meat for many hours. For those days when you don't have the time to slaughter a steer, chop down a tree, gather large stones, and dig a three-foot deep and three-foot wide pit, here is a tasty recipe for a version of barbacoa that can be cooked in your home kitchen.

3- to 4-pound boneless chuck roast
1 or 2 chipotle peppers, chopped
1 cup water
1 (4 ounce) can chopped green chilis
½ large white onion, chopped
2 garlic cloves, chopped
1 to 2 tablespoon chili powder, to taste
1 to 2 tablespoons adobo sauce from the chipotle peppers, to taste
1 tablespoon reduced sodium beef base
1 tablespoon reduced sodium chicken base
1 tablespoon olive oil
1 tablespoon brown sugar
1 tablespoon apple cider vinegar
Juice of ½ lime
1 teaspoon sweet paprika
1 teaspoon onion powder
1 teaspoon dried Mexican oregano
1 teaspoon ground cumin
2 bay leaves
¼ teaspoon table salt, per pound of beef
black pepper and red pepper flakes, to taste

(continued on folloing page)

Cut the roast into 1- to 2-inch chunks. Add olive oil to a hot skillet and sear the beef until browned. Place the browned meat in a Dutch oven. Add the remaining ingredients (except for the vinegar and lime juice). Cook covered in a 350°F oven for 2 hours or until the meat is pull-tender.

Remove the bay leaves, add the lime juice and vinegar. Mix well with the meat and broth, cover and place back into the oven. Reheat for 10 to 15 minutes. Remove from the oven and adjust the seasoning to taste.

Serve with lettuce wraps, rolls, tortillas, or taco shells. Toppings can include anything you like, such as diced tomatoes, radish slices, guacamole, cheese, salsa, sour cream, diced white onion, and chopped cilantro. This recipe can also be cooked for 6 to 7 hours in a Crock-Pot set on low or for about 35 to 45 minutes in a pressure cooker.

TWO

HERBERT'S PATTA

The Birth of Jamaican Jerk

When the mass media discusses the history of Jamaican jerked chicken, the narrative invariably goes back to Jamaican Maroons and their jerked pork. That creates the mistaken assumption among some that barbecue traditions in the United States were also influenced by Jamaican jerk and might even have been imported from that island. This chapter presents a history of Jamaican jerk how it has changed over the centuries.

JAMAICAN MAROONS

In 1509, Spain established its first colony in Jamaica. As early as 1517, enslaved people from western Africa were brought to the island. Some were able to escape to freedom by hiding in the remote mountains where they, with Indigenous people who also escaped slavery, formed communities. Spaniards continued to dominate the island until the English admiral Sir William Penn (1621–70) forcibly took it from them in 1655. After that event more enslaved people were freed, and others escaped to take refuge among the communities in the mountains. Anglos referred to the people in those communities as Maroons, using a word derived from the Spanish *cimarron*, which means *living on the peaks*, presumably because Jamaican Maroons lived in mountainous areas. The word was also used to refer to wild animals.[1] The popularity of charqui among sailors created a business opportunity for Jamaican Maroons, who, sometime in the sixteenth century, started hunting the wild pigs that lived in Jamaica's mountains to make pork jerky for trade in villages and seaports. Anglos also referred to Maroons as hog hunters, which is a term they used to refer to just about all groups who made their living hunting feral pigs.[2]

By the end of the sixteenth century, most of Jamaica's population resided in the island's southern region. Yet Maroons found a thriving market for their jerked pork and cowhides on Jamaica's northern coast that was, as one Spaniard put it, "infested with illegal traders." Those "illegal traders" included English, Dutch, and French pirates who often raided Spanish ships.[3] An account of Jamaica written in 1611 by the island's Spanish Abbot offers the following details of how people there hunted and cured meats and hides, "Nearly the whole year is taken up in killing cows and bulls only to get the hides and fat, leaving the meat wasted. There are also large herds of swine raised in the mountains, which are common to all who may wish to hunt them as is ordinarily done, obtaining therefrom a great quantity of lard and jerked pork."[4]

By the middle of the sixteenth century, the practice of salting and drying meat was widespread in the Americas. Although buccaneers (French hunters in Tortuga and Hispaniola who made their living trading hides and smoked-dried meat, discussed in detail in Chapter 3, "Jean-Baptiste's Boucan") and Maroons get all of the press for their way of curing and trading cured meats, several other groups also engaged in that form of commerce.

HOW JAMAICAN MAROONS JERKED PORK

For obvious reasons, Jamaica's ruling class's language changed from Spanish to English in 1655 after Jamaica came under the rule of the king of England. Presumably, that's when Jamaicans started to shift terminology away from the Spanish charqui to the English *jerk*. Unfortunately, seventeenth-century Anglo's barbecue terminology was anything but clear and precise. Although Anglos called wooden grills "barbecues" and a pig cooked in an earth oven "a barbecue," Maroons of the early modern period didn't.[6] To this day, the word barbecue in Jamaica refers to concrete or stone slabs on which coffee and spices are dried.[7] Moreover as far back as 1750, bridges on Jamaican plantations were called "barbecue bridges."[8] That's similar to how Spaniards referred to bridges in South America using the noun *barbacoas*.

FIRSTHAND ACCOUNTS OF JERKING PORK

Herbert Theodore Thomas (1856–1930) was a Jamaican-born police inspector, lecturer, naturalist, and explorer, and was the first person known to have crossed the John Crow Mountains. Thomas's accounts of jerked pork in Jamaica are relatively straightforward

"INNUMERABLE" WILD HOGS

English explorer Captain John Poyntz (1606–?) described the vast number of wild hogs and the thriving Caribbean pork jerky industry in the seventeenth century:

> And now we present you with the Classes of Flesh, give me leave therefore in the first place to begin with the Wild-Hogg, of which sort of cattle their numbers are innumerable; when yearly the people cut off at least twenty thousand, and yet they increase so prodigiously fast, that neither Gun, nor Engin [weapon], nor any other Artifice can be found to destroy them. It's truth beyond suspition [suspicion], that the Barbadians kill some of them, but the rest of the Caribes [unfriendly Native Americans] and others are daily visitants; who to save it for their own accommodation, commonly Jerk, and dry salt it in the Sun, or in Bulk or Pickle.[5]

(continued from page 50)

because of his clear and precise language. For that reason, they provide a baseline for understanding the process of making jerked pork and for clearly understanding earlier written accounts of making jerked pork. The following is Thomas's firsthand account published in 1890 that described how pork was jerked in Jamaica:

> On arriving at our Barracks at 3:30 the men set to work at once to prepare for "jerking" the pigs. Outside the hut they constructed a gridiron of green sticks about two feet from the ground. This is called about the Blue Mountain Valley a "patta," while among the Maroons, and in the Cuna-Cuna district it is known as a "caban"—a word that has a distinctly Spanish flavour. Underneath this a fire is kindled, into which the carcase [*sic*] is first thrust in order to singe the hair, which is then easily scraped off with a knife. This done, the animal is disembowelled [*sic*], split open down the back, the bones extracted, and the carcase laid skin downwards upon the sticks and subjected to a slow grilling during which it is plentifully sprinkled with black pepper and salt. This process lasts from six to eight or nine hours, according to the size of the animal. The adding of pimento

Drying coffee on a barbecue in Jamaica. By H. C. White Co., ca. 1904. Library of Congress.

> leaves, or those of the pepper elder to the fire imparts an improved flavour to the meat, which, when properly done, is as gamey and toothsome a dish as a hungry man can desire. We had wild pig chops, fresh, for dinner that night, and jerked the greater portion of the two animals for the next day, the dogs receiving their reward in the shape of the offal.[9]

According to Thomas, the hunters ate the best parts of the hog for dinner, thus indicating that some of the meat was eaten before it became pull tender or dried. The rest of the carcass remained on the wooden grill and was jerked "for the next day." Thomas provided a second account of the process in 1927 in which he makes it clear that the jerked meat was dried and smoked:

> The favourite occupation of the Maroons was the hunting of the wild hogs with which the mountains abounded, and the flesh of which they sold in the markets after curing it by a process which they call, 'jerking.' The so-called Maroons of the present day prepare and sell the flesh of the wild hog just in the same way. After being killed, the animal is cleaned and cut longitudinally into two halves, the hair being removed by singeing. The halves of the carcase are then laid with the skin-side downwards upon a gridiron made of sticks over a slow fire, which

> slowly grills or dries it. During this process the meat is sprinkled with salt and pepper; and the placing of the aromatic leaves of the pimento tree, or the pepper elder, upon the fire greatly improves the flavour of the meat ; which, when properly done, is exceedingly gamey and toothsome.[10]

Notice the significant differences between the Original Southern Barbecuing Technique (OSBT) and the way Maroons jerked pork. Maroons burned the hair off pig carcasses before splitting them in half lengthwise and removing the bones. The offal was given to the dogs. The two halves of the deboned carcasses were then placed on "a gridiron of green sticks" raised about two feet from the ground and seasoned with salt and black pepper. Rather than using pimento and pepper elder as a seasoning on the pork, the cooks put the herbs and spices into the fire to create aromatic smoke that flavored the pork as it was broiled, dried, and smoked for as long as nine hours. Another account of Maroons' jerked pork describes the seasonings that included bird peppers and wild cinnamon.[11] Notably Thomas, a native-born Jamaican, didn't use the word barbecue to describe the patta, the jerked pork, or the process of making jerked pork. Neither did Maroons refer to their wooden hurdles made "of green sticks" as barbecues. Instead, according to Thomas, they had their own names for the wooden hurdles, patta in the Blue Mountain Valley or caban in the Cuna-Cuna district.[12]

The English mathematician John Taylor (1664–?) spent several months in Jamaica in 1687. His description of how Jamaican hunters killed as many as thirty hogs in a single day and jerked the meat is remarkably similar to what Thomas described over two hundred years later. Taylor wrote: "Now the hunters having kil'd their game, saveth only the two sides, giving the doges the rest. These sides they sindge the hair off from, and then bone them, and after they have slash't them here and there with their knives they put some little salt theron, after which with smoke they dry it on a barbaque (as we doe red herrings in Europe), and afterward pack it up in cabbage leaves, and this they call jerck't hog, which proveth excellent food, will keep long and yeildeth a good price at Port Royall."[13]

Clearly Maroons didn't jerk whole hogs using a cooking method that's similar to the OSBT. Both Thomas and Taylor mentioned the use of salt and the offal that was given to the hunting dogs. They both noted how the hair was singed off the split and deboned carcasses. Conspicuously, Taylor didn't use either of the Jamaican words caban or patta to refer to the wooden hurdle on which the pork was cured. Instead he used the word that was most familiar to his readers in Europe, which was *barbaque*. That's reminiscent of how sixteenth-century Spaniards used barbacoa among societies that didn't have the word in their vocabularies. Although Britons used the word barbecue when describing several ways that foods were cooked or preserved in the Americas, it's not proof that the people they observed used the word.

There are several notable eighteenth-century accounts of Jamaican *jerked hog*, and not all of them agree on the facts of how it was done. Hans Sloane (1660–1753) was an Irish physician and naturalist who lived in Jamaica from 1687 to 1689. In 1707, a record of his experiences in Jamaica was published in which he included the following account of how Jamaicans jerked pork, "[The hog is] cut open, the Bones taken out, and the flesh is gash'd on the inside into the Skin, fill'd with Salt and expos'd to the Sun, which is call'd Jirking [*sic*]. It is so brought home to their Masters by the Hunters, and eats much as Bacon, if broil'd on Coals."[14] Although similar in some respects to the method used to jerk pork described by Thomas and Taylor, Sloane's account neglected to include the step of broiling and smoking the meat. The absence of broiling and smoking implies that Sloane was describing air-dried pork rather than jerked pork.

On at least one occasion during the First Maroon War during the 1730s, British soldiers reported finding "jerked hog still broiling upon the coals" left behind by Maroons who fled from them into the densely wooded mountains.[15] Such accounts support the assertion that the Maroon process for jerking pork using heat and smoke was different than the process for making charqui, which was typically salted and dried in the air. In 1760, an account of how people in Santo Domingo (the Dominican Republic) "jerked" pork stated, "[They] shoot beeves [cattle] for their hides; and the Pork they strip the Flesh from the Bones, and jerk it as in Jamaica."[16] Does "strip the Flesh from the Bones" mean they deboned the carcasses or does it mean they cut the flesh away from the bones in strips? It's hard to say. Of course, as is the case in other accounts, the author may not have bothered to learn the details. That's the case in an 1839 account published in a British periodical that reported, "'Jerked hog' is the name given to the flesh of the wild hog prepared by the maroons; the process of curing I know not, but this I know, that it is most excellent eating, neither salt nor hard, but tender, juicy, and of a smoky, peculiar flavor."[17] At any rate old accounts of how Maroons' jerked pork make it clear that smoke was a vital part of the process. In 1790 the Jamaican-born Anglo William Beckford of Somerley (1744–99) recorded, "The negroes smoak and dry this animal, from whence the pieces thus smoaked, obtain the appellation of jirked [*sic*] hog; and it is, when thus cured, a very savoury and a pleasing relish."[18] That description indicates that Jamaican jerk was still made the same way in 1790 as it was in 1690.

As early as 1803, the Jamaican-born poet Robert Charles Dallas (1754–1824) observed Maroons using aromatic herbs and spices to create smoke and wrote, "The men cure as much of the flesh as they think they will have occasion for, by scoring it internally to the skin, sprinkling it with salt, and smoking it; over the smoke they throw some aromatic leaves, which not only add flavor, but assist in preserving it. The meat thus cured will keep for months, and is esteemed a very great dainty by the most refined Epicures. It is in fact the jirked [*sic*] hog."[19]

EMBELLISHED ACCOUNTS OF JERKING PORK

In addition to an imprecise use of language, some accounts of Jamaican jerk are clearly not based upon firsthand knowledge. For example, in 1864 the Irish-born American novelist Thomas Mayne Reid (1818–83) called the flat slabs on which berries and spices were dried in Jamaica barbacoas while referring to wild boar meat that had been jerked and put up for sale as "barbecued flesh." Reid wrote, "We Maroons have no other way of raising money, except by hunting the wild hogs, and selling their barbecued flesh . . . Well, that to begin with—the white gentry are rather partial to our barbecued hog!"[20] There is no evidence that Reid ever visited Jamaica. Therefore his writing reflects the way people in nineteenth-century United States used the word barbecue to refer to smoke-dried meats, but not how Jamaicans used the word.

All too often eighteenth- and nineteenth-century authors simply recycled something previously written about barbecuing regardless of its credibility. Some even repeated questionable descriptions of "barbecuing" as their own eyewitness account. That practice introduces an additional layer of complexity to the study of the history of barbecuing. For example, Scotsman Sir Sibbald David Scott (1814–85) visited Jamaica in 1874. His account was published in *To Jamaica and Back* in 1876, which includes the following about the word barbecue:

> Barbecue is, I find, a term used in the West Indies for dressing a hog whole, by splitting it to the backbone and laying it upon a large gridiron, raised about two feet above a charcoal fire, with which it is also surrounded. This may be described as "going the whole hog." Hence it may have come to be applied to anything spread out to be dried or cured by the action of heat. I cannot discover the derivation of the word, but the process may be derived from the Maroons, who were ardent hunters of wild boars; and it was probably a primitive manner of dressing pork al fresco; it appears, moreover, to have been a successful one.[21]

Because Scott was writing about his experiences in Jamaica, it's easy for his readers to assume that he was describing what he learned about barbecuing by watching Jamaicans. Unfortunately, he wasn't. He also seemed to be unaware that barbecuing was also a tradition in the United States. It turns out Scott lifted the definition of the word barbecue almost word for word from Samuel Johnson's (1709–84) *A Dictionary of the English Language* published in London in 1773. That dictionary defines barbecue as, "A term used in the West-Indies for dressing a hog whole; which, being split to the backbone, is laid flat upon a large gridiron, raised about two foot above a charcoal fire, with which it is surrounded."[22] Johnson took his "West-Indies" assertion from eighteenth-century English satirist Edward Ward (as discussed in Chapter 8, "Ned's Barbacue"). The rest of the dictionary's entry about barbecuing came from British cookbooks, such as *The Compleat City and Country Cook* published in 1736, which states in its A Hog Barbicued whole, and grill'd recipe, "[Y]our Gridiron must be two Foot high, and your Charcoal spread the Breadth of your iron Frame."[23]

Scott's account of barbecuing in Jamaica is an embellishment based on information he found in questionable sources. That fact reduces the value of Johnson's account as an authoritative source for barbecuing history in Jamaica. Scott's statement that barbecue "may have come to be applied to anything spread out to be dried or cured by the action of heat" seems to be his way of trying to reconcile the dried and cured Jamaican jerked pork that he may have eaten in Jamaica, with what he read about barbecuing in Johnson's dictionary and cookbooks. Cleary Johnson and several other eighteenth-century British lexicographers knew very little about how barbecuing was done outside of Britain.

JAMAICAN BARBECUED HOG

In 1835, the Jamaican plantation owner Bernard Martin Senior (ca. 1788–ca. 1860) anonymously authored *Jamaica, as it Was, as it Is, and as it May Be.* In his detailed account of hunting wild boars in Jamaica he commented, "The flesh is uncommonly fine; and, when *barbicued,* is considered dainty food."[24] It's difficult to determine if Senior was praising smoke-dried pork or pork cooked in an earth oven. However, because he used the word "dainty" to describe it, he may have had Robert Charles Dallas's 1803 account of smoke-dried pork in mind. As previously discussed, until the twentieth century Maroons had two ways of jerking pork: One was a broiling, drying, and smoking method that employed a wooden grill and the other was cooking it in an earth oven. Anglo observers sometimes referred to both of those cooking methods as barbecuing. However, some who witnessed it referred to pork cured on wooden grills as being jerked hog, while pork cooked in an earth oven was referred to as being barbecued.

Maria Nugent (1771–1834), the daughter of a prominent New Jersey loyalist, left the United States for England soon after the end of the American War of Independence and lived in Jamaica from 1801 to 1805 while her husband, Sir George Nugent

(1757–1849), served there as governor-general. In her journal, Nugent wrote about formal dinners in Jamaica and made a distinction between Jamaican barbecued hog and Jamaican jerked hog. She wrote, "A long table was spread on the green, with all their most favourite dishes, of barbecued hog, jerked hog, pepper-pot, yams, plantains, etc." In another passage, she mentioned, "jerked hog . . . which is the way of dressing it by the Maroons."[25] Based on Nugent's firsthand account, barbecued hog and jerked hog were two different foods, but she offered no details of the differences.

Briton Matthew "Monk" Lewis (1775–1818) recorded the details regarding Jamaican barbecued hog in is his eyewitness account written in 1817: "It was dressed in the true Maroon fashion, being placed on a barbecue, or frame of wicker work, through whose interstices the steam can ascend,—filled with peppers and spices of the highest flavour, wrapped in plantain leaves, and then buried in a hole filled with hot stones, by whose vapour it is baked; no particle of the juice being thus suffered to evaporate."[26] Lewis, who owned a plantation in Jamaica, didn't use the Maroon terminology jerked pork in his account.[27] Like other Britons, he referred to cooking pork in earth ovens as barbecuing. Lewis's "barbecue" was a platform of wicker work used to support the pork and make it easier to remove from the earth oven.

Apparently Maria Nugent's jerked pork was salted, broiled, smoked, and dried. The "barbecued" pork she enjoyed was cooked in an earth oven, not over an open pit as was done with the OSBT. Lewis's statement that pork cooked in an earth oven that was "dressed in true Maroon fashion" also sheds light on a passage written by an eighteenth-century British bookkeeper J. B. Moreton who lived in Jamaica. He wrote, "I have sometimes shot a fat cattle of this kind [wild cattle], and frequently wild hogs; the latter are excellent when barbacued maroon fashion."[28] In this case, when taking Lewis's account of barbecuing in Jamaica, Moreton's reference to "barbecued maroon fashion" was describing pork cooked in an earth oven.

The Jamaican-born historian Edward Long (1734–1813) left us this murky account of Jamaican jerk: "The fame of our Jamaican barbecue and brawn is so well established, that it would serve no purpose to reiterate their praises, except to tantalize the reader."[29] According to other writers—such as Monk Lewis, John Bradbury, and Maria Nugent—it's clear that Long's "Jamaican barbecue" was a pig cooked in an earth oven. Because Long defined the term to jerk as "To salt meat, and smoak-dry it," it's clear that he wasn't using the word barbecue to refer to jerked pork. Long referred to jerk as *brawn*, which was a reference to pork that had been smoked and dried. More clarity is provided by the English author William Walton (1784–1857), who wrote in 1810 about the flesh of wild hogs in Argentina that was "jerked with salt" and smoked to "form a kind of brawn."[30] When Walton described jerked pork as "a kind of brawn," he was indicating that it was a preserved product. Therefore Long's "Jamaican barbecue" refers to a whole pig cooked in an earth oven. His Jamaican brawn is jerked pork cured on a patta or caban.

The "long resident in the West Indies" John Stewart (d. 1832) was a planter in Jamaica. In his firsthand account he defined what he meant by the phrase "a barbecue":

> Hunting the wild boar was a favourite diversion both of the hardy active white creole of the interior and of the Maroons. It is not now so often practised these animals having retired into the remote recesses of the woods where it is difficult to come up with them: so that when their [wild pig's] flesh is desired for what is called a barbecue (considered as a great delicacy here, being the hog's flesh smoked with a certain odoriferous wood, which communicates to it a peculiar flavour).[31]

When reading Stewart's account, the urge to interpret it in light of modern definitions of the words barbecue and smoked must be resisted. He didn't use "smoked" like people in Texas do today to refer to meat that's been cooked in a smoke roaster. He was describing jerked hog, which would be known today as smoked-pork jerky. Stewart's reference of "a barbecue" is a wild boar's carcass (the "hog's flesh") that was dried and smoked," which is "a great delicacy."

MAROONS VERSUS HOG HUNTERS AND BUCCANEERS

Some scholars believe Jamaican Maroons were inspired to make their jerked pork by French hunters in Tortuga and Hispaniola (known as buccaneers) who made their living trading hides from feral livestock, discussed in detail in Chapter 3, "Jean-Baptiste's Boucan."[32] However, it appears that Maroons were trading their jerked pork to people in local villages and passing sailors long before buccaneers got into the business. For example, before the first buccaneer settled in Tortuga, charqui was being made in Iberian-dominated colonies at least by the 1560s, which is earlier than extant accounts of buccaneers.[33] Jerked hog appears to be the Maroons' original contribution to the market.

Although the way sixteenth- and seventeenth-century Maroons hunted animals and cured their hides and flesh was similar in some ways to how hog hunters (people in the Caribbean who hunted feral livestock to make hides and dried meat for trade) and, presumably, buccaneers did those things, there were some significant differences. For example, the buccaneer word boucan was used to refer to wooden grills and huts, but the Maroon word for the devices is patta.[34] Maroons, hog hunters, and buccaneers used salt in their recipes. The hog-hunter process included skinning the pig carcasses and cutting the flesh into strips, which is much like the method that was used by many groups in Santo Domingo.[35] One firsthand account describes how hog hunters smoked meat on boucans that were placed inside sealed huts. Another report claims that buccaneers burned pigskin in the smoking fire to give "a peculiar relish to the meat."[36] All that being said, the fact that the most credible sources describe buccaneers as cow killers instead of hog hunters (see Chapter 3, "Jean-Baptiste's Boucan"), strongly argue that buccaneers didn't actually trade buccaned pork.

In contrast to how hog hunters smoke-dried pork, Maroons didn't skin the pig carcasses. Instead they removed the bones from pig carcasses after they had burned off the hair in a fire and split them in half lengthwise. They placed the deboned pig carcass halves on wooden hurdles they called patta or caban after they scored the flesh side with a knife, which made it easier for the salt to penetrate the meat. Instead of using pigskins in the smoking fire like others, Maroons burned spices and herbs to add flavor to the jerked pork. People in Venezuela had a way of jerking pork that shared elements of both the Maroon and hog hunter methods. They cut pork into strips like hog hunters. However, instead of using the pig's skin in the smoking fire, they burned citrus leaves to impart flavor, similar to how Maroons used pimento and pepper elder leaves.[37]

THE AFRICAN CONNECTION

Although smoke-dried meats were made all over the Americas during the early modern period, Maroons in Jamaica stand out because of their unique way of hunting, broiling, drying, and smoking wild pork in a single operation and their way of cooking pigs in earth ovens. Like so many other foods in the Western Hemisphere, the original version of Jamaican jerked pork was created through the process of creolization. When enslaved people of African and Native American descent and poor Europeans were brought to Jamaica in the sixteenth century to serve there, the early generations of people born to them blended their cultures in a way that created a new culture and new cooking traditions. Europeans were familiar with salted and smoked meats, and people in England were known to occasionally singe the hair off hog carcasses before roasting them. Of course, Indigenous people in the Americas cured meats by drying and smoking them on hurdles, cooking foods in earth ovens, and burning hair off carcasses before they were cooked. The enslaved people who were brought to Jamaica from West Africa had similar techniques for curing meats on hurdles, cooking in earth ovens; and, they may have also observed the practice of using fire to burn the hair off of carcasses.[38]

People in sixteenth- and seventeenth-century Africa may have had a tradition of selling smoked-dried meat and fish they cured "on stages over slow fires" in a single

(continued on page 61)

OTHER AFRICAN COOKING TECHNIQUES

The Scottish physician and missionary David Livingstone (1813–73) witnessed people in central Africa who "came to sell the dried [elephant] meat." He wrote, "His people bring sanjika, the best Lake fish, for sale; they are dried on stages over slow fires." In another passage, he documented, "This custom of drying fish, flesh, and fruits, on stages over slow fires, is practiced very generally: the use of salt for preservation is unknown." He also recorded how Africans used "stages" for beds much like the "Borbecu's" mentioned by English Sea Captain William Dampier (1652–1715) and how Native Americans slept on hurdles set over smoky fires.[41] He wrote, "Besides stages for drying, the Makonde use them about six feet high for sleeping on instead of the damp ground: a fire beneath helps keep off mosquitos, and they are used by day as convenient resting places and for observation."[42]

The British explorer Richard Francis Burton (1821–90) investigated regions around the Great Lakes of East Africa from 1856 to 1860 in search of the source of the Nile. While there he kept detailed notes on the customs and languages of the people he encountered. Like Livingstone, he witnessed Africans drying meats on wooden platforms set over live embers. Commenting on how people in central Africa preserved meats on what today would be recognized as a wooden barbecue grill, he wrote:

> One of the inducements for an African to travel is to afford himself more meat than at home. His fondness for the article conquers at times even his habitual improvidence. He preserves it by placing large lumps upon a little platform of green reeds, erected upon uprights about eighteen inches high, and by smoking it with a slow fire. Thus prepared, and with the addition of a little salt, the provision will last for several days, and the porters will not object to increase their loads by three or four pounds of the article, disposed upon a long stick like gigantic kababs.[43]

The French explorer Georges Révoil (1853–94) also visited the region around the Great Lakes of East Africa, though in 1886. There he witnessed men making what he called "viande boucanée" that their wives sold in the surrounding villages. Although Révoil used the adjective *boucanée* to refer to the smoke-dried meats and the verb *boucanent* (*boucaner*) to refer to the process of smoking and drying them, he didn't record whether or not there was an African name for the process or the food. He wrote, "To preserve the meats they want to sell, they buccan [boucanent] it and carry it from village to village offering it for sale. Boucanage is, as our readers know, the process of drying long, thin strips of meat on racks using the smoke of great fires" (author's translation).[44] Although Révoil referred to the African way of making jerky using the verb boucaner, it shouldn't be assumed that it was learned from buccaneers or that Africans called the cured meat viande boucanée.

(continued from page 59)

operation similar to how it was done in the Americas.[39] Firsthand accounts of such practices in eastern, central, southern, and western Africa go back to at least the eighteenth century and archeological evidence dates back to the Ice Age. For example, after exploring the upper Niger River in 1796, the Scottish explorer Mungo Park (1771–1806) wrote about people there who were "[R]oasting a great quantity of flesh on temporary wooden stages erected for the purpose." He continued, "This half roasting and smoaking [*sic*] makes the meat keep much longer than it would do without it."[40] Such accounts might be further evidence that Maroon jerked pork and the way it was used for trade was not inspired by *boucanage*.

Both Native Americans and Africans cooked meats in earth ovens. During his travels through Africa, Livingstone recorded, "[O]vens are made in anthills. Holes are dug in the ground for baking the heads of large game."[45] The English explorer Samuel W. Baker (1821–93) and others who visited Africa mentioned the earth ovens used there, and one observed how Africans cooked elephants' feet, "[T]roughout all regions from the Nile to the Zambesi—that is, by burying them in a hole previously heated, like an oven, with hot rocks and stones."[46]

Livingstone, Burton, and Révoil (see box, "Other African Cooking Techniques") provide evidence that people in Africa used scaffolds to dry and cure meats in much the same way as people in the Americas. However, there is evidence that those preservation and cooking techniques were practiced in several other regions, including western Africa. In her firsthand account of West Africa, the English explorer Mary H. Kingsley (1862–1900) mentioned how people there either dried fish in smoke, boiled it, or cooked it underground in buried pits. They also wrapped fish in leaves and "buried them in hot embers," which is a cooking technique Reverend John Clayton (1657–1725) of Virginia called "barbecuting" in 1687.[47]

Dried fish is still an important food in West Africa. For example, a significant portion of the population of Nigeria in West Africa still preserve foods by drying them in the sun.[48] Of course, smoking and drying fish is important in Africa just as it is in Jamaica because it will spoil quickly in hot climates.[49] Although Livingstone's, Burton's, and Kingsley's accounts of Africans drying meat and fish in smoke were recorded in the nineteenth century, its plausible that they bear witnesses to an ancient African meat and fish curing practice that's similar to that used by Maroons and hog hunters.

Archeological evidence suggests that hunters in eastern Africa removed bones from game carcasses before curing the meat on hurdles as long ago as the Ice Age. After the hunters returned home from the successful hunt, the meat was cut into strips or sheets, and the bones were cooked for their marrow. Some of the meat was roasted and consumed. The rest was dried to preserve it for later consumption or trade, similar to Herbert Thomas's description of the Maroon practice.[50] Ethnographic analogy strongly supports the notion that similar practices also existed in West Africa.[51]

Additional evidence of West African influence on Jamaican jerk is found in the word patta used by Maroons who lived in the Blue Mountain Valley. In Jamaica's creole language, patta refers to things such as the wooden grills on which pork is jerked, huts, tables, baskets, and beds much like Spanish speakers used barbacoa and English speakers used the word barbecue. Patta (sometimes spelled *patá* or *pada*) is derived from the language spoken by the Akan people of Ghana and the Ivory Coast in West Africa. There the word was used to refer to beds used by kings and wooden frames used to dry foods. The use of patta among people in western Africa is strong evidence that people there had a tradition of drying meat and fish on wooden hurdles.[52]

MODERN JAMAICAN JERK

The American author and anthropologist Zora Neale Hurston (1891–1960) visited Jamaica in the late 1930s. She wrote about Maroons in the village of Accompong and described how they hunted wild hogs and jerked their flesh. After a successful hunt, the hunters started a fire in which they singed the pig's carcass to make it easier to remove the hair. The hunters discarded the offal, which she called *the fifth quarter*. All bones were removed from the carcass. The deboned boar's carcass was then "seasoned with salt, pepper, and spices and put over the fire to cook." The hunters cooked the pork all night while occasionally turning it over to prevent it from scorching. After the pork

Jamaican-style jerked chicken with fried plantains. Photo by the author.

was finished cooking, everyone enjoyed a hearty meal of "jerked pork." In this case, the pork wasn't dried or preserved. It was broiled, and there is no indication that it was pull-tender as is the case with southern-style barbecue. After the meal, the meat and bones were "packed up" and taken to the village to share with family and friends. Hurston commented, the hunters "never sell it because they say they hunt for fun."[53]

Hurston's account of Jamaicans jerking pork is strikingly similar to Herbert Thomas's accounts published in 1890 and 1927, though with notable exceptions. Thomas stated that as late as 1927, jerked hog was a preserved pork product and that it provided an essential income source for hunters: "A great number of the men still follow their favourite pursuit of hog-hunting and selling the 'jerked' meat in the markets of the different towns," just as their ancestors had done as far back as the sixteenth century.[54] Hurston's account, which was published eleven years after Thomas's, implies that the jerked pork wasn't cooked and smoked long enough to preserve it. Instead, it was merely "cooked." Unlike in earlier times, the hunters in Hurston's account didn't sell the jerked pork.

By the end of the nineteenth century, demand for jerked meats was diminishing. Several factors were involved, including competition from bacon imported from the

An advertisement promoting tourism in Jamaica, ca. 1910.

United States and the abolition of slavery in the Caribbean and South America. This is apparently because enslavers were no longer buying jerked meats to feed the people they enslaved.[55] Although demand for Jamaican jerked pork declined, Hurston reported that people still hunted wild hogs "for fun" and made jerked pork for home use.

By the end of the 1950s, Jamaican jerked meats had changed with the times. Over the last few decades of the twentieth century, the modern version of Jamaican jerk became famous all over the world. Many modern recipes for Jamaican-style jerked chicken and pork call for the application of a paste made with ingredients such as onions, allspice, aromatic herbs and spices, scotch bonnet peppers, and salt. The paste is applied to the meat and allowed to marinate for several hours. Jerked chicken is cooked in kettle grills. Deboned pork carcasses are often cooked on large covered grates made with pimento wood. Unlike southern barbecue, the finished pork product—though delicious—is not required to be pull-tender.

Government officials in Jamaica began developing a tourism industry in the 1890s. However, the lack of adequate infrastructure, services, and the fact that most visitors had to arrive by sea hindered its growth. Of course, the first forty-five years of the twentieth century wasn't a good time to start a tourism industry because of World War I, the Spanish flu epidemic, the Great Depression, and World War II. Only after the end of World War II would Jamaica's tourism industry finally be in a position to thrive.

The modern version of Jamaican jerk is a product of the twentieth century. It took hold after World War II ended when Americans chose Jamaica as a favorite vacation destination. By the 1950s, eight international airlines were serving the island. That resulted in an unprecedented growth in the number of tourists. By the end of the 1960s, as many as 400,000 tourists—many of them Americans—visited the island each year.[56] With money to spend, the thousands of Americans also brought their definitions for the word barbecue, which included cooking just about anything outside, and they wanted something more to eat than pork jerky. That fueled the development of modern versions of Jamaican jerk.

According to firsthand accounts, before the 1970s the scarcity of indoor kitchens in Jamaica made year-round outdoor cooking necessary for a large portion of the population. In those days, Jamaicans referred to the act of cooking meats outside as roasting. During the late 1950s, the use of the word barbecue among Jamaicans grew after American influence entered Jamaican culture.[57] As previously discussed, by the 1950s events called "backyard barbecues" were growing in popularity in the United States to the point that "barbecuers" were "popping out like daisies" in backyards all over the country. Consequently many Americans were being convinced that any kind of cooking outdoors was a form of barbecuing.[58] Therefore when American tourists started visiting the island in the 1950s and 1960s and witnessed families and food vendors cooking outdoors, they associated it with barbecuing. As a result, people in Jamaica started to refer to roasting and grilling foods in a way that's similar to how Americans cook outdoors at backyard barbecues as "barbecuing."[59]

By the 1960s Jamaican jerked pork had been transformed from a cured wild-pork product into grilled pork made from deboned, domestic pig carcasses.[60] At the same time, Jamaicans started cooking chicken in covered grills and calling it jerked. Jerked chicken is also known as *drum chicken* because it's often cooked in old barrels that have been cut in half lengthways to make grills. Jamaicans consider jerked chicken to be fast food, indicating that it isn't necessarily cooked using the southern barbecuing method.[61] Indeed, American barbecuing and cookouts have had more influence on modern Jamaican jerk than West Indies barbecuing ever had on barbecuing in the United States.

SOUTHERN BARBECUE VERSUS JAMAICAN JERK

The way some in the mass media discuss Jamaican jerked chicken in the same context as the Maroons and their jerked pork conveys the impression that Jamaicans have cooked jerked chicken for centuries. However, modern Jamaican jerked chicken and the modern version of Jamaican jerked pork are relatively new foods that were inspired by backyard barbecuing in the United States rather than the other way around.

Although there are some similarities between the OSBT and how Jamaicans jerk pork, the differences between the two techniques are far more significant. For example, although both call for grills set over coals, there are no records of anyone in Jamaica digging a pit to contain the coals under the grill. There are no known accounts of people in the southern United States deboning pig carcasses before barbecuing them during the Original Southern Barbecuing Period (OSBP).[62] Also, there are no credible records of anyone in Jamaica barbecuing a whole animal carcass sitting on a grill directly over coals in a pit while basting it with a mixture of butter, vinegar, or citrus juice, salt, spices, and herbs.

Unlike in the southern United States, there are no credible records from the early modern period of people in Jamaica hosting large outdoor social events that featured barbecued meats cooked in a way that's similar to the OSBT. Rather, records indicate that jerked pork was served at meals and banquets.[63] Although Jamaicans discarded offal from the pigs they killed, people in the southern United States used it to make barbecue hash or, in the case of Georgians, used it to make their version of Brunswick stew.[64] All of that strongly supports the assertion that the OSBT and Jamaican jerk developed independently. The similarities exist because of the they both have elements from the three primary loaner cultures that existed in both places.

It's significant that Maroons didn't adopt the Spanish word barbacoa to refer to their way of jerking pork using wooden grills even though the island was under Spanish

“A model kitchen in Jamaica.” By Griffith & Griffith, ca. 1900.

control for over 145 years. The Jamaican word jerk is an Anglicized version of charquini, not barbacoa. That fact doesn’t comport with one of the main premises of the COT, which claims barbecuing is directly descended from the Taíno’s barbacoa. The Jamaican word jerk is also strong evidence that proponents of the COT have misinterpreted and overemphasized the role played in the history of barbecuing in the Western Hemisphere by the Taíno in Haiti and their barbacoa.

Jamaican jerked pork developed among Maroon communities consisting of Africans and Native Americans who combined their food preservation techniques in a way that produced something new while appealing to Europeans who were accustomed to eating salted pork. In that way Jamaican jerked pork demonstrates creolization in the Americas at work.

Jamaican-Style Jerked Pork

Although real-deal Jamaican jerked pork cooked over pimento wood can only be found in Jamaica, that doesn't mean its flavors can't be enjoyed at home. This recipe won't take you to Jamaica, but it can bring a little bit of Jamaica to you.

1 (8-pound) pork butt roast
6 scallions, cut into 1-inch pieces
2 scotch bonnet or habanero peppers
2 garlic cloves
1 onion, chopped
Juice of 1 lime
2 tablespoons brown sugar
1 tablespoon dried thyme
2 teaspoons table salt
1 teaspoon dried ginger
1 teaspoon ground allspice
1 teaspoon ground cinnamon
½ teaspoon ground black pepper
½ teaspoon ground cayenne pepper

—

Put all ingredients (except the pork) in a food processor and blend until smooth. Place the pork butt into a roasting pan fat-side down. Using a knife, make shallow cuts on the surface of the pork. Using food-safe gloves to protect your hands from the hot peppers, rub the pork with a generous portion of the marinade. Cover and refrigerate for 24 hours.

When ready to cook, bring your smoker up to 275°F. Place the pork in the smoker uncovered and cook for 3 hours. Snuggly wrap the pork in foil and continue to cook for about 3 more hours, or until the internal temperature is 205°F or until the meat is pull tender. Remove the pork from the smoker and let it rest for 30 minutes. If you don't have a smoker, cook it in the oven at 300°F uncovered for 2 hours; wrap, then cook it for another 3 hours or until the pork is pull tender. Serve the pork with beans and rice and Jamaican-style fried sweet plantains.

THREE

JEAN-BAPTISTE'S BOUCAN

A Seventeenth-Century "Buccaneer" Picnic

The fascinating history of French buccaneers is riddled with contradictory accounts that make it difficult to determine fact from myth. Almost all sources agree that there were sea-faring buccaneers and there were buccaneers who made their living hunting feral livestock for their hides. Sources disagree on whether the *true* hunting buccaneers were cow killers or hog hunters.

At any rate, the prevailing theory regarding buccaneers and their boucanage leads some who assert that the Original Southern Barbecuing Technique (OSBT) was imported from the Caribbean to cite the memoirs of a French monk in St. Martinique named Père Jean-Baptiste Labat (1663–1738).

In 1698, Labat hosted a picnic that featured a pig he claimed was cooked buccaneer-style on a boucan (a wooden grill) sat over embers. He also served sauce on the side. Some take Labat's picnic at face value and cite it to support the assertion that the OSBT was imported from the Caribbean. A detailed analysis of Labat's picnic and the process he used to cook the pig considered in the context of buccaneers and their boucanage reveals striking details that strongly argue against the Caribbean Origins Theory (COT).

BOUCANAGE IN THE FRENCH CARIBBEAN

Unlike most people who remained in France, French-speaking people in the Americas adopted the creole word boucan and its variants to refer to salted and smoke-dried

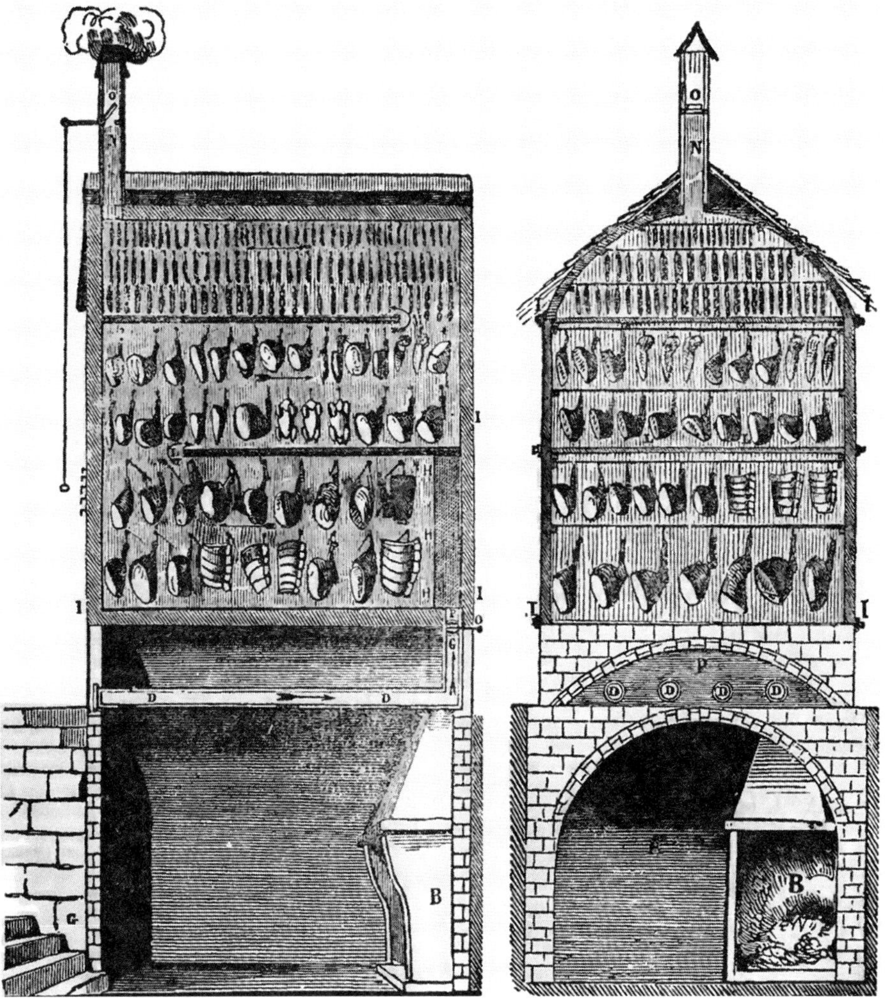

A Chambre de boucanage, which is a French smokehouse referred to as a "A rustic house of the 19th century." *Maison Rustique Du Xix' Siècle.*

meats and the act of smoking them. Consequently boucanage (preserving meat and fish with salt and smoke) became a cultural trait of French Creole culture.[1] That explains why people in France nowadays are more likely to use boucan to refer to a loud, annoying noise than to barbecuing, grilling, or smoking foods. When speaking of smoking meats and fish they prefer *fumer*.[2] Buccaned foods, such as poulet boucané, can be found in several places where French Creole cultures developed, including Réunion Island in the Indian Ocean, Madagascar, and Martinique in the Caribbean.[3] Although Canadians have a "barbecuing" tradition, its origin traces back only to the 1950s after the American backyard barbecue fad spilled over the United States' northern border.[4]

Nevertheless Canadians did adopt a form of the word boucan to refer to smoking meats in smokehouses. For example, the Acadian French word *boucanière* is spoken in the region around Cap-Pelé in New Brunswick, Canada, and refers to a smokehouse used for smoking fish.[5]

During the first three decades of the seventeenth century, French settlers in Tortuga and Hispaniola made their living by trading hides from feral cattle they hunted on the islands. Some claim buccaneers adopted and tailored a Native American process for preserving meat with salt and smoke called boucanage.[6] It's not clear whether buccaneers specialized in dried beef or dried pork.

BOUCAN

At least one scholar claimed the word boucan can be traced to the ancient Celtic language root *bouk* and the smoked meats found in the region of Northern France around Bockange and Bouconville.[7] However, the most widely accepted etymology of boucan asserts it was derived from *moquém*, a South American Tupinambá word for smokehouses and wooden hurdles, or another Tupinambá word that sounds like boucan.[8]

By the 1560s, the adjective boucanées (the source has a typographical error spelled "boucauées"), which means smoked, had been adopted by French speakers in the Americas.[9] The word boucan was first included in a published work in 1578 by Jean de Léry. The first time *Boucanniers* shows up in literature is in the French explorer Jean de Laon's *Relation du voyage des François fait av cap de Nord en Amériqve* published in Paris in 1654. He described Boucanniers as people who were "not religious and spend much of the year in the woods eating beef and pork without bread" (author's translation).[10]

BUCCANEERS, MAROONS, HOG HUNTERS, AND COW KILLERS

The people in the Caribbean who made their living hunting feral livestock for hides, fat, and flesh during the seventeenth century were known by several names, such as *monteros* (Spanish for hunters), *chassuers* (French for hunters), boucanier*s*, boucaniers Espagnoles, or *bucaneros* (Spanish for buccaneers). To English speakers they were hog hunters if they hunted wild hogs and cow killers or hunting Marownaes if they hunted wild cattle. English speakers eventually anglicized boucaniers into buccaneers. Other settlers included the planters, who settled on farms and plantations and the indentured servants who were often cruelly mistreated, known as "engagés." Sailors who made their base in Tortuga were called *flibustiers* by the French, *freebooters* by the English, and *zee-roovers* by the Dutch. Eventually people who made their living trading hides and cured meats developed a symbiotic relationship with pirates and privateers.[11]

Identifying accurate details regarding buccaneer boucanage is difficult because historical accounts of buccaneers and their use of the boucan are at best convoluted and at worst contradictory and unreliable. For example, in contrast to the common belief that buccaneers hunted wild hogs to make smoke-dried pork for trade, some accounts of buccaneers claim their primary occupation was hunting feral cattle. According to those sources, they occasionally hunted feral pigs, but only for sport and amusement.[12] At any rate the contradictory claims might explain why, as will be discussed, some rely on an account of an outdoor dinner hosted by a French priest in 1698 in attempts to connect boucanage to southern barbecuing.

BRETHREN OF THE COAST

After seventeenth-century Spanish authorities noticed the growing presence of foreign settlers in the Caribbean, they responded by harassing them and killing the wild cattle and hogs on the islands that was the source of their livelihoods. In 1638, Spanish forces took the opportunity to attack settlements in Tortuga when the men were away hunting. They destroyed homes and property and killed as many as 300 people, which outraged the hunters. That prompted buccaneers to take to the seas in large numbers seeking revenge against Spain. They organized a confederacy that would become known as the Brethren of the Coast, with the mission of inflicting retribution upon Spanish interests.[13] Spanish forces continued to harass them throughout the seventeenth century, but they failed to extinguish them. In 1661, Edmund Hickeringill became the first to use the terms "buckaneers" and "hunting Marownaes" (Maroons) in English literature.[14] In *Jamaica Viewed* he wrote:

> A thousand *English* Soldiers being now an overmatch to all Power, that the *Spaniards* in *Hispaniola*, can bring into the field; unable at this day to ferrit [ferret] out a few *French Buckaneers*, or Hunting *Marownaes*, formerly mentioned; who live by killing the wild Beeves [cattle] for their Hides; and might grow rich by the Trade, did not their lavish Riottings in expence (at the neighbour-*Tortudoes* [Tortuga]) exceed the hardship of their Incomes. Their comfort is they can never be broke whilest they have a Dog and a Gun; both which, are more industriously tended then themselves. The *Acteon* [hero] straglers (that

> seldome number above five or six in a company) are often affronted with the *Spanish* Rounds (consisting of about one hundred Fire-locks) that once a year compass the Island, yet dare they never cope with these resolute Champions, and wandring Knights; who, setting back to back, would make sure to sell their lives at a double rate, and in that posture bid defiance to the enemy.[15]

After England took control of Jamaica in 1655, they feared a Spanish counterattack. Consequently, English authorities made the short-sighted decision to invite pirates and buccaneers to Jamaica to defend the island. By that time, most people who were called buccaneers were not in the business of hunting feral livestock. They were privateers (authorized by a European government) or outright pirates ("enemies to mankind"). Buccaneers, pirates, and privateers soon made Port Royal their base of operations. Soon after Port Royal gained the reputation of being "the wickedest city on Earth." As the English lexicographer Elisha Coles (1640–80) commented in his *English Dictionary: Explaining the Difficult Terms*, published in London in 1676, buckaneers were "the rude rabble of Jamaica."[16]

By 1670 there were barely 300 buccaneers left who hunted wild cattle and hogs. The rest had moved on to farming or freebooting. Still, the freebooter buccaneers remained a formidable force in the fight against Spain until 1697.[17] That's when the Treaty of Ryswick was signed, which ended the Nine Years' War fought between France and an alliance between Britain, Spain, Portugal, the Dutch Republic, and Savoy. At that time all European governments with interests in the Caribbean declared buccaneers to be criminals. By 1730, buccaneers had faded into history.[18]

NOTABLE ACCOUNTS OF EARLY MODERN BUCCANEER BOUCANAGE

JEAN BAPTISTE DU TERTRE

Jean Baptiste Du Tertre (1610–87) was a French priest and botanist who served as a missionary in the Caribbean from 1640 to 1658. His *Histoire generale des Antilles habitées par les François* (*General History of the Antilles inhabited by the French*) was published over thirty years after his first visit to the Caribbean in 1671. He wrote, "Buccaneers received their name from the word *boucan*, which is a wooden grill with several grates resting on four forks on which the buccaneers roast whole pigs that they eat without bread" (author's translation).[19] It appears that Du Tertre's knowledge of buccaneer cookery was second-hand. Although Du Tertre used the word "roast" (rotissent), he

A depiction of a buccaneer roasting a pig on a spit—not on a boucan. Exquemelin, *Histoire des avanturiers*.

neglected to mention whether or not buccaneers skinned hogs, cut the meat into strips, or how they, ostensibly, roasted, smoked, and dried it. Although he may have glossed over the details of buccaneer boucanage, it's more likely that he didn't fully understand it. Like other Europeans, there is little doubt that buccaneers roasted pork and beef for their own consumption.[20] Still, roasting was so common, it seems implausible that it could explain why buccaneers' culinary practices garnered so much attention from authors who wrote for a European audience.

Du Tertre also authored *Histoire générale des isles de Christophe, de la Guadeloupe, et le Martinique et autre*, which was published in Paris in 1654. That work was written during the period during which he was serving in the Caribbean. Nowhere in it does he mention how buccaneers received their name, nor did he include a firsthand account of buccaneers "roasting" a pig on a boucan and one can only speculate as to why that is the case.

ALEXANDER EXQUEMELIN

In 1666, after studying medicine, French-born (presumably) Alexander Exquemelin (1645–1707), sometimes spelled Esquemeling, Exquemeling, or Oexmelin, embarked on a journey from Europe to the Caribbean where he would spend three years as an

Native Americans in Brazil curing fish on a boucan, ca. 1550. Schmidel, *Vierte Schiffart*.

indentured servant (engagés) on the island of Tortuga.[21] After being released from his indenture, Exquemelin joined a band of buccaneers led by the Welsh privateer Sir Henry Morgan (1635–88). By 1674 Exquemelin had left buccaneering and was back home in Europe. In 1678 his record of time spent with the buccaneers was published in Dutch under the title *De Americaensche Zee-Roovers* (*History of the Buccaneers of America*).[22] The book was translated into German in 1679, Spanish in 1681, and twice into English—via the original Dutch and the Spanish translation—in 1684. Boucan appears in the Dutch version spelled *boulan*. It's found in the phrase "deza Boulan," which, according to Exquemelin, is what buccaneers called their camps. The translators of the Spanish version, and at least one English version, preserved that spelling.

Exquemelin wrote that there were two kinds of French hunters in Hispaniola: There were the hog hunters and there were cow killers who hunted feral cattle for their hides and smoke-dried beef. The cow killers, according to Exquemelin, were the true buccaneers (boekaniers), not the people who hunted hogs.[23] Nevertheless a passage that appears in an English version of Exquemelin's work describes how hog hunters cut meat into long strips, salted it, and let it rest for "three or four hours" before hanging it on "sticks" over a slow fire. The meat was smoked until it became "dry and hard."[24] The German version has a similar passage.

In 1686, Jean de Frontignières translated the Spanish version into French titled *Histoire des Avanturiers qui se sont signalez dans les Indes* (*History of the Adventurers Who Distinguished Themselves in the Indies*). That version contains much spurious material that doesn't appear in any of the others.[25] In fact it contains so much additional material, English author George Walter Thornbury (1828–76) was convinced that it was a completely different work written by a French buccaneer named Exmelin. Thornbury complained that Exquemelin was "constantly mistaken by booksellers and in catalogues for Exmelin."[26] The following is a spurious passage in de Frontignières's translation that's relevant to the study of barbecuing history: "When some natural Indians of the West Indies, named Caribs, make prisoners of war, they have become accustomed to cutting them into pieces and putting them on racks under which they make fire; they call these 'Barbacoa racks' and the place where they are 'Boucan,' which is where they buccan them, which means to roast and smoke them at the same time. That is where our Buccaneers took their name with the difference that they do to animals what the Caribs do to men" (author's translation).[27] That account correctly points out that buccaning means to dry meat while simultaneously roasting and smoking it. The claim of cannibalism among Island Caribs is disputed.[28] Additionally de Frontignières mistakenly attributed the words barbacoa and boucan to a single Native American language family. However, barbacoa was adopted from people who spoke a language from the Arawakan family of languages. Boucan was adopted from people who spoke a language from the Tupi–Guarani family of languages.

PIERRE FRANÇOIS XAVIER DE CHARLEVOIX

Pierre François Xavier de Charlevoix (1682–1761) was a French priest and historian. He traveled to the Americas multiple times and wrote several volumes about his experiences. Of particular interest is his *Histoire de l'Isle espagnole ou de S. Domingue* (*History of the Spanish island of S. Domingue*) published in Paris in 1730. Charlevoix's version of the origin of buccaneers is similar to Exquemelin's. He wrote that when English and French adventurers realized Spain had abandoned the northern portion of Hispaniola, they decided to settle there because it was remote and was "swarming with pigs and oxen everywhere" (author's translation). Although Exquemelin claimed the cow killers were the real buccaneers, Charlevoix claimed buccaneers received their name not from pork or hides, but from the buccaned beef they made "in the manner of Savages" (author's translation) that they called "Boucan."[32]

IGNORING DIVERSITY AMONG NATIVE AMERICANS: AN UNFORTUNATE ERROR

Virginia-born planter and historian Robert Beverly (1667–1722) made a similar error to de Frontignières's in 1705. He described how Indigenous people in Virginia cured meat on wooden hurdles: "This they, and we also from them, call Barbacueing."[29] By referring to Native Americans as "they," it appears that Beverly made no distinction between different nations of Indigenous peoples in the Americas or their languages. The Algonquian, Iroquoian, and Siouan languages, spoken by Native Americans in colonial Virginia, didn't include barbecuing, barbacoa, or boucan. Therefore, Beverly's reference to "they" must be a reference Native Americans in general rather than specifically to those who inhabited Virginia in the late seventeenth century. Further, it is fairly well established that the word barbecue was not directly derived from a Native American language.

Another confusing situation was created by the French explorer Andre Pénicaut (1680–ca. 1720). He wrote of seventeenth-century Native Americans in Louisiana, "Their meat is usually smoked or otherwise *boucanée*, as they say in this country. They, however, have some kind of grill, on which they put it, but little fire underneath, making it dry with smoke contributing as much as the heat of the fire."[30] Of course the languages spoken by Native Americans in seventeenth-century Louisiana didn't include the word boucan.[31] If they did use it, they most likely learned it from French speakers.

WILLIAM DAMPIER AND LIONEL WAFER

Two famous seventeenth-century buccaneers, English Captain William Dampier and Welsh explorer Dr. Lionel Wafer (1640–1705), wrote detailed accounts of their exploits. However, they never used the word boucan in their writings. The contrasting ways the word barbecue was used by them sheds light on how seventeenth-century English speakers understood it. Even though Dampier and Wafer were colleagues, each had his own way of using barbecue. Dampier favored definitions for barbecue and jerk that were similar to the definitions Spanish speakers have for barbacoa and charqui. Wafer used the word barbecue similar to how French speakers in the Americas used boucan and Dutch speakers used *berbekot*.

Portrait of William Dampier. Russell, *William Dampier.*

Dampier was the first man to circumnavigate the globe three times. In 1699, the record of his adventures was published in *A New Voyage Round the World.* Dampier started his sailing career around the year 1670. After several years of buccaneering, Dampier made his way to a plantation in Hampton, Virginia, in 1683 and lived there for at least a year. It was there that he joined buccaneer Captain John Cook (d. 1684), who was described as a "cirole" (Creole) and native of St. Kitts. Virginia's eastern shore became their base of operations.

Dampier's use of the noun barbecue doesn't indicate an exclusive association with cooking or a grill. He even alluded to the definition of barbacoa. On one occasion when Dampier and his companions had trouble crossing a river, they had to spend the night on "low swampy ground." He described how they dealt with the wet conditions around the river, "We built Hutts upon its Banks and lay there all night, upon our Borbecu's, or frames of sticks, raised about 3 foot from the ground."[33] Dampier also described a Native American "couch" covered with animal skins as a "Barbecu of Sticks lying along about 2 foot distant from the Ground."[34]

Early modern Native Americans all over the Americas used wooden hurdles as beds. The Belgian missionary Louis Hennepin (1626–1704) recorded how Native Americans who lived around the Ohio River slept on hurdles, "They drive into the Ground big Poles, very near one another, which support a large Hurdle, which serves them instead of a Floor, under which they make their Fire; and the Smoak drives away those Creatures, who cannot abide it. They lay upon that Hurdle, the roof whereof is cover'd with Skins against the Rain, and serves also to shelter them against the Heat of the Sun."[35]

Dampier referred to meats dried on barbecues not as barbecued or buccaned, but as "jerk'd." Writing about hunters in Cuba, he recorded, "Here are also Hunters that gain a Livelihood by killing wild Hog and Beef." Those Cuban hunters were making their living much as we are told hunting buccaneers made theirs. On another occasion, Dampier wrote about crew members who were sent out to hunt hogs. Some of the pork from the hunt was "corn'd," and some was "jerk'd and salted."[36] Nevertheless Dampier was no doubt aware of the use of the word barbecue as a verb to describe how meat and fish were dried on hurdles. For example, in 1680 when Dampier was serving under Captain Bartholomew Sharp (ca. 1650–1702), Sharp's diary entry for Sunday, August 15, reads, "Our men feasted on Shoar [shore] with Barbakude, Goats and Fish, &tc."[37] In this instance the adjective *barbakude* indicates that the meat and fish were jerked.

In 1698, England's government gave Dampier his first command for a voyage to study Australia (then known as New Holland). He reported seeing several "barbecues" in New Guinea during that voyage. Dampier wasn't sure if the barbecues there had been erected by Europeans or Indigenous peoples because of the precision with which the sticks used to make the hurdles were cut, thus indicating the use of iron tools. He also didn't specify whether the barbecues he saw in New Guinea were used for sleeping or drying meat and fish.[38] At any rate, the expedition was a failure, and Dampier returned to England in disgrace. In spite of that, Dampier was offered the job of pilot on a ship named *Dutchess*. While serving on that ship in 1709, Dampier rescued Alexander Selkirk (1676–1721), who had been marooned on an island in the South Pacific for over four years. Selkirk's story was the inspiration for English author Daniel Defoe's (1660–1731) *Robinson Crusoe*. Dampier returned to England from his last adventure in 1711 and died there in 1715.

Dr. Lionel Wafer was a buccaneer and companion of Dampier's. In 1680, Wafer met Dampier after joining Captain Sharp and his flotilla of approximately 12 ships with which they raided Spanish assets. During a mission across the Isthmus of Darien in Panama, Wafer was injured in a gun powder accident. His injuries were so severe, his crewmates left him behind to be cared for by the local Kuna people. While living with the Kunas he learned their language and many of their customs, including their way of curing meats on wooden hurdles. In Wafer's *A New Voyage and Description of the Isthmus of America*, he wrote of the barbecues—not boucans or barbacoas—that the Kuna people used. Like Dampier, Wafer used the noun barbecue to refer to furniture. He described how the Kuna people made dinner tables by constructing "a great Barbecue, ten, twelve, or twenty Foot long, or more, as the Company is, and broad proportionally."[39] Unlike Dampier, Wafer used the word barbecue in the context of food preservation. He described how meat and fish were preserved on a barbecue being a "Grate of Sticks made like a Grid-iron" to "keep any of it longer."[40]

Wafer's career as a buccaneer ended in Virginia in 1690. The last two sentences in *A New Voyage* are: "[W]e carted our Chests, with other Goods, over a small Neck of Land in *Bohemia*-River, which leads down the great Bay of *Chisapeek* (Chesapeake) to Point-*Comfort* in *James*-River in *Virginia*. There I thought to settle: But meeting some Troubles, after about three Years residence there, I came home for *England* in the Year, 1690."[41] There are some details about his stay in Virginia that Wafer left out of his book. The "troubles" he mentioned were directly rooted in his life as a buccaneer. In June of 1688, Wafer and some companions were rowing a boat through the Chesapeake Bay with three large chests filled with silver and Spanish gold. When they reached the James River, they drew the attention of authorities who arrested them and imprisoned them in Jamestown. Wafer confessed that he was a pirate and requested amnesty under a pardon the king offered pirates who surrendered. The authorities in Virginia were in no mood to entertain his offer. They reminded Wafer that he was in custody not because he surrendered but because he was arrested. After the English captain who arrested Wafer failed to show in court, Wafer was released to England for trial in 1690. Because authorities sent his buccaneer loot to England a year earlier, he was penniless. Eventually Wafer's loot was returned to him after he agreed to purchase his freedom with 300 pounds sterling, which was sent back to Virginia where it was used to help found the College of William and Mary.[42]

JEAN-BAPTISTE LABAT

Père Jean-Baptiste Labat was a French missionary who lived in Martinique from 1694 to 1705 and provided spiritual leadership in the French Caribbean colonies. In 1722 his account of his adventures in the Americas was published in several volumes titled, *Nouveau voyage aux isles de l'Amérique* (*New trip to the Isles of America*). More volumes were

Portrait of Jean-Baptiste Labat by André Bouys, ca. 1742.

later added in 1742. Labat's memoirs reveal that he was energetic, curious, quick-witted, well-read, and had a keen eye for details.

Like Exquemelin before him, Labat asserted that the true buccaneers were the cow killers. People who hunted hogs were merely chasseurs (hunters). Flibustiers, according to Labat, were the sailors who raided Spanish vessels.[43] In contrast to Charlevoix who claimed buccaneers were named for their buccaned beef, and Du Tertre who claimed they were named from wooden boucans, Labat claimed they received their name from their huts and smokehouses called boucans. Seventeen years before Exquemelin published *De Americaensche Zee-Roovers*, and 61 years before Labat published his memoirs, Edmund Hickeringill also confined the name "buckaneers" to the cow killers in Hispaniola. Apparently, buccaneers were exploiting the strong demand for dried beef. John Smith was acquainted with West Indies "jerkin beefe." Richard Ligon mentioned "Jerkin Beef" (not barbycu'd beef). Therefore in spite of the Jamaican Abbot's 1611 report (see Chapter 2, "Herbert's Patta") that people in Jamaica killed cows for their hides and left the meat rotting in the field, it appears that some in the seventeenth-century Caribbean and South America were hunting wild cattle for their hides and flesh.[44]

A strong case can be made that Labat was the Western Hemisphere's first foodie.[45] His descriptions of recipes and cooking techniques for making New World dishes, such as *boucan de tortuë* (tortoise cooked in an earth oven), *cochon boucanné*, and *mouton en robe de chambre* (sheep in a dressing gown; i.e., a sheep cooked in an earth oven) are of particular interest.[46] According to Labat, he nor his French colleagues made smoke-dried meats, even though they were a standard shipboard offering.[47] At any rate, he was fascinated by the hog hunters he encountered in Santo Domingo (the Dominican Republic). His firsthand account of their camp and of how they made cochon boucanné reveals some surprising details.

LABAT'S HOG HUNTERS

Labat wrote a detailed account of his encounter with hog hunters (he didn't refer to them as buccaneers) in Santo Domingo. He negotiated a trade with them for *viandes boucannées* (buccaned meats) that he described as "viande sechée àpetit feu et à la fumée" or meat dried over a low temperature, smoky fire.[48]Labat followed the hog hunters to their "boucan" he described as a hut roofed with leaves. He witnessed men hot smoking wild hog meat in a smaller boucan (hut) that was used like a smoky oven:

> After the hunters kill a hog, they skin it and cut all the meat into long strips that are about an inch & a half thick. The strips of meat are then lightly sprinkled

> with beaten salt and allowed to rest for twenty-four hours, after which they remove the salt and spread the strips of meat out on stages inside the boucan. They build a smoky fire on the floor of the boucan using the hogs' skins and bones to produce smoke. The boucan is then sealed up like an oven, and the meat continues to smoke until it is as dry and hard as a piece of wood. This meat can be stored for years, as long as it is kept in a dry place. When it's dry, it's an unappetizing brown color. But when put in warm water, it turns red and develops a pleasant smell like fresh meat. It can be heated on a grill, on a spit, or in a pot of stew as if it were fresh pork. However, it's infinitely more favorable & more delicate because of the salts imparted by the burning skins & bones (author's translation).[49]

There are several critical details in Labat's account of the hog hunters. He described their boucan as being what is otherwise known as a smokehouse that was sealed up like an oven (*maniere d'étuve*) with stages (*étages*) in it to hold the strips of meat while they were simultaneously baked, smoked and dried. It appears that Labat's "stages" were structures made with sticks mounted horizontally on which strips of meat, not whole carcasses, were hung.

Labat's description of the hog hunters' cochon boucanné indicates that it differed from Jamaican jerked hog that was "neither salt [meaning not excessively salty] nor hard, but tender, juicy, and of a smoky, peculiar flavor" (see Chapter 2, "Herbert's Patta"). The cochon boucanné, on the other hand, was dry and hard.[50] Labat's hog hunters skinned the hogs, cut the flesh into strips, and hot-smoked it in a smokehouse until it was dry. Although Labat was fond of tortoise and sheep cooked in earth ovens similar to how Maroons "barbecued" pork, there are no records of buccaneers or Labat's hog hunters cooking in earth ovens.

LABAT'S BUCCANEER FEAST

In 1698, Labat held a picnic for his friends at which he served a "cochon boucanné dans le bois," which means a buccaned pig in the forest.[51] Labat explained that the *boucan de cochon* (boucan of pig or buccaned pig) was served "in imitation of Boucanniers (buccaneers) or Chasseurs" (hog hunters), but attendees were expected to pretend to be buccaneers.[52] Labat's buccaneer feast and the way he imagined buccaneers cooking whole pigs on boucans reflects the claim that *true* buccaneers only hunted wild pigs for amusements and sport, rather than for making dried pork for trade.

Some today interpret the phrase *cochon boucanné dans le bois* to mean a pig barbecue in the forest, based upon the American use of the word barbecue to refer to an outdoor social event that features barbecued meats. Nonetheless based upon the context of the passage, it's clear that Labat was only stating that he buccaned a pig in the forest and served it there to his guests. Although some today might refer to that event as a barbecue, Labat and other French speakers of his era didn't use boucan in that way. In John Eaden's famous 1931 English translation, *The Memoirs of Père Labat*, the phrase boucan de cochon wasn't translated. Instead, the French-language phrase *cochon boucan* (pig boucan) was substituted for it.[53] Be that as it may, this author hasn't found the phrase "cochon boucan" in the original French version of Labat's memoirs. Unfortunately, Eaden's "cochon boucan" makes it appear that French speakers have used boucan for hundreds of years to refer to outdoor social events where buccaned meats are featured just as people in the United States have used the word barbecue. However, French dictionaries don't define boucan as an event. If there are French speakers today who use boucan in that way, they learned it from how Americans use barbecue (see Chapter 1, "Hernando's Barbacoa").

Some have suggested English translations for the phrase boucan de cochon, such as pig barbecue and pig roast.[54] However, those suggestions are no more accurate than Eaden's cochon boucan. Because Labat referred to the picnic as *festin boucanier*, which means buccaneer feast, that would have been a good option for Eaden to use.[55] A better option would have been the definition of the phrase found in the glossary of Labat's memoirs, which is "festin champestre" or *country feast*.[56]

The French lexicographer Emile Littré (1801–81) correctly interpreted boucan de cochon. In his *Dictionnaire de la langue française*, which was published in Paris in 1863, it's defined as, "repas champêtre fait dans les bois à l'imitation des boucaniers" or a "country meal held in the woods in imitation of buccaneers."[57] Although the phrase boucan de cochon may have been used one time by one person to refer to an outdoor social event that featured a buccaned pig, the noun boucan itself never has been used in that way. Additionally, Labat is the only person in recorded history to host a boucan de cochon and his festin boucanier never became a tradition in the Americas or in Europe.

After complaining that he had to cook a domesticated pig instead of a wild boar, Labat described the party in great detail.[58] He had a hut (what he called an "ajoupa") built close to the bank of a nearby river in which he had stashed some wine at daybreak to ensure that it would be chilled in time for the festivities. His guests arrived at around 9:00 and he immediately put them to work. The ablest guests received the honor of constructing the 4-feet-long by 3-feet-wide boucan (wooden grill). Curiously Labat's boucan bore no resemblance to the smokehouse he saw at the hog hunters' camp in Santo Domingo.

Labat had his helpers butterfly the pig and put it on the boucan lying on its back. He used sticks to hold the pig's belly open so it could be used as a cooking vessel. Enslaved people built a fire, and when it had burned down to hot embers they placed them under the pig. Labat seasoned the pig by filling the cavity with citrus juice, salt, crushed chili peppers, and black pepper. As the pig cooked, its flesh was pierced with a sharp stick to ensure the seasonings penetrated the meat. The cooks were careful to avoid cutting the pig's skin so the citrus juice, seasonings, and natural juices of the pork wouldn't leak out of the pig's belly cavity. Labat speculated that the buccaneers would put birds killed during the morning hunt inside the pig's open cavity so they'd be cooked by the time the pig was done.

When the pig was ready to eat, it was up to the *maître du boucan* (master of the boucan, a play on the phrase *maître de cuisine* (master of the kitchen), as *chef de la troupe* (leader of the troop) and *pere de famille* (father of the family) to cut the first piece.[59] While the pig was still resting on the boucan, Labat, the chef de la troupe, approached it holding a large fork in his left hand and a large knife in his right hand with which he cut slices of pork being careful to not damage the skin. After the first serving was eaten, the older "buccaneers" in attendance served the others, followed by the youngest who served the remaining pork to the other guests.

The pork, which Labat called boucan, was served with two sauces. One was the *jus* (gravy) that collected in the pig's belly cavity. The other was made with the same combination of citrus juice, crushed chili peppers, salt, and pepper used in the braising liquid. Guests mixed the pork jus and the tangy, spicy sauce to their taste in bowls made of leaves. Labat and his twenty guests enjoyed the boucan so much none of it was saved for the enslaved people who did the hard work to make Labat's buccaneer feast a success.

Contrary to some claims, Labat's writings don't contain any accounts of buccaneers or chasseurs roasting or buccaning whole pigs on boucans.[60] Exquemelin, a real buccaneer, didn't record any occasions like Labat's pleasant buccaneer feast, either. During a campaign led by Captain Morgan, the buccaneers happened across a "great quantity of cattle." The following is Exquemelin's firsthand account of the buccaneer feast that ensued:

> Here while some were employed in killing and slaying of cows, horses, bulls and chiefly asses, of which there was greatest number, others busied themselves in kindling fires and getting wood wherewith to roast them. Thus, cutting the

> flesh of these animals into convenient pieces, or gobbets, they threw them in the fire, and, half carbonadoed or roasted, they devoured them with incredible haste and appetite. For such was their hunger that they more resembled cannibals than Europeans at this banquet, the blood many times running down from their beards to the middle of their bodies.[61]

If buccaneers liked to buccan whole carcasses during pleasant picnics like Labat's, they missed a perfect opportunity to do so on that occasion. However, they didn't build boucans, they didn't buccan whole carcasses, they didn't cook the meat until it was pull-tender, and there were no sauces served on the side.

THE EUROPEAN ROOTS OF LABAT'S COCHON BOUCANNÉ

Labat's fanciful buccaneer feast held "in the woods in imitation of the Buccaneers or Hunters" wasn't based on a firsthand account of buccaneers or hog hunters. For that reason, it may have been inspired by Du Tertre's unsubstantiated claim of buccaneers "roasting" pigs on boucans. At any rate Labat's active imagination coupled with European recipes and cooking techniques certainly came into play.

Labat's way of cooking a pig on a boucan differs significantly from the OSBT. For example, rather than pulling the pork he cut it with a knife, he didn't dig a pit to contain the embers, nor did he *mop* the carcass with sauce as it cooked, in spite of modern claims to the contrary.[62] Most significantly Labat didn't barbecue the pig. He cooked it using a French technique known as braising, which is a way of slowly simmering meat in a small amount of liquid with or without a lid on the cooking vessel.[63] Labat's comment, "dans le ventre du cochon, qui servoit de marmitte" (the belly of the pig, which served as a pot), reveals that he braised the pork using the pig's body cavity as a vessel to hold the braising liquid made of citrus juice and seasonings.[64] That wasn't the first time Labat employed a European cooking technique in one of his Caribbean culinary creations. He took full credit for his sheep in a dressing gown (*mouton en robe de chambre*) writing that he feared "the English will rob us [the French] of the honor of a cooking invention, in which our Nation [France] had the best share."[65] That statement indicates that although cooking in an earth oven was a Native American and creole technique, Labat employed many European culinary practices in the use of it.

The assertion that Labat's pig was braised and not barbecued is also attested to by the fact that he never flipped the pig's carcass over while it cooked. When using the OSBT, pitmasters flipped animal carcasses from time to time as they barbecued and basted the meat with a vinegary sauce. Labat didn't baste his pig or flip it over in a continuous performance because he was braising the pig, not barbecuing it. Markedly, there are no records of anyone cooking pigs for a barbecue event in the South (southern United States) using Labat's European cooking method during the Original Southern Barbecuing Period (OSBP). The notion that Labat's cochon boucanné inspired southern barbecuing is rebutted by the striking differences between the two cooking techniques.

There were many European sources available to Labat that could've provided inspiration for his cochon boucanné. One example is the first-century Roman cookbook *Apicius*, which contains a recipe for roast suckling pig that calls for filling its belly with small birds and generous amounts of pepper. That recipe is reminiscent of Labat's imaginative claim that buccaneers cooked birds in the pig's open belly.[66]

The similarities between Labat's sauce made with citrus juice, chili peppers, salt, and pepper, and the original southern barbecue sauce made with vinegar, butter, salt, pepper, and spices are not the result of the latter being inspired by the former.[68] Those recipes are similar because they were inspired by the same sources: sixteenth- and seventeenth-century European cookbooks. The primary four flavors in both Labat's sauce and the original southern barbecue sauce are fatty, tangy, spicy, and salty. Labat filled those roles in his sauce with pork jus for the fatty, citrus juice for the tangy, crushed chili peppers for the spicy, and salt. Of course, citrus fruits are another European contribution to Labat's cochon boucanné as they were brought to the Caribbean by Columbus in 1493.[69] Colonists in the colonial United States filled the essential four flavor roles in their original barbecue sauce with butter for the fatty, vinegar for the tangy, red or black pepper for the spicy, and salt. Over time, people in the South added other ingredients to the basic southern barbecue sauce recipe. However, the original foundational formula of fatty, tangy, spicy, and salty is still almost universally observed.

The sauce formula used by Labat and by southern barbecue cooks has been around for centuries. *Le Ménagier de Paris* (*The Parisian Household Book*), which was published in 1393, includes a recipe for wild boar ("Bourbelier de Sanglier") that calls for a sauce made of vinegar, verjuice (a tangy liquid made from unripe grapes or other sour fruit), ginger, cinnamon, cloves, and nutmeg. The Italian cookbook *Libro della cocina*, which was published in the early fifteenth century, contains a "Sauce for Roasts" that includes verjuice, herbs, and black pepper. The author points out that orange juice or lemon juice can be substituted for the verjuice. *The Accomplisht Cook*, first published in London in 1660, offers several sauce recipes with the option of making them with either citrus juice mixed with gravy (jus) or vinegar and butter.[70] "Similar examples can be found in many other European cookbooks from the fifteenth through the eighteenth centuries."[71]

The earliest known British "barbecued pig" recipe is found in *The Country Housewife* published in London in 1732. It calls for a European braising technique similar to the one Labat used to cook his pig. The recipe is titled "An Hog barbecued, or broil'd whole. From Vaux-Hall, Surrey," and includes the following instructions, "Cut the Belly in a strait Line down to the Bottom, near the joining of the Gammons [hams]; but not so far, but that the whole Body of the Hog may hold any Liquor we put into it." The reader is then instructed to season the pig with salt and pepper before placing it on a gridiron raised about 3.5 feet above a "good clear Fire of Charcoal," with the carcass's meat side facing the live coals. When the chef is satisfied that the pig's "belly side" has cooked enough, it should be "turn'd upwards." Fill the "Belly of the Hog" with white wine, salt, sage, an ounce of fresh cloves, and the peels from 6 to 8 lemons. The author continued, "The Skin must not be cut before you lay it on the Gridiron, to keep the Gravey; neither should any of the Skin be cut, when you have any Pork roasted for the same Reason." The pig should be broiled for seven to eight hours. When the pig is done, pour the sauce from the pig's cavity into a dish and serve it with the pork.[67]

The old British recipe includes several European practices that were exhibited in Labat's boucan de cochon. The braised pig, the citrus, the gravy (jus), the grill, and the sauce on the side are a few. It's doubtful that pitmasters in the South during the OSBP would consider either of those European ways of cooking a pig to be barbecuing.

(continued from page 88)

Labat didn't record any eyewitness accounts of people in the Caribbean barbecuing a pig in a way that's similar to the OSBT. If he had witnessed such an event, it's doubtful that foodie Labat would have neglected to mention it.

MOREAU'S BARBARO

Médéric Louis Élie Moreau de Saint-Méry (1750–1819), referred to hereafter as Moreau, was born in Fort-Royale, Martinique.[72] He was a writer, a lawyer, and held public offices in France, the French colonies of Martinique, and Saint-Domingue (Haiti). He was also instrumental in founding the Museum of Paris and eventually became its president in

1787. In 1794 he moved to Philadelphia and opened a bookstore. Shortly after President John Adams signed the *Alien and Sedition Acts* in 1798, he returned to Paris.[73]

On his way to Philadelphia, Moreau passed through Norfolk, Virginia, and happened to witness the residents enjoying themselves at a Virginian barbecue that he referred to as a "*Barbaro* or Barbecue."[74] It appears that barbaro contains a typographical error. Based upon Moreau's other writings, the correct spelling should be *barbaco*, which refers to an outdoor religious event that was popular in Haiti. In Haiti the word is spelled *barbasco* but the letter *s* is silent. Therefore it is likely that Moreau meant to use the phonetic spelling of the word which is barbaco. Moreau described a barbaco as "[an] entertainment that we host in the countryside in a place where the pleasure of bathing can be combined with other amusements" (author's translation). The word barbaco comes from the name of a chemical extracted from a plant that Indigenous people in South America used to intoxicate fish to make them easier to catch. Therefore Moreau made the mistaken assumption that barbasco was borrowed from Native Americans.[75] Nevertheless, modern scholars tell us the word barbaco is a distortion of *verbasco*, the Spanish name for mullein: a fuzzy-leaved plant used by Native Americans for thousands of years to intoxicate fish and to make medicines. Some believed that it also had the ability to ward off evil spirits. The *v* was replaced with *b* because *barba* (beard) is an allusion to the beard-like appearance of Mullein's fuzzy leaves.[76]

Another source defines the Haitian word barbaco as a feast, as in the Haitian phrase *Donner Un Barbaco*, which means to give a feast.[77] That definition was used in the 1960s by a hotel in Haiti that referred to a feast as a barbaco that also included a "barbecue buffet."[78] It's interesting that people who live on the island that's ostensibly the source of the word barbacoa chose to use the English word barbecue in that advertisement. Apparently, using the word barbecue in the context of a barbaco was an attempt to entice American tourists to dine on grilled foods at the hotel's restaurant.

The word barbaco is associated with Haitian Vodou, which is an Afro-Haitian religion that's been practiced in Haiti since the sixteenth century. In that context, it refers to foods offered to gods. After the offering was accepted, the foods were shared with the poor.[79] Barbaco picnics weren't barbecues in the American sense of the term. They were religious ceremonies meant to appease a god and emphasize the importance of the individual.[80] The religious nature of the events is reflected in this passage that was published in 1835 about Haitians, "Some neighbors resolved this year to lend themselves to a popular superstition by reviving the old barbaco, or party at the spring (author's translation)."[81] Based upon this additional context, some of which was provided by Moreau himself, it's safe to conclude that Moreau's barbaro is a typographical error where the letter *c* in the word barbaco was accidently replaced with the letter *r*.

Père Labat hosted his buccaneer feast in Martinique 96 years before Moreau arrived in Virginia. According to the COT, barbecues were supposedly common in the West Indies and were the inspiration for southern barbecues in the United States. If that's so, the eyewitness account of an eighteenth-century Virginian barbecue provided by the Martinique-born Moreau raises an important question: If outdoor social events called barbecues and boucans that featured hogs barbecued "in the West Indies manner" were common in the Caribbean (the supposed "birthplace of barbecue"), is it not reasonable to assume that the French-speaking Creole Moreau would have recognized the event and possibly even used the word boucan somewhere in his account of the Virginia barbecue? The answer is, of course, he most likely would have. However, he didn't. Furthermore Moreau's reaction implies that the practice of barbecuing oxen and pigs on hurdles set over a pit full of live coals wasn't a cultural trait in Martinique or Haiti during the eighteenth century. Not only did Labat's buccaneer feast not inspire or influence the OSBT or the custom of holding barbecues, it didn't even inspire a similar barbecuing tradition in three of the places it had the best chance to do so, which were the French colonies of Martinique, Saint-Domingue, and Canada.

Poulet Boucané

Americans never really embraced the word boucan, but that's not necessarily the fault of buccaned foods. This recipe is a tasty and easy-to-do version of poulet boucané (buccaned chicken).

1 whole chicken
5 scallions, cut into 2-inch pieces
2 garlic cloves, sliced
1 onion, chopped
Juice of 2 limes
2 teaspoons kosher salt
2 teaspoons red pepper flakes
1 teaspoon dried poultry seasoning
1 teaspoon ground allspice
1 teaspoon brown sugar
1 teaspoon black pepper
1 cup low-sodium chicken broth

—

Put all ingredients (except the chicken and chicken broth) in a food processor and blend until smooth. Apply a generous amount of the marinade to the exterior of the chicken. Refrigerate the chicken overnight. When it's time to cook, bring your smoker or oven up to 325°F. Wipe excess marinade from the surface of the chicken. Place the chicken in a roasting pan and season its skin with salt and pepper. Cook uncovered for 1 hour. Add the chicken broth to the roasting pan and cover with a lid or foil. Let the chicken continue to cook for about 2 hours. Do not remove the chicken from the cooker until the internal temperature is at least 190°F in the legs and thighs and at least 180°F in the breast. Cooking time will vary based upon the size of the chicken. When done, let the chicken rest for 20 minutes before carving.

Sauce Chien

¼ cup low-sodium chicken broth
¼ cup parsley, chopped
2 scallions, chopped
1 small tomato, seeded and diced
1 garlic clove, minced
Juice of 1 lime
2 tablespoons olive oil
½ teaspoon ground allspice
Salt, black pepper, and red pepper flakes, to taste

—

While the chicken is cooking, combine the ingredients and mix well. The sauce should have a texture similar to pico de gallo. Refrigerate until it's time to serve with the poulet boucané.

FOUR

BEAUCHAMP'S BARBECADO

Native American Food Preservation

Smoke-dried foods were important sources of nourishment in the times before refrigeration. Although Europeans who came to the Americas during the sixteenth and seventeenth centuries were acquainted with smoked and dried foods, they weren't familiar with the process Indigenous people in the Americas used to dry and smoke foods using wooden grills.

EARLY GERMAN, FRENCH, AND ENGLISH ACCOUNTS OF BARBECUING

Based upon the COT, one would think sixteenth-century Spanish chroniclers of the Americas played a prominent role in providing the details of how Native Americans preserved foods on barbacoas during the sixteenth century. However, they didn't. In fact, they demonstrated a remarkable lack of curiosity for it. An example of this attitude is seen in a very brief description of how Aboriginals boiled iguanas, "But this is enough about cooking recipes. Let us pass on to other subjects."[1] Iberian explorers were more focused on foods found in the Americas that could be grown and sold in Europe, Africa, and Asia for profit, such as chili peppers, potatoes, and maize. It was 65 years after Columbus first set foot in Haiti before a detailed description of how Native Americans used wooden hurdles to preserve foods was published in Europe.

A bearded Hans Staden depicted with purported cannibalistic Native Americans in sixteenth-century Brazil. *Americae Tertia Pars Memorabilē Provinciæ Brasiliæ Historiam Continē*, 1597.

HANS STADEN

Hans Staden (1525–76) was born in Homberg, Germany. In 1547, he traveled to South America and returned home safely in 1548. In 1549, he set sail for Río de la Plata in South America. His ship was wrecked, and he didn't reach his intended destination until 1552. Soon after he was captured by Tupinambá warriors and enslaved. Staden claims he feared he was going to be cooked and eaten by his captors. He was spared, he claimed, because he could facilitate communication between the Tupinambá and the Portuguese. He also claimed to have healed the Tupinambá king and his household through prayer, which resulted in him being embraced as a friend before returning to Europe in 1555.

Staden's account of his ordeal titled *Warhaftige Historia und beschreibung eyner Landtschafft der Wilden Nacketen, Grimmigen Menschfresser-Leuthen in der Newenwelt America gelegen* (*True History: An Account of Cannibal Captivity in Brazil*), was published in 1557. Although Staden didn't tell us the Tupinambá name for the hurdle on which meats and fish were preserved, he did record the earliest detailed accounts of the process and the name of the preserved foods, which is "Mockaein." He wrote,

> They also make a meal from fish and flesh, and do it in this way: they roast the flesh or fish above the fire in the smoke, and they allow it to become quite dry;

> then they pull it to pieces, dry it once again on the fire in pots called Yueppaun. Thereupon they pound it small in a wooden mortar, and they pass it through a sieve, reducing it in such a manner to powder. This lasts a long time; for they have not the custom of salting fish and meat. . . . When they want to cook any food, flesh or fish, which is to last some time, they put it four spans high above the fireplace, upon rafters, and make a moderate fire underneath, leaving it in such a manner to roast and smoke, until it becomes quite dry. When they afterward would eat thereof, they boil it up again and eat it, and such meat they call Mockaein.[2]

Staden's "Mockaein" was recorded by sixteenth-century Portuguese chroniclers as moquém. Moquém refers to wooden hurdles, the meat and fish preserved on them, earth ovens, and certain foods that are stewed in pots. The verb *moquear* refers to the act of cooking moquém.[3] An early description of the moquém (with the spelling *moquén*) is found in a letter written in 1554 by a Portuguese priest named Luis de Grã (1523–1609). He mentioned "[S]moked meat they bring from a moquén" (author's translation).[4] In 1584, a Portuguese priest in Brazil named Fernão de Cardim (1549–1625) mentioned the *peixinhos de moquem assados* (fish roasted on a moquem), potatoes, and fruits used in the Tupinambá recipe for *moquecas*. When Staden's passage is compared to that one, it's clear that the fish weren't only "roasted," they were broiled, dried, and smoked. A passage from 1610 describes how meat was cooked in an earth oven called a moquém as it was being "roasted in a moquém, which is done by making a hole in the ground, filling it with coals and placing a layer of banana leaves over them, which are taller than a man and two or three inches wide, and, after covering it with another layer, cast dirt on it, so that the hole is covered" (author's translation).[5]

JEAN DE LÉRY

Jean de Léry was a French explorer who lived among the Tupinamba people in Brazil near Rio de Janeiro from 1557 to 1558. The account of his experiences was published in France in 1578 titled *Histoire d'un voyage faict en la terre du Bresil, autrement dite Amerique* (*History of a Voyage to the Land of Brazil)*. Like Staden, de Léry also claimed that some Native Americans in South America were cannibals. De Léry's disturbing passages about cannibalism and the "strange" way Native Americans preserved foods on wooden grills also demonstrates why Europeans adopted words such as boucan, berbekot (English speakers preferred *barbacot*), and barbacoa.

De Léry described the boucan as a "store-house." That's reminiscent of how Spanish chroniclers described barbacoas as being used to store corn and valuables. Unlike barbecuing during the OSBP, the carcasses in Staden's and de Léry's accounts were "cut in pieces." Moreover the Tupinamba didn't dig a pit under the grills to contain burning embers, and instead of cooking the meat to tenderize it—such as was done using the OSBT— they let it remain on the grill until it was thoroughly dried. His statement that meats were placed over "a soft fire of dry wood, that there may be no smoke almost at all" is curious. Nevertheless he may have been referring to the first phase of the Native American meat preservation process when the meats or fish were roasted or broiled. That part is clear from the description of how Indigenous women supposedly reacted during the process: "The old women sit beside the boucan collecting the grease that drips off the big wooden grills and they say, '*Yguatou*,' which means, 'It tastes good' as they lick the grease from their fingers."[7]

FRANCIS DRAKE

When English explorer Francis Drake visited the Americas in the 1580s, a French chronicler who accompanied him wrote a firsthand account of a Native American preserving fish and meat on a hurdle complete with a watercolor illustration, titled "Come Les Yndes Boucquane Ou Rotissent Le Poisson Et La Chair" ("How the Indians Buccan or Roast Fish and Meat"). He described how the cook made a big fire and allowed it to burn down to embers before building a wooden grill that rested on four forks stuck in the ground. After the meat and fish were placed on the grill, the cook turned them often to prevent them from scorching. As the meat and fish continued to cook, grease was rendered out and dripped into the fire, thus creating smoke and steam that flavored the food. The process continued until the meats and fish were cooked, smoked, and dried.

The dripping grease indicates that during the first stage of the process the food was being cooked at a high temperature. By the time the meats and fish were fully cooked, the temperature of the burning coals started to drop. The meats and fish remained on the wooden grill until they were dry and cured with smoke, which imparted a red color to them.[8] Like other early modern Europeans, Drake's chronicler struggled to adequately describe the buccaning process and resorted to the phrase *boucaner ou rotir* (buccan or roast) and *cuite* (cooked.) Nonetheless he described the same food preservation process as de Léry's boucaner, which combined broiling (or roasting), drying, and smoking.

JEAN DE LÉRY'S ACCOUNT OF BOUCANAGE

De Léry wrote detailed accounts of how Indigenous people in South America used boucans during the sixteenth century. Whatever the reasons (we can only speculate) he not only associated the boucan with preserving game and fish, but also with cannibalism as recorded in the following passage:

> And if they set upon the Enemy unawares, as many men, women and children as they meet with, are not only brought away, but also slain by the Enemies returning in their Country, and put upon Boucan in pieces, and at length devoured. . . . The Americans [Native Americans] fastening four wooden forks in the ground, of the thickness of an arm, three foot asunder, in the figure of a square, and almost of the equal height of three feet, lay sticks across over them two fingers distant each other from the other, and so make a wooden Grate: this, in their language they name Boucan. They have many such Grates in their houses, whereon they lay flesh cut into gobbets or pieces, and making a soft fire of dry wood, that there may be no smoke almost at all, they suffer them to be broiled as long as they please, after this manner, having twice turned them in the space of an hour. And because they do not powder meats with salt, as [in France], they use the only remedy of broiling, for the preserving of them.
>
> Therefore although they had taken thirty whole beasts in one day, (such as we will describe in this Chapter,) they would lay them all cut in pieces, upon those Grates, as soon as it might be done, lest they should be tainted and corrupted: and there, being often turned, they are sometimes broiled and scorched above four and twenty hours together, until the inside of the flesh be as well roasted as the outside, and by this means they are all preserved from corruption. Nor is there any other manner of dressing or preserving fish, which when they have gotten, they dry them in great plenty, to make Meal, especially those which in the Country language they call Piraparati, which are the very true and natural Mullets, of the which I shall hereafter speak in another place.

> And the Grates among the Barbarians are rightly to be accounted the Shambles, and Store-house: and therefore you shall scarce come to their Villages, but you may see them laden with the flesh of wild beasts, and fishes: and it usually happened also very often, as we shall hereafter speak, if you come unto the Barbarians, that you shall behold these Grates filled with man's flesh, which, I think, they bring as spoils taken from the conquered enemies, to be slain, and eaten.[6]

THOMAS HARRIOT

The earliest eyewitness account of Native Americans preparing food on wooden hurdles recorded in English was published in 1585 by the English scientist and ethnographer Thomas Harriot (1560–1621). Writing of Indigenous cooks in what is today North Carolina, Harriot states: "After they have taken a store of fish, they move them into a place fit to dress them. There, they stick up in the ground 4 stakes in a square room and lay 4 posts upon them and others over them like a hurdle, of sufficient height, and laying their fish upon this hurdle, they make a fire underneath to broil them, not after the manner of the people of Florida, which do but scorch, and harden their meat in the smoke only to reserve for the winter."[9]

Harriot's claim that the Native Americans he visited didn't preserve fish on hurdles "after the manner of the people of Florida" is curious because other old accounts of Indigenous people in that region indicate they did preserve fish in that way.[10]

JOHN SMITH

Another early English-language account of Native Americans in North America preserving and cooking foods on hurdles was recorded by the English explorer John Smith (1580–1631). Smith referred to the process used by Native Americans in Virginia as being "after the Spanish fashion . . . they turne first the one side, then the other, til it be as drie as their jerkin beefe in the west Indies, that they may keepe it a month or more without putrifying." The term "Spanish fashion" refers to the charquini process that was employed in Spanish colonies. That implies jerked meats were known in the Caribbean and Jamaica at least several years before the Abbot of Jamaica mentioned jerked hog in his 1611 report to Spain's king.[11] *Jerkin* eventually became *jerked*, presumably

How sixteenth-century eastern Algonquians cooked fish. By John White, ca. 1585.

first in Jamaica after England took control of the island in 1655. Smith also described how Powhatans cooked meats and fish, writing: "Their fish and flesh they boyle either very tenderly, or broyle it so long on hurdles over the fire."[12]

BEAUCHAMP PLANTAGENET

The first verbs used by non-English speaking Europeans to refer to the Native American way of preserving meats and fish included the Spanish charquini, the Portuguese moquear, and the French boucaner. Later Dutch and English speakers shifted the function of the nouns berbekot and barbacot to verbs. By 1607 English speakers had added the verb jerkin (from the Spanish charquini).[13] By at least the 1640s, English speakers added the verb *barbecado*. Although the word barbecue (see Chapter 5, "Richard's Barbycu") was in use during the 1640s, no accounts of it being used as a verb has been found in literature earlier than 1661.

Barbecado first appeared in a pamphlet that was ostensibly authored by a man named Beauchamp Plantagenet titled *A Description of the Province of New Albion* and published in London in 1648. Some parts of the pamphlet have been in dispute since at least 1840. Scholars claim the actual author is the English explorer Edmund Plowden (1590–1659). Even so, the date of the pamphlet's publication nor the author's claims regarding Native Americans have been disputed.[14] Describing how Indigenous people who lived near the Chesapeake Bay cured fish on hurdles, the author wrote, "The Indians in stead [*sic*] of salt doe barbecado or dry and smoak fish."[15] Barbecado is the earliest known variant of the verb barbecue in English literature. It appears to be an attempt among English speakers to shift the function of the English *barbycu* or the Spanish barbacoa from a noun to a verb by blending it with the English word *carbonado*, which is both a noun that refers to grilled meats and a verb that refers to grilling.

The author who wrote under the name Beauchamp Plantagenet gave us the only known appearance of the word barbecado in early modern literature, and it's hard to determine how widespread its use may have been during the seventeenth century. However, it's clear that the verb was short-lived as English speakers eventually preferred the verbs jerked and barbecued.

EDMUND HICKERINGILL

Edmund Hickeringill (1631–1708) was born in the English village of Aberford. During the First English Civil War, he joined the staunch supporter of the Parliament of England Colonel Robert Lilburne (1613–65) as a chaplain. Later he served as a soldier in Scotland and the Swedish service. After Britain took control of Jamaica in 1655, Hickeringill visited the island and was inspired to author a pamphlet titled *Jamaica Viewed with all the Ports, Harbours, and their Several Soundings, Towns, and Settlements,* which was published in 1661. That pamphlet is significant because it includes the earliest use of the verb barbecued in English literature found in the following excerpt:

> But usually their Slaves, when captive ta'ne [taken],
> Are to the English sold; and some are slain,
> And their Flesh forthwith Barbacu'd and eat
> By them, their Wives and Children as choice meat.
> Thence are they call'd *Caribs*, or *Cannibals*.[16]

Hickeringill has been quoted by many who write about barbecuing. However, the context in which Hickeringill wrote the verb barbecued is rarely, if ever, examined. Although the passage appears in a pamphlet titled *Jamaica Viewed*, Hickeringill was writing about what he believed to be cannibals in South America, not Jamaica. Hickeringill clarified that fact by commenting about the "Native Indians" and "Guiana and Charby Indians, that cohabit with the English in Surinam" and added, "But this Diversion is somewhat out of our way to Jamaica."[17] Other early modern works written by Hans Staden and Jean de Léry that associate cannibalism with Indigenous people in South America, in which Hickeringill had read, shed light on his terms "their Slaves" and "Barbacu'd." Consequently Hickeringill's verb Barbacu'd referred to the Native American meat preservation technique grotesquely applied to human flesh, not a process similar to the OSBT.

BARBECUING "IN THE INDIAN MANNER"

Indigenous people who live today within the borders of the Guiana Amazonian Park still preserve foods on wooden hurdles using what is claimed to be the same process implemented at the time of first contact with Europeans. Modern conservationists created video documentation of how the Indigenous peoples of Guiana roast, smoke, and dry meats and fish with a process that combines all three techniques. The video depicts the following: After meat and fish are placed on a wooden grill made of sticks, a fire is kindled under it. At first, flames from the fire roast the meats and fish resulting in rendered fat dripping into the coals that creates smoke and steam that flavors the food on the grill. When fully cooked the food can be safely eaten, yet it remains on the grill for the next phase of the process. As the fire dies down, its temperature drops and the foods on the grill above begin to tenderize much like how southern barbecue becomes tender after long cooking. The foods remain on the hurdle while being constantly flipped one side to the other during the entire process. Eventually the coals smolder and smoke with more intensity, which preserves the foods while repelling insects. Smoke, together with the acute reduction of moisture in the meats and fish, preserve them so they can be safely stored for future use.[18]

That video reveals why the Native American way of preserving foods on hurdles was as unfamiliar to Staden and de Léry as it was to Iberian chroniclers before them. In fact, de Léry, who was born in the country that gave us the culinary arts, stated, "*Buccaning* is a way of roasting meat that is unknown to us in France" (author's translation).[19] Clearly the way Native Americans combined broiling, drying, and smoking in a single process was something new to the Europeans who visited the Americas in the sixteenth and seventeenth centuries.[20] The unfamiliar nature of Native American barbecuing explains why early modern Europeans had such a hard time describing the process. The best English words available to describe were *roast*, *smoke,* and *broil,* none of which was adequate because Native Americans preserved foods using a unified process that combined all three techniques. Speakers of other European languages had the same difficulty. That's ultimately why the verbs boucaner, berbekot, charquini, and barbecue were added to European languages.

NORTH AMERICAN JERKY

Settlers in the North American frontier didn't learn to make venison jerky from Indigenous people in Brazil, Spaniards, buccaneers, or Jamaicans. They learned it from Native Americans in North America.[21] Pemmican (a food made with fruit and dried meat) was also adopted from Native Americans in North America. Many of the enslaved Africans brought to the Americas were familiar with preserving meat and fish in Africa with salt and smoke, as was discussed in Chapter 2, "Herbert's Patta." The similarities in how Africans, Native Americans, and Europeans preserved meats was the foundation on which charqui, Jamaican jerk, and North American jerky independently developed.

Robert Beverly observed that the Native American way of barbecuing meat on a hurdle "drys up the Gravy." "Gravy" refers to the "running juices of roast meat," according to culinary historian Karen Hess (1918–2007). Therefore Beverly was describing a meat preservation technique.[22] The Native American way of barbecuing was important because it prolonged the shelf life of food without the use of salt. It was also important because Native Americans didn't observe the custom of mealtimes. In those cultures, people ate meals whenever they pleased; if food was available, of course.[23] Cooking and holding soups and stews in simmering pots was a way of making sure a safe-to-eat meal was always available. Cooking and holding meat and fish on grills set over a low-temperature bed of coals was another convenient way to keep meat and fish warm and ready to eat for hours while preventing them from spoiling.

During the seventeenth century, Anglos in the Americas adopted the Native American way of barbecuing but modified it according to their preferences. Those preferences weren't always culinary in nature. In 1665, a man who had attempted to murder the captain-general of Guyana, Lord Willoughby (1605–66), was brutally punished by being dragged naked from his jail cell and "dry barbicued or dry roasted after the Indian manner" on a barbacue erected specifically for his torture and execution. After he expired, his body was quartered and his head was placed atop a pole.[24] Anglos in Guyana weren't the only ones to distinguish between barbecuing and barbecuing "after the Indian manner." George Washington (1732–99) also made such a distinction.

In 1758, during the French and Indian War, Colonel George Washington wrote a letter to his British commander in which he complained about not having salt to

(continued on page 105)

TWO ACCOUNTS OF HOW JERKY WAS MADE

In 1778, the Irish-born Pennsylvania politician George Bryan (1731–91) wrote to a newspaper under the penname Agricola. He argued that the leaders of the Continental Army should serve soldiers jerked beef dried on hurdles without the use of salt.[27] Bryan's detailed instructions for jerking meats are as follows:

> The mode of curing it in this way is easy and certain; in summer it may be dried in the sun, making a smoke to keep off the flies, but in winter it is done by fire. Erect a stage, large or small, according to the quantity you have to cure, about four feet from the ground, this you may do by planting posts with crotches in the earth, and laying poles or sticks across so as to admit the heat, and let them be so small, as not to cover too much of the surface of the meat; make your fire under this stage, so as to distribute the heat equally, and let it not be so great as to roast or broil, but gently to dry the flesh; and when the pores are sufficiently stopped, and both surfaces dry, hang it up in the smoke to dry through. The Hunters, and Indians, of choice take provisions of this kind with them, as the carriage is light, one pound being of equal nourishment with six pounds of salted meat.[28]

After traveling through the American West on a diplomatic mission in the 1830s, American lawyer, painter, and author George Catlin (1796–1872) wrote of Native Americans who lived on the Great Plains: "Their mode of curing and preserving the buffalo meat is somewhat curious, and in fact, it is almost incredible also; for it is all cured or dried in the sun, without the aid of salt or smoke! . . . This seems almost an unaccountable thing, and the more so, as it is done on the hottest months of the year, and also in all the different latitudes of an Indian country."[29] Catlin's reaction to the "almost unaccountable" way Native Americans dried and cured meats was similar to the reaction early explorers in the Americas had when they witnessed it among Native Americans. Because firewood was scarce on the open plains, the use of smoke wasn't always a part of the process used by Native Americans who lived there.[30]

(continued from page 103)

preserve beef, "We have not an Oz. of Salt Provisions of any kind here, and that it is impossible to preserve the Fresh, (especially as we have no salt neither) by any other Means than Barbacuing it in the Indian manner; in doing which it loses near a half; so that a Party who receives 10 days Provisions will be obliged to live on little better than 5 days' allowance of meat, kind—a thing Impracticable."[25] Although the denture-wearing Washington often enjoyed Virginia-style barbecue that was tender and delicious, he disapproved of beef jerky—referred to as being barbecued "in the Indian manner"—because it lost half its weight, which made it more difficult for him to provide each soldier with their promised daily pound of meat.[26]

Bryan's process for making jerky (see box, "Two Accounts of How Jerky Was Made") was apparently influenced by how Native Americans in North America preserved meats and fish without salt. George Washington never mentioned barbecuing in the Caribbean fashion and Beverly didn't reference Native Americans in the Caribbean or South America when he described Native American barbecuing. That in combination with the differences between Bryan's North American meat jerking process and the charquini process used in the Caribbean and South America that calls for salt supports the assertion that although the verbs jerk and barbecue were imported into North America, they were used to refer to different meat curing methods.

The American author Lettice Bryan (1805–77) shared instructions for barbecuing venison hams in her cookbook *The Kentucky Housewife* published in 1839. She explained how to debone and salt venison hams before hanging them up in a smokehouse to "smoke them till dry." She warned, "Plan to salt fresh venison and barbecue it immediately. . . . Dried venison makes excellent chip for the table."[31] The definition of the verb barbecue in *A New English Dictionary on Historical Principles*, published in 1888, is "to dry cure (flesh, etc.) by exposure upon a barbecue."[32] That indicates even as late as 1888 drying meat to preserve it was known as barbecuing. The London-born author and artist Everett Watson Mellor (1878–1965) shed more light on the subject in 1906. He wrote, "The name 'barbecue' is derived from the aboriginal Indian name for the places on which they dried fruit and fish and hogs. Hence, we have the term 'barbecued pig' for dried pig."[33] Americans expanded the definition to include all dried meats, not just pork.

In 1902, a reporter in Georgia wrote about "a large heap of fat barbecued briskets, rumps and tongues of buffalo and deer, as well as plenty of bear ribs, which are piled on large racks." He went on to describe how traders "make bacon" that they "barbecue over a slow fire." It's clear that the barbecued brisket described in the passage was smoked and dried like Lettice Bryan's venison hams, not the tender and juicy brisket that made central Texas famous.[34]

Native American woman in South Dakota drying meat on a hurdle, ca. 1908. Library of Congress.

Powhatan-style barbecue grill. Photo by the author.

According to a few seventeenth-century accounts, Native Americans also had a way of barbecuing that wasn't a preservation method. In addition to John Smith's description of how Powhatans broiled meat "so long on hurdles over the fire," in 1687, the aforementioned Reverend John Clayton recorded how Native Americans in Virginia wrapped venison in leaves while "barbecuting" it in embers.[35] Robert Beverly described how Native Americans in Virginia barbecued meats "by laying the Meat itself upon the Coals," which is apparently a reference to slowly broiling meat or fish. Beverly may have been describing the same cooking technique as Clayton, but neglected to mention the leaves.[36]

Europeans and Americans were still associating barbecuing with Native Americans as late as the early nineteenth century. John M. Duncan (ca. 1795–1825) was born in Scotland, and visited Virginia in 1818. While there he was invited to attend a barbecue in Alexandria. He described the enslaved African American cooks laboring to prepare the foods as, "a scene by the way which suggested a tolerable idea of an encampment of Indians preparing for a feast after the toils of the chase."[37] After watching pitmasters near Richmond, Virginia, in the early nineteenth century, Colonel Thomas H.

Ellis (1814–98) compared Virginia's barbecuing technique to the Powhatan method of cooking on wooden barbecue grills. He wrote, "The mode of roasting, too, was primitive—reminding one of the picture in Captain John Smith's *True Travels, Adventures, and Observations*, wherein is given the Indian method of cooking fish, which was simply to build a platform by laying sticks across four stakes driven in the ground, and make a fire beneath the platform, and place the fish upon it to be broiled."[38]

Beef Jerky

This recipe for beef jerky is a modern version of what Beauchamp Plantagenet might call barbecado.

4 pounds beef, top round
5 tablespoons brown sugar
4 tablespoons seasoned salt
2 tablespoons white sugar
2 tablespoons coarse ground black pepper
1 tablespoon table salt
1 teaspoon granulated garlic
1 teaspoon granulated onion
1 teaspoon smoked paprika
ground cayenne pepper, to taste

—

When making jerky at home, follow all US Department of Agriculture safety recommendations.[39] *Trim as much fat and membrane from the surface of the meat as possible. Place the meat in the freezer for about 30 minutes. (Slightly freezing the beef makes it easier to cut into thin slices.) Slice the beef against the grain into ¼-inch-thick steaks. If any of the steaks turn out thicker than a ¼ inch, pound them with a meat mallet until they are the correct thickness.*

Combine all seasoning ingredients in a bowl and mix well. Place the meat in a sealable, food-safe container, and add the seasonings making sure all of the meat is well coated. Seal the container and refrigerate for 2 to 8 hours.

When it's time to cook, bring your smoker up to 185°F to 190°F. Use your preference of wood chunks for smoke. Place the steaks on the grill grates or on a flat pan making sure they don't touch each other. After the steaks cook for 1½ hours, flip them over and let them continue to cook for another 1½ hours. After 3 hours total cooking time, raise the temperature of the smoker to 275°F, and let the meat cook at that temperature for 20 minutes and its internal temperature is at least 180°F. Remove the meat from the smoker and let it cool. Slice the jerky into strips and it's ready to eat. Place the jerky in an airtight container and refrigerate it. Consume it within 3 to 5 days.

Beef Jerky. Photo by the author.

FIVE

RICHARD'S BARBYCU

The English Word Barbecue

The assumption made by some that the English word *barbecue* has always had the definitions it has today is not supported by historical sources. The origins of the word barbecue are murky, and it has had many definitions over its (approximately) 400 years of existence. This chapter investigates the word barbecue starting with its first known appearance in English literature to modern times while highlighting its changing definitions.

SOMETHING BORROWED, SOMETHING NEW

Although sixteenth-century Spaniards borrowed the noun barbacoa from Native Americans, they preferred the verb charquini when referring to the process of preserving meat on barbacoas. French speakers in Brazil borrowed the Tupinambá noun boucan and shifted its function to be a verb (boucaner) and an adjective (*boucané*).

Dutch speakers in South America adopted the noun berbekot (also spelled *barbequot* and *barbracot*) and shifted it to a verb and an adjective, ostensibly, after they established colonies in the Americas during the late sixteenth century.[1] English speakers, on the other hand, borrowed words to refer to barbecuing from other Europeans.[2] For example, *buccaneer* was adopted from the French boucanier, not from Native Americans.

English speakers in South America possibly borrowed the noun barbacot from the Dutch and shifted its function to a verb (*barbecute*) and an adjective (barbecuted).[3]

The earliest published theory for the origin of the English word barbecue goes back to at least 1820. Because barbecuing in the United States during the Original Southern Barbecuing Period (OSBP) was associated with cooking whole animal carcasses, some assumed that the French language phrase *de la barbe à la queue*, which translates to English as *beard to tail*, is the origin of the word barbecue. Hence the sentence, "The pig was roasted barbecue," meaning "the pig was roasted beard to tail."[4] In 1856, an alternative theory was offered. Instead of a French phrase, a Bostonian argued that the word barbecue came from a "slight corruption" of *barbecutt*, which he claimed was an Arabic word that referred to a roasted horse carcass.[5] In the early twenty-first century, it was suggested by an American author that the word barbecue was derived from syllables in an Arawakan-language phrase that means "sacred fire pit."[6] The problem with all of those arguments is they favor modern definitions of the word barbecue without considering the many other meanings it has had over the last roughly four centuries.

The French anthropologist Pierre Grenand, who specializes in Native American populations in Guyana, has claimed that English speakers adopted *barbacot* from Native Americans in South America after Sir Walter Raleigh's (1552–1618) first visit there in the 1590s. The word barbacot, according to Grenand, eventually evolved into the word barbecue after England had established colonies in the Americas during the early seventeenth century.[7] The most widely accepted etymology of the English word barbecue comes from the aforementioned Edward Tylor who asserted in 1865 that barbecue was derived not from a Native American word, but the Spanish word barbacoa.[8]

Linguists tell us it's rare for words from two different languages to be fully equivalent in all situations.[9] The words barbecue, boucan, berbekot, and barbacoa bear witness to that fact. Of those four words (referred to hereafter as *barbecue et al.*), the Spanish noun barbacoa is the only one that wasn't used as a verb and an adjective until Americans starting using it that way in the twentieth century. Therefore barbecue et al. are more like cousins than quadruplets. To maintain clarity and precision, barbecue et al. should never be considered synonyms and shouldn't always be used interchangeably.

Evidence that barbacoa is not an accurate Spanish translation of boucan is found in the 1863 edition of the Spanish *Diccionario Militar* (*Military Dictionary*). It states that French buccaneers got their name from "una especie de parrillas para asar carne" or, in English, "a kind of grill used to roast meat," and the word barbacoa is never mentioned. If barbacoa were the equivalent of boucan, it stands to reason that the compilers of the *Diccionario Militar* would have used barbacoa instead of parrilla in their definition. The fact that they didn't supports the assertion that the way Americans use barbacoa today doesn't reflect the word's traditional Spanish definition.[10]

"A LITTLE PLATFORM OF GROUND"

After several failed investments in England, Richard Ligon (ca. 1585–1662) set sail for Barbados in 1647. He remained there until 1650. The earliest appearance of the word barbecue in English literature is found in his *A True and Exact History of the Island of Barbadoes,* which was published in London in 1657, with the archaic spelling of barbycu. Ligon's "barbycu" was not a barbecue grill, and it wasn't jerked or barbecued pork. It also had nothing to do with horses, cooking, beards, tails, or fire pits. It was a noun that referred to a structure used to temporarily store sugar cane. Ligon described it as "the place where they unload, is a little platform of ground, which is contiguous to the Mill-house, which they call a Barbycu; about 30 foot long and 10 foot broad; done about with a double rayle [rail] to keep the Canes from falling out of that room."[11] Therefore Ligon's barbycu was a structure similar to a barbacoa used to store corn and valuables.

England colonized Barbados in 1625, which was 18 years after the Virginia colony was established. Initially planters in Barbados attempted to replicate Virginia, but their efforts to cultivate tobacco failed. By 1637 they had successfully transitioned to cultivating sugar cane. By 1640 Dutch traders from Brazil had brought their sugar cane to Barbados along with enslaved people who were skilled in growing and processing it.

Ligon probably never heard the word barbycu until after he arrived in Barbados in the 1640s. By that time the term could have been in use for as long as several decades. According to the laws of culinary history identified by Karen Hess, "print always lags behind practice" and "the first appearance of a word or recipe doesn't necessarily indicate first use."[12] Therefore barbecue may have been in use much earlier than the 1640s, and Barbados may not be the word's place of origin. However, we can be relatively sure that by the early 1640s English speakers were using the word in Barbados. According to Ligon, barbycu was used by enslaved people who toiled on sugar plantations that included people from Africa and their descendants born in the Americas and enslaved Native Americans from South America, Mexico, and North America.[13] Therefore enslaved Creoles from different backgrounds, ethnicities, and who spoke different languages very well could be the ones who gave us the word barbecue.

Plantations in the sixteenth- and seventeenth-century Americas were often populated by groups of people who didn't share a common language. That sometimes resulted in the development of a second language called a *pidgin,* which is a simplified form of a new, shared language spoken by groups of people who speak different

A Cocoa Drying House in Granada called a "bocan.." *Illustrated London News,* March 28, 1857.

languages. Many linguists believe creole languages developed among the children of people who spoke pidgins.[14] That means it's possible that the English word barbecue developed from either a creole language or a pidgin spoken by enslaved people. That supports the assertion that the word barbecue evolved from English and Dutch variations of barbacot as well as the Spanish barbacoa. For example, Ligon's use of barbycu only as a noun supports Tylor's assertion that the word was derived from the Spanish noun barbacoa. Influences to language and culture introduced by people from Dutch Brazil in Barbados in the early 1640s support Grenand's assertion that barbecue evolved from babracot.

DIFFERENT PEOPLE, DIFFERENT PLACES, DIFFERENT DEFINITIONS

Definitions for the word barbecue have always depended on where the word was being used and the speaker's place of origin. For example, although Maroons in Jamaica referred to wooden grills on which they jerked pork as patta or caban, visitors and immigrants in Jamaica who came from the British Isles referred to pattas as barbecues (see Chapter 2, "Herbert's Patta").[15] People in some colonies that cultivated coffee called the flat slabs on which coffee and spices were dried "barbecues." In British Grenada, the slabs and the associated drying houses were referred to as *bocans*; in British Guiana, the slabs were called barbacots.[16] How Ligon's "platform of ground" and the flat slabs used for drying foods became to be known as barbecues is not clear. Because early modern Europeans associated barbecuing with Native Americans, Creoles, and barbarians, it might be rooted in the Native American method of drying foods on mats spread over the ground. For example, in 1648 Native Americans in the Chesapeake Bay region "sun dried on the rocks, Strawberries, Mulberries, Symnels, Maycocks and Horns like Cucumbers."[17] The Powhatan people in the Tidewater Virginia region had a similar practice, according to John Smith.[18] The Irish-born John Brickell (1710–45) wrote of how Native Americans "commonly barbecu or dry their Venison on Mats."[19] Based upon those accounts, it's clear that early modern European Anglos had a different understanding of the word barbecue than North American Anglos before and after the War of Independence. There is no known evidence that North American Anglos have ever used the word barbecue to refer to flat slabs used to dry foods or to refer to bridges, beds, porches, or corn cribs.

The verb *barbacu'd*, or a form of that verb, may have been used among some English speakers at least as far back as the 1630s. Barbacu'd refers to the process of curing and drying foods on hurdles or flat slabs, as discussed in Chapter 4, "Beauchamp's Barbecado." Around the turn of the eighteenth century, the word barbecue, and its variants, started to show up in literature referring to carcasses cooked over hot coals or cooked in earth ovens. Examples include Robert Beverly's account of Native Americans barbecuing over coals, also discussed in Chapter 4, and the *Rising Sun*'s 1726 advertisement for "a fine hog barbyqu'd." The Scottish Botanist John Bradbury (1768–1823) traveled through the United States between the years 1809 to 1811. In 1818, the first edition of Bradbury's *Travels in the Interior of America* was published in London, followed by a second edition in 1819. Writing of the significant number of settlers who started arriving in the Midwest from the East after the end of the American War of Independence, he described how they "occasionally give what they call a 'a barbique' in the woods." He wrote, "The hog is killed, dressed, and roasted after the Indian method; this consists in digging a hole, the bottom of which they cover with hot stones; on these the hog is laid, and covered over also with heated stones."[20] Bradbury's account of barbecuing in earth ovens reflects another eighteenth- and nineteenth-century British understanding of barbecuing. His description of how early settlers in Ohio roasted pigs "after the Indian method" in an earth oven is almost certainly an embellishment. The early settlers in Ohio came from states that barbecued hogs on grills set over pits of live embers. Bradbury's description of the "barbecuing" process is consistent with eighteenth-century and early nineteenth-century European accounts of how people in Jamaica "barbecued" pork in earth ovens. Therefore although Bradbury knew that settlers in Ohio barbecued hogs, he probably never personally witnessed a barbecue there. Americans only warmed up to the practice of referring to cooking meat in earth ovens as barbecuing after California became a state, as discussed in Chapter 7, "Juba's 'Cue."

BURNABY'S ROSETTA STONE

Although European Anglos used the word barbecue to refer to chairs, couches, beds, roasted or baked pigs, and flat slabs during the OSBP, those definitions were not adopted by North American Anglos. Furthermore before World War II, the practice of referring to an outdoor social event that featured barbecued meats as a barbecue was virtually unknown among people outside the United States. During the eighteenth and nineteenth centuries, people in England referred to roasted beef as a roast, to carbonadoed steak as a carbonado, and to a barbecued pig as a barbecue.[21] An 1884 British publication titled *Notes and Queries* even defined barbecue as "a roast hog."[22] At first glance that may appear to be insignificant. Upon closer examination, however, it turns out to be a critical clue to interpreting passages about barbecuing written by early modern European Anglo authors. Dampier and Wafer demonstrated that a person's understanding of the word barbecue during the seventeenth and eighteenth centuries depended on where they were from, where they visited, and their personal experiences. Fortunately, a British author left us the "Rosetta Stone" for understanding the eighteenth-century British phrase: a barbecue.

Clergyman Andrew Burnaby was born in Leicestershire, England, in 1732. He died 80 years later in London. During the years 1759 to 1760, he toured the colonial United States. While there he cultivated a friendly relationship with George Washington and authored a vivid account of life in the American colonies in his travelogue titled *Travels Through the Middle Settlements in North America in the Years 1759 and 1760*. Writing of Virginians, he noted their love of outdoor festivals and Virginia-style barbecued pork with the following passage, "The Virginian ladies, excepting these amusements, and now and then going upon a party of pleasure into the woods to partake of a barbacue."[23]

In the 1770s, Burnaby's book was translated into French. Realizing that most people in France didn't know what a barbacue was, the editor added a footnote erroneously explaining barbecue (not a barbecue) as, "A barbarous amusement where they beat pigs to death to tenderize the meat. I don't even think cannibals do such a thing" (author's translation).[24] Clearly even the French editor didn't know what a barbecue was, and his attempt to explain it only made matters worse. Notably the French editor also didn't make a connection between barbacue and boucan. In the 1798 edition of *Travels*, Burnaby corrected the record by adding this footnote to the passage, "In justice to the inhabitants of Virginia, I must beg leave to observe, that such a cruel and inhuman act was never, to my knowledge at least, practiced in that country. A barbacue is nothing more than a porket [a young pig] killed in the usual way, stuffed with spices and all rich ingredients, and basted with Madeira wine."[25]

Even though Burnaby tried to set the record straight, he didn't reference the Virginian barbecue recipe that called for vinegar, butter, salt, and red pepper. Instead, he cited the prevailing British recipe of stuffing a pig and basting it with Madeira wine. Nevertheless his footnote provides the key to understanding how eighteenth-century Britons defined the noun barbecue, which is as follows:

1. A whole, young pig that has been barbecued or baked in an oven.
2. The pig must be stuffed with spices (not dry rubbed).
3. The pig must be basted with Madeira wine (not a southern-style vinegar-based sauce).

Based upon Burnaby, it's clear that Britons of his era had their own understanding of barbecuing that was different than in the American colonies. There are no records of southern pitmasters stuffing pigs with spices before barbecuing them or basting them with Madeira wine during the OSBP. In addition to pork, Americans have always considered game meats, mutton, lamb, beef, and poultry to be appropriate meats for barbecuing. When passages written by Britons are analyzed in light of Burnaby's definition of the word barbecue, British notions of barbecuing become much clearer. The differences between how people in the South (the southern United States) understood barbecuing compared to how eighteenth- and nineteenth-century Britons understood it means old British passages about barbecuing are not directly applicable to the history of southern barbecuing. That also underscores the uniqueness of the southern barbecuing tradition.

Burnaby's British understanding of the phrase "a barbecue" was shared by many Britons who wrote on the subject of barbecuing. The London newspaper *The General Advertiser* printed an advertisement for the Sun Tavern on Fish Street on December 5, 1750, that stated, "A Barbicue to be ready at Half an Hour after Two o'Clock." That advertisement demonstrates how the phrase "a barbicue" in eighteenth-century Britain referred to the barbecued pig, not the event where it was served.[26] That understanding was also reflected in the British dramatist Samuel Foote's 1764 play, titled *The Patron*. In it a character states, "I am invited to dinner on a barbicu [*sic*], and the villains have forgot my bottle of chian [cayenne]."[27] Notice that the character was not invited to a barbecue. He was invited to dine "on a barbecue," which was a young pig that had been barbecued or baked whole. The Scottish doctor and poet James Grainger (1723–66) settled on the island of St. Kitts in 1759. In 1764, he published a poem titled *The Sugar Cane* in which he revealed his British barbecue knowledge:

> Both on the Avon and the banks of the Thame.
> Be thrifty, planter, e'en they skimming save:
> For, planter know, the refuse of the cane
> Serves needful purposes. Are barbecues
> The cates thou lovest?[28]

A careful reading of that poem reveals that Dr. Grainger's "barbecues" were not social events. He described them as "cates," which is another word for delicacies. Therefore another version of the passage can be, "Are barbecued pigs the delicacies thou lovest?"

When Captain Cook visited the Society Islands in French Polynesia during his second voyage to the Pacific (1772–75), the local chief honored him and his officers by serving two whole hogs that had been cooked in an earth oven. One of Cook's officers later wrote of the hogs, "They tasted better than an English barbecue: the equal degree of heat with which it stews underground, had preserved and concentrated all its juices; . . . and the skin, instead of being very hard, which is the case of roasted pork with us, was as tender as any other part."[29] It's clear that the "English barbecue" mentioned in that passage doesn't refer to a social event. The writer was contrasting a whole hog cooked the English way (an English barbecue) to the whole hog cooked in an earth oven (the Polynesian way).

The eighteenth-century British actor John Singleton also held to Burnaby's belief. Singleton composed a poem titled "The Barbecue," which was published in 1767. The poem's title refers to a whole pig carcass that was cooked in an earth oven after the "Maroon fashion." That was made clear in the passage, "[T]he verdant earth Spreads forth her matted carpet, sylvan feat; And lo! the smoaking Barbecue appears! Escorted by a train of sable guards."[30] Clearly, it was the piping hot pig that was "smoaking," not the event.

The seventeenth-century English explorer John Lawson (1674–1711) referred to animal carcasses being cooked by a Native American woman as *barbakues*. Lawson didn't reveal the kind of meat she was cooking. However, he did mention that she baked "white-bread" as well as any English cook. Because she was cooking bread made with wheat flour which was brought to the Americas by Europeans, it's possible that the "barbakues" were pig carcasses.[31]

In 1784, Lawrence Butler (of Westmoreland County, Virginia) wrote a letter to Mrs. Anna F. Cradock, who resided in Andrew Burnaby's birthplace: Leicestershire, England. Notice how Butler had to explain to Cradock what a Virginian barbecue was:

> I have been very happy since my arrival in Virginia, I am continually at Balls & Barbecues (the latter I don't suppose you know what I mean) I will try to describe it to you, it's a shoat [young pig] & sometimes a Lamb or Mutton & indeed sometimes a Beef splitt into & stuck on spitts & then they have a large Hole dugg in the ground where they have a number of Coals made of the Bark of Trees, put in this Hole, & then they lay the meat over that within about six inches of the Coals, & then they Keep basting it with Butter & Salt and Water & turning it every now and then, until its done.[32]

Although Butler compared barbecues to balls, indicating that he understood them to be social events, he didn't actually describe them. Instead he described the meats and the process used to barbecue them.

The Irish author, artist, and explorer Isaac Weld (1774–1856) visited Virginia in the late 1790s. One aspect of life in the United States that he felt compelled to explain to his European readers was "an entertainment which they call a barbacue." He went on to describe it as "a large party meeting together, either under some trees, or in a house, to partake of a sturgeon or pig roasted in the open air, on a sort of hurdle, over a slow fire."[33] Notice that Weld was careful to point out that the entertainments that featured barbecued sturgeons or pigs is what "they" (Americans) call "a barbacue."

Briton Francis Asbury (1745–1816) was the bishop of the Methodist Episcopal Church of America. In 1800 he visited Loudon County, Virginia, and attended a barbecue there. In typical early modern British fashion, Asbury didn't refer to the event as a barbecue. He referred to it as "a green-corn feast, with a roasted animal, cooked and eaten out of doors under a booth."[34] John Bradbury was also introduced to the uniquely American use of the word barbecue when he visited the United States in 1809 to 1811. Commenting on the outdoor festivals hosted by farmers in frontier communities in Missouri, he wrote, "the farmers occasionally give *what they call* 'a barbique.'"[35]

The aforementioned John M. Duncan wrote of the barbecue he attended in Alexandria, Virginia, "The very term [a barbecue] was new to me; but when explained to mean a kind of rural fête which is common in Virginia it was not difficult to persuade us to accept the invitation."[36] In 1858 a correspondent for the *Daily News London* felt compelled to explain what a barbecue in the United States was. He wrote, "Do our readers ask what a barbecue is? It is (or was) a feast, the piece de resistance of which is a boar, or other savory animal, cooked in a pit."[37] At least he tried to explain it. In 1858, an English journalist clumsily compared an American barbecue to a "ball" in an effort to explain it to British readers.[38]

The fact that a barbacue referred to a whole pig in eighteenth-century Britain and not an event is also supported by old dictionaries. *A New, Complete and Universal English Dictionary,* published in London in 1764, doesn't define barbecue as a noun. It defines it as a verb that means, "[T]o dress a whole hog." The noun barbecue shows up in the 1774 edition of *A Complete and Universal English Dictionary* and is defined as "a hog dressed whole after the West Indian manner."[39] That stands in contrast to the definition of the word barbecue found in Noah Webster's (1758–1843) *American English Dictionary of the English Language* published in 1828. Like many other English-language dictionary compilers, Webster accepted the British definition of the noun barbecue at face value and included it in his definition: "In the West Indies, a hog roasted whole." Although he may have relied on British dictionaries for that definition, he knew it didn't adequately describe the meaning of the word as used in the United States. Therefore he added, "It is with us [Americans], used for an ox or perhaps any other animal dressed in like manner" and "to roast any animal whole."[40] Somehow Webster neglected to include the other American definition, which is an outdoor social event that features whole, barbecued animal carcasses. *The Licensed Traders' Dictionary,* which was published in London in 1903, was apparently inspired by Webster. It defines barbecue with the British definition of "a West Indian dish, consisting of a hog roasted whole, stuffed with spice, and basted with Madeira wine," and Webster's American definition of "any animal roasted whole."[41]

By the late nineteenth century, British dictionaries were beginning to include the unique American usage of the word barbecue to refer to outdoor social events that featured barbecued meats. In *New Hazell Annual* published in London in 1888, we find, "'A barbecue' has been adopted *in America* [emphasis added] as a term to express any great gathering of people, where a large animal, such as an ox or hog, is dressed whole and partaken of by those assembled."[42] One of the definitions of the word barbecue given in *A New English Dictionary on Historical Principles* published in 1888 is, "In *U.S.* a large social entertainment, usually in the open air, at which animals are roasted whole, and other provisions liberally supplied."[43]

In spite of the updated definitions in those dictionaries, many people around the world remained unaware of the unique barbecue parlance used in the United States. That was demonstrated when hundreds of reporters from all around the world

A barbecue in New York City. *New York Tribune,* April 13, 1919.

converged in Washington, DC, in 1921 to cover the Conference of the Limitation of Armament, which was an international effort to regulate weapons of war. The wealthy publisher of the *Baltimore Sun*, Van Lear Black (1875–1930), invited all of the visiting foreign reporters to a barbecue that was held just outside of Washington, DC, "so that these foreign gentlemen would have the opportunity to witness a characteristic American entertainment." A correspondent for *The Washington Times* reported, "The word 'barbecue' was unfamiliar with the foreigners, and so it was inevitable that they should give it the most difficult and least phonetic pronunciation. They referred to the event as a berbeek."[44]

Briton Henry W. Nevinson, special correspondent at Washington for *The Manchester Guardian,* was invited to Van Lear Black's barbecue. He wrote the following account of the event, "When I first heard of the Barbecue, I thought it was some kind of animal—probably some kind of porcupine. But I was wrong." The matter-of-factness of that passage adds to the humor of it. Even with firsthand experience, Nevinson didn't fully understood how Americans used the word barbecue to refer to an event. To him, "the barbecue" was the carcass being barbecued. He continued, "Out in the open field a large trench fire was blazing, fed by forest logs. And over the flames hung in chains a huge mass of roasting flesh, dropping odours, dropping fats. It was the Barbecue. Not, as I had supposed, a fretful porcupine, but all that was mortal of a gentle ox."[45]

As late as the early 1950s barbecuing wasn't widely known among Britons. In the March 4, 1951, edition of the *Omaha World-Herald,* Columnist Frank Colby wrote, "The word barbecue and that method of preparing meat are generally unknown in England." In the October 12, 1947, edition of the same newspaper we find, "An Englishman visiting the western cattle country writes: 'Your word barbecue interests me. I have never heard it in England. Tell me about it so that I may take it home and introduce it (and the delicious way of preparing meat) to my friends.'"[46]

THE WORD *BARBECUE* IN THE UNITED STATES

The word *barbecue* was originally confined to describe things in the Americas. The practice of referring to outdoor social events that feature barbecued meats as "barbecues" emerged in the colonial United States and largely remained a uniquely American practice until the twentieth century. Unlike people in the United States who embraced barbecuing during their country's earliest history, Europeans didn't widely embrace the word barbecue until after World War II. Although there are a few accounts of people in England barbecuing pigs during the eighteenth century, the barbecuing technique was looked upon with suspicion or, at least, skepticism (see Chapter 8, "Ned's Barbacue"). People in France don't hold events they call boucans. They adopted the word barbecue from Americans. No one in the Netherlands hosts events called berbekots. Instead people in the Netherlands prefer the word barbecue, which they adopted from Americans sometime after World War II ended.[47] Dutch speakers in Suriname prefer the word *brabakoto.* The word barbacoa was little more than a distant memory in Spain until after the end of World War II.[48]

James Hammond Trumbull (1821–97) explained that barbecue is a Virginian word, which means it gained many definitions familiar to Americans today first in colonial Virginia.[49] Compilers of *A New English Dictionary on Historical Principles* also recognized Virginia's significant contributions to barbecuing in the United States. The compliers implied that barbecue was as Virginian as boucan was French: "The Virginia *barbacue* and the French *boucan* 'dried meat' were all derived from the names of the high wooden gridiron or scaffolding on which Indians dried, smoked, or broiled their meats."[50] Pierre Grenand added, "The barbecue is a cultural trait of the English colonies of America, just as the boucan is in French Creole culture" (author's translation).[51] Recognizing that barbecue is a term that's long been associated with the United States, a correspondent wrote in *The Western Star and Roma Advertiser* on April 30, 1887, "A hog barbecued is a West Indian and old Virginian term."[52]

It's difficult to determine exactly how the word barbecue was introduced in Virginia. Sailors or even well-read settlers from England could have brought it to the colony. However, there is a possibility that it was introduced to southeastern Virginia from Barbados through the intercolonial trading network that existed between the two colonies. After Barbados was established in 1625, colonists in North America started trading enslaved Native Americans and enslaved people of African descent in Barbados.[53] The fact that the trading network was bi-directional appears to be ignored by people who write about the history of barbecuing. The emphasis is almost always placed on the assertion that the exchange of things like language and food traditions only occurred from the Caribbean to North America with little or no consideration of the possibility that language and food traditions were also imported from North America to the Caribbean. One instance of that occurrence is the Jamaican use of the word *hominy* which was derived from *rockahomen*, a Virginian Algonquian word for maize.[54] Another example is Ligon's description of how Native American women in Barbados made cornbread using a pan they called a *pone*.[55] Pone is derived from the Virginian Algonquian word *apone*, which is the Powhatan name for cornbread cakes (i.e., corn pones).[56] Ligon was fascinated by the strange griddle the Native American women in Barbados used to cook their flat corncakes. Virginian colonists cooked hoecakes on a similar griddle they called a *bread hoe* (not to be confused with a European baking hoe).[57] It appears that Virginian bread hoes were exported to Barbados along with the word pone when enslaved Native Americans from North America were sold to plantation owners in Barbados. In like manner it's possible that when enslaved people from Barbados were traded to Virginian plantations, they may have introduced the noun barbycu.

BARBECUE SLANG

The use of the word barbecue as slang is an American innovation that goes back to at least 1783 when people who lived around the Chesapeake Bay used the word barbecued to refer to being robbed at sea.[58] As early as 1833, barbecue was used to refer to beautiful women. A woman's admirer wrote of her, "[She is] the belle of Williamsburg, the toast of Norfolk, and the barbacue of all that part of Virginia."[59] That practice continued into the 1930s. Louis Armstrong recorded the song "Struttin' with Some Barbecue" in 1927. The "barbecue" he was strutting with was his girlfriend.[60] In the 1938, Cab Calloway included barbecue in *The Hepster's Dictionary*, with the definition of "the girl friend, a beauty."[61] During President Ulysses S. Grant's (1822–85) administration, political corruption that lasted from 1869 to 1877 was called "the great barbecue" where "the government supplied the beef."[62] In 1892, an advertising for a clothing sale described it as a "Barbecue of Bargains."[63]

BARBECUE RESPELLINGS

Americans also invented the practice of using abbreviations, acronyms, initializations, and respellings of the word barbecue. The earliest known respelling occurred in 1856 when a reporter criticized a local political barbecue held in support of James Buchanan's presidential campaign. With an unmistakable tone of sarcasm, the correspondent described the "barbykew" and the undercooked meats. He went on to denigrate an attendant who was wearing a hat with "BUCHANIER" engraved on the front and a placard on his overcoat "bearing the hieroglyphics 'Bar B Q.'"[64]

By the turn of the twentieth century, acronyms, abbreviations, respellings, and initialisms of the word barbecue were no longer considered hieroglyphics. For example, in 1916 a dance was held in Marion County, Ohio, at "Bodley's Bar B-Q."[66] Of course, Americans have never agreed on a standard spelling for barbecue. At the time of this writing, there is a barbecue restaurant in Richmond, Virginia, that's served Virginia-style barbecue for 85 years. A careful reading of the menu and signs inside and outside the restaurant reveals no less than three different spellings of the word barbecue. Or should it be barbque, bar-b-cue, or bar-b-que? Although *BBQ* is the most popular initialization of the word barbecue today, its use didn't become prevalent in newspaper advertisements until the around the 1930s to reduce character-based fees.[67]

BARBECURIOSITY

In addition to Britons, Americans who didn't live in a region where barbecues were popular also didn't fully understand them. A correspondent for the New Orleans *Times-Picayune* noticed that fact in 1876 and commented, "Everybody has heard of barbecues in the South, but very few persons in the Northern States have any clear

Top: A menu with barbecue spelled "BAR-B-CUE" and "BAR-B-QUE." Photo by the author.

Bottom Left: An advertisement for a Chicken "B-B-Q." Photo by the author.

Bottom Right: A menu with two spellings of barbecue: "BAR-B-QUE" and "Barbques." Photo by the author.

idea of what a barbecue really is."[68] An article that appeared in an 1892 edition of the *Chicago Daily Tribune* highlights the lack of barbecue knowledge among people in the northern regions of the United States. A columnist for that paper wrote, "A New York man who had never seen a barbecue went all the way to Kentucky to attend one. He must have had a great deal of barbecuriosity."[69] Although the story may be fiction, it was based on fact. Often northerners' understanding of barbecues came from dictionaries and newspapers rather than personal experience. In 1825 an observant editor of a Virginia newspaper commented, "We would bet a pumpkin that our New England friends think a barbecue is what our lexicographers define it to be."[70] It's not clear if that editor knew how correct he was.

The New England statesman John Pickering (1737–1805) lived in London from 1799 to 1801. While there, he noticed how American English differed from British

BARBECUED WALRUS

The ways Americans spelled and defined the word barbecue changed significantly in the twentieth century. The use of the word barbecue to refer to the process of smoking venison in smokehouses and for making dried meats—such as beef jerky— fell out of fashion. One of the last accounts of referring to the process of making jerky as "barbecuing" came from Arctic Explorer and American meteorologist Evelyn Briggs Baldwin (1862–1933). In 1909, Baldwin described his plan to settle the North Pole. His idea was to sail there across the Arctic Ocean from the Bering Strait. The first North Pole settlers would live in portable houses and use balloons to scout territory. He also proposed that the pioneers should barbecue "the walrus seal and polar bear" for food.[65] What Baldwin had in mind wasn't pull-tender, juicy southern-style barbecue. He was referring to what we would call today walrus jerky and polar-bear jerky.

(continued from page 126)

English. That inspired him to author *Collection of Words and Phrases which Have Been Supposed to be Peculiar to the United States of America* published in 1816. He included the word barbecue in the book because he noticed that it wasn't widely used in London. Apparently he wasn't fully aware of how people in the southern United States used the word. Instead of offering the American definition of the word, he reprinted Burnaby's British definition.[71]

John Edwards Caldwell (1769–1819) was born in New Jersey. Even though he conducted business in the West Indies, he wasn't introduced to barbecues until later when he visited Virginia. Caldwell's parents were killed during the War of Independence. When he was 12 years old, the Marquis de Lafayette (1757–1834) took the orphan to France where he was educated. He returned to the United States in 1791 and became successful in the mercantile trade with the West Indies. Because of British sanctions against American trade in the first decade of the nineteenth century, Caldwell's business was lost. That prompted him to travel. While passing through Virginia in 1808, he came across a crowd of about 400 Virginians at a barbecue. Even though Caldwell was an American, the event he witnessed in Virginia was new to him. He wrote, "I witnessed a scene to me altogether novel and equally pleasing" . . . I understood these merry meetings (termed Barbicues) were very frequent during the summer, and I observed that the hope of soon assembling at another, took the sting from adieu when about to part." He closed with, "A Virginia Barbicue seems a day of rejoicing and jubilee to the whole of the surrounding country."[72] Caldwell witnessed a barbecue during his first visit to Virginia. He conducted business in the West Indies for over ten years and yet he never witnessed a barbecue there. If they were imported from the Caribbean as is asserted by some proponents of the COT, one would think he would have witnessed many barbecues in that part of the world.

Edward Hooker (1785–1846), born in Farmington, Connecticut, is another example of someone from the North who wasn't acquainted with southern barbecues. After graduating from college, he moved to Columbia, South Carolina, to study law with his brother who had a successful practice there. On Independence Day in 1806, he attended his first southern barbecue. He commented, "The dinner was in a little thicket not far from the village, and consisted chiefly of roast beef and pork—cooked over fires that were kindled in a long trench dug in the ground, about a foot deep." It appears that he wasn't impressed with the event. He certainly wasn't impressed by how all of the guests were served by enslaved people. Apparently he was the only person there who noticed the contradiction and wrote, "What an incongruity! An Independence dinner for freemen and slaves to wait upon them. I couldn't keep the thought out of my mind, the whole time I was there feasting."[73]

Though not widespread in the New England colonies, there were some there who were familiar with barbecues—at least their versions of them. The earliest known use of the word barbecue in literature that refers to a social event is found in the diary of the chief justice of the Massachusetts Superior Court of Judicature, Benjamin Lynde Sr. (1666–1749). He recorded the following on August 31, 1732, "Came home this afternoon; and Coz. S. Browne from a barbacue at Browne's Farm with my sons W^{lm} and Benjamin, coming home in the evening, his coachman was thrown off the coach box, and Coz. S. Browne leapt out, but over him, and his coachman hurt."[74] Although the first occurrence of the word barbecue used to refer to an outdoor social event is found in a diary written in Massachusetts, compelling evidence that Virginians were the first to refer to outdoor social events as barbecues is discussed Chapter 6, "George's Barbicue."

Sauce for Barbecues

From *Mrs. Hill's Southern Practical Cookery and Receipt Book*, 1872, by Annabella P. Hill

Even though the OSBP is long gone, there is no reason why the flavors of barbecue from that time can't be enjoyed today. The following is an authentic recipe for a nineteenth-century barbecue baste and sauce. It was formulated for basting meats while they are being barbecued directly over burning embers. It's a tasty sauce served on the side with meats cooked in a modern smoker-style pit.

2 cups apple cider vinegar
½ pound butter
1 tablespoon prepared mustard
½ teaspoon ground red pepper
½ teaspoon ground black pepper
salt to taste

—

Melt the butter. Stir the melted butter with the mustard, red pepper, black pepper, and salt. Add the vinegar until the sauce has a strong acid taste (the quantity of vinegar will depend on the strength of it.) As soon as the meat becomes hot, begin to baste and continue basting frequently until it's done. Pour any sauce that remains over the meat.

SIX

GEORGE'S BARBICUE

The Beginnings of Southern Barbecue

The United States is the only nation in the world that associates barbecuing with politics and just about every national celebration and significant national achievement. From as far back as the Virginia House of Burgesses, barbecues have played a critical role in American-style democracy. No other people in the world have sung more songs about barbecue, produced more barbecue-themed television shows, established more barbecue-themed websites, written more newspaper and magazine columns about barbecue, has more members of barbecue clubs and associations, or published more books about barbecuing than people in the United States. Clearly barbecuing holds a special place in the hearts of Americans. The unique conditions that existed in the thirteen American colonies contributed to the independent invention of southern barbecue and the South's barbecuing tradition.

THE PURSUIT OF LIFE, LIBERTY, AND BARBECUE

The history of southern barbecuing is intertwined with the history of the United States. Barbecuing is so prominent in American culture and history, a case could be made for changing the national emblem of the United States to a bald eagle with a barbecued rib in its beak. That's not as farfetched as it might sound. Lynton Yates "Stag" Ballentine

Ferry Farm, George Washington's boyhood home, as imagined by H. Rosa in 1886.

(1899–1964), who served as lieutenant governor of North Carolina from 1945 to 1949, once proposed changing the symbol of the Democratic Party from a donkey to a barbecued pig.[1]

In 1758, a large crowd of Virginians gathered at the home of James Wood (ca. 1697–1759)—the founder of Winchester, Virginia—to celebrate George Washington's first election to Virginia's House of Burgesses.[2] On August 4, 1770, Washington wrote in his diary, "Dined at the Barbicue [*sic*] with a great deal of other Company, and stayd [*sic*] there till Sunset." He attended that barbecue during an extended visit with his mother in Fredericksburg, Virginia, just across the Rappahannock River from Ferry Farm (his boyhood home).[3] The barbecue was most likely hosted by Colonel Fielding Lewis (1725–81) at his estate named Kenmore. From 1769 to 1774, Washington attended at least six Virginia barbecues, including one he hosted and one that he stayed at all night in Alexandria. In 1793, Washington presided over the ceremonial laying of the cornerstone for the US Capitol in Washington, DC. The elaborate event, which included military processions and a Masonic ceremony, was concluded with a barbecue. One newspaper reported, "The whole company retired to an extensive booth, where an ox of 500lbs. weight was barbacued, of which the company generally partook, with every abundance of other recreation." The festival concluded with fifteen successive volleys from the artillery.[4]

During the Original Southern Barbecuing Period (OSBP), Virginia planters hosted weekend barbecues in turns during the barbecue season: May through October. Barbecuing whole carcasses and inviting people from neighboring plantations and farms to partake meant there would be no leftovers, which was crucial in times before ubiquitous refrigeration. One family hosted a barbecue this weekend, another the next. By the end of the season, everyone who provided livestock had been paid back with barbecued meats from a neighbor.[5]

The Virginian way of hosting barbecues was enthusiastically practiced by people who lived in and around Fredericksburg. Records indicate that frequent "barbecues, fish-fries and fox hunts" were held in the area well before the city of Fredericksburg was established in 1728.[6] Plantations in the area—such as Augustine Washington's Ferry Farm, Colonel Fielding Lewis's Kenmore, George Washington Lewis's Marmion, Hazel Hill, Hopyard, Spring Hill, Belle Grove, and James Madison's Montpelier—participated in the summertime barbecues.

When he was six years old, George Washington and his parents, Mary and Augustine, moved from his birthplace in Westmorland County, Virginia, to Ferry Farm in Stafford County, Virginia, located just outside of the city of Fredericksburg on the Stafford County side of the Rappahannock River. Washington's parents were enthusiastic devotees of Virginia barbecues. They even celebrated their wedding in 1731 by hosting not one but several Virginia-style barbecues.[7] Of course, they didn't give up barbecues when they moved to Ferry Farm. The family regularly hosted or attended barbecues all around the area. Washington's parents passed their Virginian barbecue traditions on to their son.

When one considers the words of the philanthropist and Virginian politician Alexander R. Boteler (1815–92) written in 1860, "It [the southern barbecue tradition] belongs to the people—theoretically, practically, and emphatically—and its social influences upon the body politic are altogether beneficial," it's fitting that a Virginian known as "the Father of His Country" was an ardent devotee of America's rich and unique barbecue tradition.[8]

THE MASON–DIXON LINE OR THE BARBECUE–NO BARBECUE LINE

Before the Reconstruction period, barbecues were relatively rare occurrences in the North. The barbecue hosted on State Street in Boston, Massachusetts, in 1793 is an example of one of those rare events. It was held in front of the Old State House where the first blood of the American Revolution was shed during the Boston Massacre of

1770. The following is a description of a barbecue Bostonians held to celebrate not only their own liberty but also the mistaken belief that liberty was sweeping France during the French Revolution:

> A thousand pound ox was killed, and its horns gilded and placed on an altar twenty feet high. Drawn by fifteen horses and preceded by two hogsheads of punch pulled by six horses, and accompanied by a cart of bread, it was escorted through the streets of Boston, and finally deposited in State Street. Tables had been spread from the Old State House to Kilby Street, and the citizens feasted upon roast ox and strong punch, to the subsequent confusion of many. Boston's fair women decked the windows of the neighboring houses, and amused themselves by throwing flowers upon the feasters, until the scene culminated in what some of the best citizens characterized as a "drunken revelry."[13]

Clearly, people at the Boston barbecue got out of hand. That brings the details behind Lynde and the "barbacue" he attended in 1733 where on his way home his "hack overset" into question. Was the carriage crash the result of drinking too many toasts at the barbecue?

Even though people who lived in the North had their share of barbecue failures, there were some successful barbecues held in colonial Massachusetts. The *Boston Evening* reported in 1767, "At the invitation of the Owner, a Number of Gentlemen, about 70, went from Town, and were entertained with an elegant Barbacue; after which a Variety of Toasts were drank, and the Afternoon spent in social Mirth: In the Evening the Cavalcade reurn'd to Town, without any Occurrence to impede their jollity."[14] The diary of Mrs. Mary Holyoke of Salem, Massachusetts, recorded that she attended two "barbeque[s]" in Boston during March of 1760.[15] In spite of the successes, barbecues in Massachusetts didn't become a lasting tradition there. In 1856, a barbecue was held in Needham, and it was said such events had "not hitherto been seen in Massachusetts, at least not by this generation." An ox "roasted whole" was served. African American pit masters from Virginia were hired to do the cooking. The author estimated that it was "doubtful whether the flesh of an ox roasted a la barbecue will be relished by Massachusetts men as . . . it is not always palatable to those who are not accustomed to eating it."[16] Apparently, it took some trial and error for northerners to consistently hold successful barbecues. The barbecued ox served in Auburn, New York, in June 1860 was described as looking like it had just been "rescued from a burning distillery, his sides dripping in blood." The attendees were "tearing the half cooked and bloody meat" from the carcass

(continued on page 136)

BARBECUE AT THE WHITE HOUSE

Although 3 of the first 6 presidents of the United States who lived in the White House were barbecue-hosting Virginians (George Washington never lived in the White House), there are no known records of any of them hosting barbecues there. The first president recorded to have hosted a White House barbecue was Andrew Jackson (1767–1845), who was president from March 4, 1829, to March 3, 1837. We know this because of an address made in August of 1829 by Kentucky congressman John Kincaid (1791–1873) who stated, "That the appeal was made both to *Jackson* and his *cabinet*, we have the testimony of Gen. McAfee, who informed several intelligent gentlemen of Mercer of the fact, at the barbecue at the White House on the 4th of July."[9]

President Jackson had a long relationship with barbecues. The city of Fredericksburg, Virginia, rolled out the red carpet when he visited to preside over the laying of the cornerstone for the Mary Washington monument in 1833. Music filled the air as military processions, parades, dignitaries, and crowds of admirers filled the streets. The occasion drew more people to Fredericksburg than Marquis de Lafayette's visit in 1824. The event was celebrated with a barbecue "in the old-fashioned Virginia style . . . prepared under an ample awning, in the beautiful grounds of Hazel Hill."[10] At least five hundred attendees partook of the Virginia-style barbecued beef. At 4 o'clock, dancing commenced and "was kept up with considerable spirit until near sunset."[11]

Andrew Jackson has always been a controversial figure. Some love him, some hate him, and that was also true while he was alive. A political cartoon published in 1824 titled "The Political Barbecue" satirized the controversy surrounding Jackson's withdrawal of federal funds from the Second Bank of the United States. Jackson is depicted as being barbecued like a hog by his critics on the fires of public opinion. Controversy aside, perhaps Jackson's most significant contributions to barbecuing history in the United States were the barbecue trees planted on the Capitol grounds during his presidency. An old newspaper account tells us, "South of the Washington Elm are the Barbecue Trees planted during Jackson's Administration by James Maher, 'a Jolly Irishman' who owed his appointment as superintendent of the Capitol Grounds to the President's personal friendship. These trees are relics of two circular groves intended for barbecue celebrations one for Democrats the other for Whigs."[12] Images of the barbecue groves on the Capitol grounds were captured by an artist in 1860. The groves were demolished when the grounds were renovated in the 1870s.

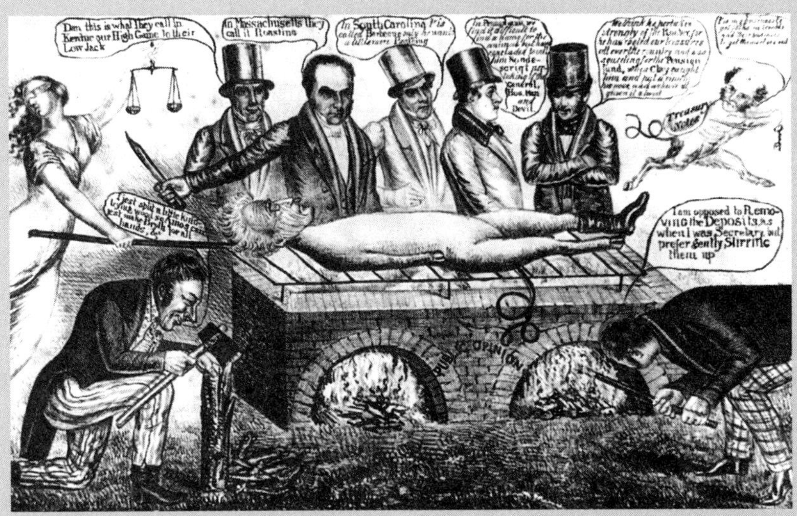

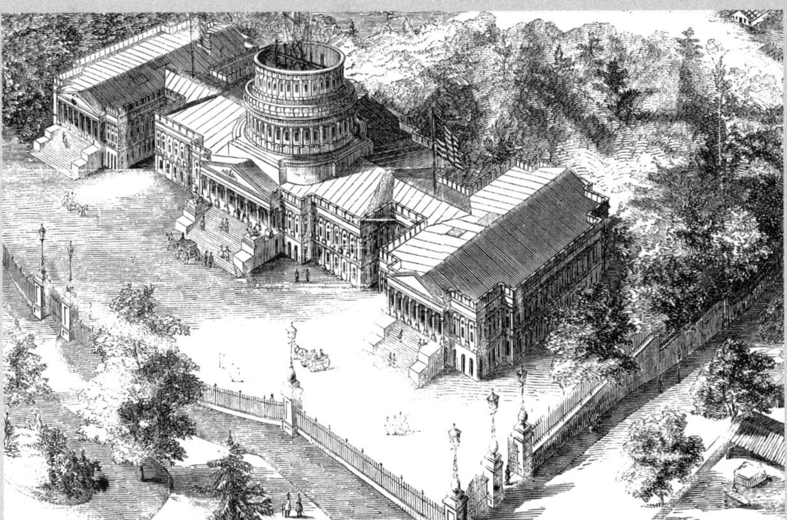

Top: "The Political Barbecue." By H. R. Robinson, 1834.

Bottom: The Barbecue Trees are depicted as two groves of trees in the lower left corner of this 1861 pencil drawing of the U.S. Capitol. *'Harper's Weekly,* July 27, 1861.

(continued from page 133)

and eating it "with the speed of famished men." As people crowded in an The First attempt to get to the ox, the whole event turned into a riotous food fight with projectiles of potatoes, bleeding pieces of ox, and chunks of bread thrown in all directions.[17] The disastrous event prompted one to humorously ask, "Who put tartar emetic [a substance that induces vomiting] on the 'ox roasted whole?'"[18] Later that same year, two large wagons drawn by four horses each made their way through the streets of New York City. The first wagon was hauling a band playing live music with banners on its sides that read "GREAT DOUGLAS BARBECUE AT JONES' WOODS." The second wagon was hauling a "Kentucky ox" festively decorated with flags.[19] The "Kentucky ox" was emblematic of the way Douglas was going to defeat Abraham Lincoln, his Kentucky-born Republican opponent, in the election.[20] A local correspondent humorously reported that the ox was barbecued whole "for the benefit of the unterrified."[21] In 1876, a Republican barbecue was attended by 50,000 New Yorkers. Barbecue sandwiches were made from two barbecued oxen, one each for the morning and evening crowds. While announcing the start of festivities, the chairman of the event commented "[barbecues] such as these were a rarity in the Northern states" as the anxious hoard was rushing forward to get a barbecue sandwich.[22] The first ox was completely served within 20 minutes.[23]

In 1895, a newspaper correspondent observed, "Whoever first thought of a barbecue, and why it should be strictly Southern, is not on record. It is just as easy to make a pit, fill it with coals, and roast meat over it in New Hampshire as it is in this State [Georgia], and yet the barbecues are associated exclusively with the life of the South."[24] The correspondent made a good point. Northerners (people who live above the Mason–Dixon Line) certainly are just as capable of barbecuing a pig or an ox as southerners (people who live below the Mason–Dixon Line). Although northerners have cooked meats hot and fast on gridirons and grills since colonial times, they didn't refer to that way of cooking as barbecuing until the twentieth century. In 1860, a journalist for the *New York Times* offered an explanation for why barbecues were popular in the South but not in the North, "The barbecue is an 'institution' peculiar to the South, and only adapted to sparsely settled regions, in which a few hundred people are all the most intense excitement can possibly collect in one spot. When an ox is roasted whole by Southern politicians, in the shades of a primeval forest, it takes all the white men within fifty miles to pick its bones. But nothing short of insanity is sufficient to account for the getting up of an entertainment of this sort by adult lawyers and bankers within the precincts of a city of 900,000 inhabitants."[25] The journalist may have made some valid points. However, there is more to the story.

LINCOLN AND JOHNSON!

GRAND UNION

MASS MEETING,

BARBECUE AND PUBLIC DINNER!

At ELKTON, Md.

Wednesday, November 2d.

The following Distinguished Speakers will be present to address the Meeting:

Hon. THOMAS SWANN,
Dr. C. C. COX.
Hon. E. H. WEBSTER,

Hon. R. STOCKETT MATTHEWS,
Hon. ALEX. EVANS,
Hon. W. D. KELLEY.

SEVERAL BANDS OF MUSIC ARE ENGAGED.

By order of the Committee of Arrangeme…

King & Baird, Printers, 607 Sansom Street, Philadelphia.

An 1864 flyer for the Lincoln and Johnson rally held in New York in 1864.

In attempts to explain why barbecuing was primarily confined to the South, some argue that enslaved people from the Caribbean introduced barbecuing to American colonies below the Mason–Dixon Line.[26] However, enslaved people from the Caribbean were also sent to New England and colonies in Canada and Mexico, but no barbecuing technique resembling the Original Southern Barbecuing Technique (OSBT) materialized in those places. The more logical conclusion is that enslaved people from the Caribbean didn't introduce barbecuing anywhere in the American colonies. That assertion is buttressed by the lack of convincing evidence in the Barbecue History Body of Knowledge (BHBoK), which supports the claim that people in the early modern Caribbean barbecued whole animal carcasses in a way that resembled the OSBT.

DIFFUSION, INDEPENDENT INVENTION, AND CREOLIZATION

The approach to discovering the origins of southern barbecuing taken by proponents of the COT is based in a concept known as *diffusion*. Diffusionists assert that humans are copycats more than they are inventors. As a result southerners, they assert, copied barbecuing from people in the Caribbean.[27] The alternative to diffusion is the concept of independent invention, which is what occurs when similar things are invented independently of each other, sometimes simultaneously, in different parts of the world.[28] Of course, diffusion has and does occur. You can see that in how ideas pass from one group to another. However, there are also instances of independent invention where two or more cultures develop similar things, sometimes simultaneously, even though they are isolated from each other. There are also documented instances of the process of creolization resulting in independent invention. For example, when people of African, Native American, and European descent were transplanted onto plantations in the Americas during the early modern period and forced to serve the rich elite, they shared their knowledge, skills, and customs with each other and sometimes experimented by exchanging the similarities and differences. Eventually a new culture or cultural element that didn't exist before was independently invented through creolization. Similarities among creole cultures in the Americas didn't occur because they all share a single birth. They exist because they were largely created from the same three loaner cultures: African, Native American, and European.

EXAMPLES OF INDEPENDENT INVENTION

Some scientists assert that agriculture was independently invented at least 11 times on at least 4 continents.[29] Just as there is no one-time invention of agriculture from which all agriculture descended, there is no one-time invention of barbecuing in the Caribbean from which the OSBT descended. Certain conditions had to exist to make the invention of agriculture possible, and those conditions existed in several places simultaneously. That's also true of the various forms of barbecuing. When the right conditions existed in various places in the Americas during the early modern period, it became possible for barbecuing to develop independently.

Hoecakes, Johnny cakes, tortillas, and arepas are examples of similar foods that were independently invented in different parts of the world. The basic recipe for all those breads is essentially corn or wheat flour, water, and fat. The recipe is based upon how Native Americans made bread using ground hominy, water, and sometimes animal fat. That recipe has been ubiquitous among maize-cultivating Indigenous societies in the Americas since pre-Columbian times. Some baked them, some griddled them on rocks, and others baked them beside the fire on logs or strips of bark. Our modern versions of that Native American bread are made with recipes that developed when people of African descent collaborated with people of European descent to modify the basic bread recipe that Native Americans shared with them.[30] Early modern Africans, Native Americans, and Europeans were familiar with bread, and each group had their own ways of making it. That set the stage for hoecakes, Johnny cakes, tortillas, and arepas to be invented. Today, hoecakes and Johnny cakes are considered the same bread. However, hoecakes were the result of creolization in the Chesapeake region; Johnny cakes were the result of creolization in New England; tortillas were the result of creolization in Mexico; and arepas were the result of creolization in South America. Although the recipes for hoecakes, Johnny cakes, tortillas, and arepas are similar, they all developed independently in different regions of the Americas.[31]

One of the most striking examples of creolization and independent invention at work in the colonial United States is colonoware. Colonoware was a locally produced pottery that archeologists find in seventeenth- and eighteenth-century plantation sites, mainly on the eastern seaboard of the United States and the Caribbean. In Virginia, where indentured servants from Europe, enslaved people of African descent, and enslaved Native Americans lived together in close quarters, archeologists have found African, European, and Native American characteristics in colonoware that identify it as a creole product.[32] The pottery was created primarily by enslaved African Americans and Native Americans. It reveals how people of different cultures combined their similar culinary traditions in colonial times to create something new that wasn't entirely African, European, or Native American. Like southern barbecue, it was a uniquely American product. According to a contributor for the *Virginia Gazette*, colonoware was "something new informed by a multicultural society."[33] The colonoware found in the Caribbean is not an ancestor of colonoware found in the American colonies.

People in both parts of the Americas created it independently. The same dynamics that created colonoware in different and unconnected parts of the Americas created various styles of barbecuing independently in different regions. The style of barbecue that was invented independently in the American colonies is known today as southern barbecue. Historical evidence supports the notion that the OSBT was also, to borrow a phrase, something new informed by a multicultural society.

AMERICAN CREOLES

Elite colonial Virginians endeavored to emulate England's upper classes, especially in regard to foods and holidays. They often modeled their barbecues after England's ox feasts. On special occasions, such as royal birthdays, it was a custom among the upper-class English to celebrate by roasting an ox. They played games such as horse races, foot races, and the gander pull, which was a cruel game where men on horseback competed to be the first to pull the head off a greased goose hanging by its feet from a cross bar or tree branch. Alcohol freely flowed at ox feasts, and men drank "healths [toasts] of the king."[34]

Try as they may, colonial Virginians never quite duplicated English traditions. Like their English counterparts, they played "rough, honest English sports" such as foot races, horse races, boat races, shooting matches, quoit games, nine pence loo, greased poles, bull-baiting, cockfights, and gander pulls.[35] Yet instead of roasting oxen, Virginians barbecued them along with pigs and lambs. Instead of roast beef, Yorkshire pudding, and gravy, Virginian barbecues featured barbecued meats, cornbread, barbecue hash, and country ham. They drank "healths" and observed their "barbecue law," which held that the only excuse for refusing a round of drinking was unconsciousness.[36] When upper-class Virginians, like Washington and Madison, dressed in their finest clothes and offered their most refined table to guests, they saw themselves as equals to their European counterparts. However, when Europeans looked at them, their cornbread, barbecued meats, barbecue hash, and smoked hams, they saw Yankee Doodles and Creoles who were born in a part of the world that made them inferior.

People in English, French, and Spanish colonies in the Americas developed their own unique and diverse ways of "barbecuing" during the early modern period. The differences in the ways they "barbecued" were the result of the various ways cultures blended to create new cultures (known as creole cultures) with new languages and culinary traditions. Thus the French word boucan and the Spanish noun barbacoa are creole words. There is strong evidence that the same is true of the English word barbecue (see Chapter 5, "Richard's Barbycu").[37]

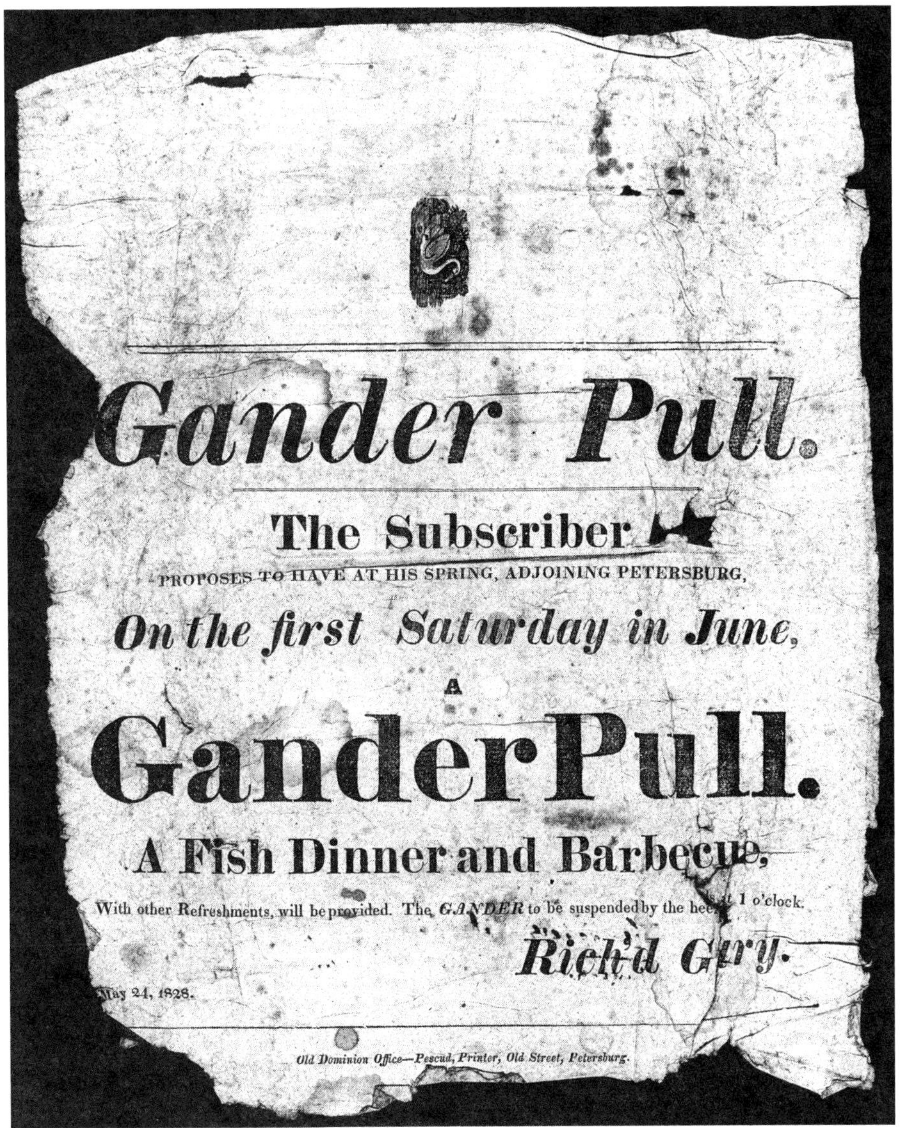

A gander pull, fish dinner, and barbecue at Petersburg, Virginia, ca. 1828. Courtesy of Albert and Shirley Small, Special Collections Library, University of Virginia.

Creole (*criollo* in Spanish, *crioulo* in Portuguese) was first used by sixteenth-century Iberian explorers to refer to the children of Europeans who were born in the Americas.[38] It's derived from the Latin word *creare,* which means to create anew. People in France (*créole* or *créolien* in French) and Britain (*creole, creolian,* or *creolean* in English) also adopted the word. They used it as a pejorative term to refer to people of any race born in the colonies, and those who transplanted to the colonies and lived there long enough to adopt colonial ways.[39] By the end of the seventeenth century, several English authors referred to the children of English colonists born in the Caribbean and the American colonies as Creoles or Creolians because, they believed, the Americas had robbed them of their British and European identities. Although people in the colonial United States resented being called Creoles, it was common for them to apply the term to people born in the British-, French-, and Iberian-dominated colonies in the Caribbean. For example, it's claimed that John Adams once called Alexander Hamilton a "Creole bastard" because of his birth in the Caribbean to an unwed mother.[40] Today, the word creole, and its variants, refer to a much larger scope of cultures than only those in Louisiana and the Caribbean. Scholars use it to describe new cultures and new cultural elements—such as language, music, food, and religion—that develop among people of different cultures who live together in societies with forced inequality.

HUMORS

Greek philosophers of the Classical period believed that location and even the constellations above different geographic areas influence humans psychologically and physiologically. That concept is known as Geohumoralism. During the early modern period, Europeans embraced the humoral theory that humans have four bodily humors that include black bile (corresponding to cold), yellow bile (hot), blood (dry), and phlegm (wet), and these are influenced by the four elements of earth, water, air, and fire.[41] According to early modern Europeans, climates in the Americas caused imbalances in peoples' humors that resulted in physical, spiritual, and cultural degeneration. They also believed that was true of plants and animals.

As early as 1626, English puritan William Prynne (1600–69) condemned English playactors in London because they dressed like Native Americans in theatrical productions and feared they had "degenerated into Virginians."[45] In 1633, Puritan clergyman John Cotton (1585–1652) warned his congregation, "[H]ave a tender care that you looke well to plants that spring from you, that is, to your children, that they doe not degenerate as the Israelites did." The spirited New England puritan preacher Cotton Mather (1663–1728), John Cotton's New England-born grandson, warned colonists against "Criolian degeneracy observed to deprave the children of the most noble and worthy Europeans when transplanted in America" brought on by what he called "Indianizing" which was imitating "the evil manners of the Indians." In a 1724 letter, he wrote about "the strange influence that climates appear to have on the humors and manners and actions of the people that inhabit them."[46]

EARLY MODERN GEOHUMORALISM

The Spanish missionary Bernardino de Sahagun (1499–1590) was one of the earliest Europeans to notice that Spaniards born in the Americas were different. He wrote, "Those who are born here [the Americas] become like the Indians, and although they look like Spaniards, in their constitution they are not; those who are born in Spain, if they do not take care, change within a few years after they arrive in these parts; and this I think, is due to the climate or the constellations in these parts."[42] The French philosopher Jean Bodin (1530–1596) wrote, "[People who are] transplanted into anreviouun-trey . . . shall not be changed so soon, as plants which draw their nourishment from the earth: yet in the end they shall be altered."[43] The English philosopher Nathanael Carpenter (1589–1628) agreed with Bodin and wrote, "This change may we find not onely [sic] in *mankind*, but also in *beasts* and *plants*, which being transported into other regions, though a long time retaining their native perfection will notwithstanding in time by little and little degenerate." Carpenter continued, "Colonies transplanted from one region into another, farre remote, retaine a long time their first disposition, though little by little they decline and suffer alteration."[44]

(continued from page 142)

The belief that people are changed by the environment in which they live was also expressed by the American historian Frederick Jackson Turner (1861–1932). He wrote, "In the crucible of the frontier the immigrants were Americanized, liberated, and fused into a mixed race, English in neither nationality nor characteristics." Turner continued, "*The wilderness* [emphasis added] puts a European in a canoe and strips off the garments of civilization" and "arrays him in the hunting shirt and the moccasin." The next thing you know, those European settlers are "planting Indian corn and plowing with a sharp stick," and the "outcome is not old Europe." What results is a "new product that is American."[47]

CREOLIZATION

Scholars tell us that new cultures developed in the Americas because of creolization that occurred when people of mainly African, Native American, and European descent mingled while serving rich oppressors through enslavement or indenture.[48] Often, when such mingling occurred, the creolization process produced a new and unique culture. In that way, creolization is much more than a fusion of cultures. It involves negotiations and exchanges between cultures that result in a new culture that didn't exist before.[49] Professor Lee Haring explained it this way, "Where societies come into a colonized, multiracial existence for the benefit of a European minority, the normal reaction of the constituent groups is to renegotiate culture."[50] The distinguished professor of anthropology Leland Ferguson asserted, "[Creolization] provides another important advantage in answering questions about the African-American past and the American past in general."[51] Unfortunately most people who write about barbecuing history have all but ignored creolization, even though it's vital for understanding how the OSBT materialized.

VIRGINIAN CREOLES

Iberian colonies in the Americas were beginning to be established approximately one hundred years before the first successful English colony was established in Virginia in 1607. As a result, creolization among people born in the North American English colonies occurred after it had already occurred among people in the Caribbean, South America, and Mexico. When Maroon communities first formed in the Americas during the sixteenth century, they were made up of people from various backgrounds with different customs and languages. A similar thing happened in Virginia during the seventeenth century. By the time England wrestled Jamaica away from Spain in 1655, much of Jamaica's population was already made up of island-born Creoles. In contrast, the Virginia-born creole population was just beginning to materialize.[52] That explains why accounts of people in Jamaica practicing their way of barbecuing were published earlier than accounts of barbecuing in Virginia. Nevertheless just as it was in Jamaica, as creole populations grew in Virginia they forged their own unique cuisine. When William Beckford of Somerley wrote his praises of Jamaican jerked pork and Monk Lewis was praising Jamaican pork cooked in earth ovens at the turn of the nineteenth century, Virginians already had a tradition of barbecuing pigs, oxen, and lambs using the OSBT. When creolization occurred in Jamaica, it resulted in Jamaican jerk made by salting and drying meats and by "barbecuing" pigs in earth ovens. When creolization occurred among the French in the Americas, it resulted in buccaneers who used boucans to salt, smoke, and dry meat. When creolization occurred in Mexico, it resulted in barbacoa cooked in an earth oven. When creolization occurred in the seventeenth-century colonial United States, it resulted in salted pork smoked in

Powhatan-style smokehouses and southern-style barbecue made by barbecuing just about any animal—be it game or domesticated.[53]

In 1732 Briton William Hugh Grove visited Virginia. Very little is known about Grove outside of the detailed journal he kept of his visit in which he commented on Virginians: "The Creolians, or Natives of European parents, are few corpulent [portly], but [are] tall and thin. In Summertime even the gentry goe Many in White Holland Wast Coat [waistcoat] & drawers and a thin Cap on their heads and Thread stockings."[54] The European-born Grove couldn't help but recognize the differences between European-born people in Virginia and people who were born in Virginia that he called "creolians." The Scottish historian William Robertson (1721–93) summed up the attitude among many Europeans toward "Creoles, or the descendants of Europeans settled in the Americas": "[because of] a sultry climate . . . the vigor of their minds is so entirely broken, that a great part of them waste life in luxurious indulgences, mingled with an illiberal superstition still more debasing."[55] The belief among many eighteenth-century Britons was that people immigrated to the North American colonies because they were incapable of achieving success in England, and that the colonies were filled with criminals, prostitutes, and money-grubbing plebeians who cultivated tobacco, which was a crop considered fitting for their inferior status.[56] The fact that male indentured servants in Virginia frequently married or procreated with Native American women during the first half of the seventeenth century also damaged the colony's reputation among people in England.[57]

Although people in the colonial United States occasionally referred to people born in the Caribbean as Creoles, they were offended when they themselves were called Creole or any name that insinuated they had a creole nature. That attitude is reflected in a letter written in 1687 by the aforementioned Reverend John Clayton: "I have noticed many gross mistakes in peoples' notions of Virginia, when discoursing of the natives, which have arisen, from the want of making a distinction in their Expressions, when they speak of the English or Whites born there & so-called Natives & the Aborigines of the Country." He was explaining that Virginians didn't like to be referred to as natives and insisted that the term should only be used to refer to the Indigenous population.[58]

As the population of native-born Virginians grew over the course of the seventeenth century, they began to fill leadership and political roles previously held by their European-born parents. In 1697, England-born Edward Chilton (1658–1707) lodged the following complaint against Virginian Creoles having political power in the colony:

> These County Courts have always been held by country gentlemen of no education in the law, so it is no wonder if the sense of the law was mistaken and the

> method of proceeding often very irregular. But of late the insufficiency of these Courts has been much more felt than in former times, while the first stock of Virginia gentlemen lasted. These having been educated in England were far better accomplished in the knowledge of the world than their children and grandchildren, who have been born in Virginia, and have had generally little more education than to read, write and cast accounts, and that very indifferently.[59]

In response to the British attitude exhibited by Chilton and others, by the time Alexander Spotswood (1676–1740) was appointed lieutenant governor of Virginia in 1710, native-born Virginians were asserting themselves by resisting British governors.[60] Spotswood responded by complaining that Virginia's constitution was defective because it "allows every one, tho' but just out of the Condition of a Servant, and that can but purchase half an acre of Land, an equal Vote with the Man of the best Estate in the Country." Privately, Spotswood referred to Virginian-born colonists who opposed his policies as "ungrateful Creolians."[61] His attitude reflected that of many other upper-class Britons who would eventually consider American colonials to be the "spawn of our [prisoners'] transports," rabble-rousers "with manners no better than Mohawks."[62]

Over the course of the seventeenth century, elite Virginia-born planters developed a creole consciousness. For example, Robert Beverly, acutely aware of the differences between Virginians and Britons, intreated his European readers: "Not to Criticize too unmercifully upon my Stile [style]. I am an Indian, and don't pretend to be exact in my Language."[63] By "Indian," he meant he was born in Virginia, which was considered to be in the Indies because of the Indigenous people who lived there.[64] Other Virginians referred to themselves as Creoles to mock the haughtiness of European officials the king appointed over them.[65] Virginian planter and founder of Richmond, William Byrd II (1674–1744), mentioned Virginians several times in his *History of the Dividing Line Betwixt Virginia and North Carolina* published in 1728. However, he never referred to himself as a Virginian or an American. Instead he referred to himself as an Englishman. In 1740 he offered advice to first lord of the admiralty Sir Charles Wager (1666–1743), who had proposed to fill the role of the clerk of the Naval Office of York River in Virginia with a British-born official. Byrd explained that such offices had always been filled by native-born Virginians. He commented with subtle sarcasm, "You will pardon me, Sir, for presuming to obtrude my Creolean notions in affairs so high above my humble sphere."[66]

Byrd had no trouble identifying what Europeans pejoratively called *Creolean degeneracy* in colonists outside of Virginia while seeming to be unaware of it in himself.

To him the border between Virginia and North Carolina was more than a border between two colonies: it was a barrier that separated Virginia's gentility from the creolean degeneracy he believed to be of people in North Carolina. He described his fellow Virginian surveyors as industrious "Knights Templars" carrying out a noble mission for the king. At the same time, he wrote of people in North Carolina that they live in "a dirty state of Nature" and grunt like pigs. Expressing his humoral thinking, he added, "[They eat] so much Swine's flesh that it fills them full of gross Humors."[67] Although Byrd may not have been fully aware of his creole nature, people from other parts of the world were. When the aforementioned Caribbean-born Creole Moreau arrived in Norfolk and witnessed Virginians holding a barbecue in 1794, he clearly recognized the *otherness* in Americans. A historian described his reaction "as a Creole to a place that to him was more Creole than either Martinique or Saint-Domingue."[68]

Factors that made American colonists deny their own creole nature include efforts of clergymen to prevent the English king's subjects in North America from experiencing Mather's "Criolian degeneracy." However, evidence suggests that their efforts were more successful in helping colonials deny their creole nature than it was in assisting them in actually avoiding it.[69] Even though they—like their parents—endeavored to replicate upper-class society in England, Virginia-born colonials had a different vocabulary, a different way of dressing, and preferred different foods than their European-born parents. The elite among them considered themselves as thoroughly English and aristocratic as their European-born counterparts. Because of that, they considered themselves as having more in common with the upper classes in England than people who were enslaved and indentured by them and the lower-class free colonials who lived around them. Ultimately the Virginia-born elite excused the striking differences between themselves and people born in Europe, but those differences weren't dismissed by Europeans. According to some Britons, it was pretentious of colonials born in Virginia to think themselves equal to Britain's upper classes and many refused to accept them as equals or as being fully British. Indeed, native-born colonials in Virginia lived in a world that was much different than Europe. In Virginia, many races and ethnicities mingled through institutions such as marriage, indentured servitude, and slavery. Therefore European Anglos referred to them as natives, Creoles, or country born, and judged them culturally inferior.[70]

THE BIRTH OF "AMERICANS"

When the British Parliament passed The Stamp Act of 1765, they imposed taxes on just about all forms of paper in the American colonies. American colonials vigorously

Colonists dumping the almost-barbecued ox and barrels of beer into a river. Lossing, *Our Country*.

opposed the tax because it was passed without their representation, which denied them the same rights and privileges as people in Britain. Adding insult to injury, British pamphleteers and press referred to American colonials as a "mixed rabble of Scotch, Irish and foreign vagabonds, descendants of convicts, ungrateful rebels," mongrels and Creoles. American colonists reacted with the first serious challenge to British rule in their history and the way American colonials saw their relationship with Britain was profoundly changed.

When news of the tax reached Wilmington, North Carolina, it created much unrest among the population. The British governor of North Carolina, William Tryon (1729–88), had his hands full. He thought the best way to appease an angry mob of Creolean American colonists was to feed them their native barbecue along with barrels of beer, so he paid the expense of providing a barbecued ox and several barrels of beer. Ultimately his plan backfired. Though there are differing accounts of the events that ensued, the most widely publicized one claims that Carolinians were so insulted by the governor's attempted bribe they dumped the kegs of beer on the ground and dragged the entire barbecued ox into a nearby river.[71]

From that time onward, although American colonials acknowledged their English roots, they started to embrace the name "Americans," which signaled that they were finally accepting at least some of the differences between themselves and their "British brothers."[72] However, many eighteenth-century Britons equated the term *American* with debased, unrefined, barbarian-like degenerates and Creoles who, in their estimation, lived too close to "slaves" and "savages." They also believed that American colonists had a questionable diet because it consisted of "Indian corn," which, one claimed, couldn't possibly make "an agreeable, or easily digestible breakfast."[73] The Massachusetts lawyer James Otis (1725–83) argued against such British notions. He asked, "Are the inhabitants of British America all a parcel of transported thieves, robbers, and rebels, or descended from such?"[74] Another asked colonists, "Was the blood of your ancestors polluted by a change of soil? Were they freemen in England and did they become slaves by a six-weeks voyage to America?"[75]

After the end of the War of Independence, many Americans were still offended by notions of British superiority. Writing under the pseudonym John Littlejohn in 1786, the American poet and clergyman Timothy Dwight (1752–1817) shared his pointed thoughts on British immigrants' attitudes toward colonials in the American colonies, "[They believe] all things European degenerate in American climates," and "No title of respect was too humble an act of inferiority, from a dirty Creole," which was a tongue-in-cheek reference to American colonists.[79]

THE FATALITY OF TRANSATLANTIC BIRTH

Ironically American colonials felt that proper English culture could flourish in the North American colonies but couldn't do so in the Caribbean. That is testified by many eighteenth-century American newspapers that were filled with references to people of any race born in the Caribbean as Creoles. The thought that their North American version of English culture might exhibit creole elements repulsed many American colonials. That fueled their resentment and frustration with being called Creole because they believed that they were superior and had avoided the cultural degeneration they perceived to exist in Caribbean colonies. Thomas Jefferson also rejected the idea that animals, plants, and humans degenerated in North American environments and argued just the opposite. In *Notes on the State of Virginia*, Jefferson wrote of how America's natural surroundings made Americans superior. He pointed to the buffalo's large size and the giant wooly mammoth fossils he had collected as proof.[80]

Joyce E. Chaplin, a respected professor of early American history, observed of American patriots in 1776, "The first surge of creole patriotism that challenged European empires in the Americas was propelled by people who emphatically rejected the name

'Creole.'"[81] That "surge of creole patriotism" can be seen in the life of George Washington. At the age of 21, he received a commission with the rank of major in the Virginia militia. Still his greatest ambition was to receive a commission in the British army. He never received one. He suffered from what the Irish historian Benedict Anderson (1936–2015) called the "fatality of trans-Atlantic birth," and, apparently, British officers weren't comfortable giving command to a "Yankee Doodle." As a result, Washington abandoned his quest for a British commission in the 1760s.[82] Like many of his contemporaries, Washington embraced the chance for independence from the British crown, and realized that he was no longer merely British; he was American. The change in attitude was also exhibited by a contributor in the May 6, 1765, edition of the *Newport Mercury*, who closed his essay with a response to the British, "I am no Smuggler, nor Creole, but a true British American." By calling themselves Americans, colonials were admitting that they were different from Britons while asserting their equality with them.

COLUMBIAN BARBECUING

Columbian barbecuing includes all styles of barbecuing that developed in the Western Hemisphere after enslaved Africans arrived in the Americas. Several of those styles of barbecuing are still practiced by people in the Americas today. The births of the different Columbian barbecuing styles coincided with the development of creole populations. During the early modern period, after European colonies were established and creole cultures formed, each of the three primary loaner cultures combined their cooking traditions. Each had their early modern period methods for preserving meats: Europeans and Africans salted and dried meats to preserve them. Native Americans had a tradition of drying and smoking meats on hurdles without the use of salt. That explains why barbecuing styles in the Americas—such as Spanish charqui, French creole boucanage, Jamaican jerk, and southern barbecuing—all exhibit traits of African, Native American, and European cooking. Barbecuing didn't emerge in all early modern creole cultures in the Americas. Nevertheless all ways of barbecuing that did materialize there during the early modern period did so among creole cultures.

As different creole populations emerged in various places in the Americas, elements of the loaner cultures' cooking traditions blended in ways that formed new creole cuisines. Some creole cultures have a more assertive African influence than others, while some cultures have a more assertive European or Native American influence. This helps explain why the styles of barbecuing in the Americas differ between cultures and regions. Yet in all cases, Europeans contributed the salt, vinegar, citrus, and livestock. Native Americans contributed the hurdle, cooking in earth ovens, and the unique herbs

FERGUSON'S FOLLY

After a London newspaper referred to American colonists as "a mongrel breed (i.e., animals of no particular breed and with no pedigree) of Irish, Scotch, and Germans leavened with convicts and outcasts," American colonials were again deeply insulted.[76] In similar fashion, the British major Patrick Ferguson (1744–80) issued a warning to Americans on October 1, 1780, "Unless you wish to be eat up by an inundation of barbarians . . . If you choose to be degraded forever and ever by a set of mongrels, say so at once, and let your women turn their backs upon you, and look out for real men to protect them." When word of that *warning* reached colonials in Tennessee and southwestern Virginia, that was all the motivation they needed to fight against the British invaders.[77] Six days after he issued his insult, Ferguson was killed in action during the Battle of Kings Mountain on the border between North Carolina and South Carolina.[78]

(continued from page 150)

and spices found in the Americas. Africans contributed their expertise in drying and roasting meats, cooking in earth ovens, and the artisan use of herbs and spices, among other traditions.[83]

THE BIRTH OF SOUTHERN BARBECUING

John Smith described how Powhatan Indians cooked meat by "[broiling] it so long on hurdles over the fire," which is an accurate way of describing barbecuing without using the word barbecue.[84] Nevertheless the Powhatan way of barbecuing wasn't the same as the OSBT. Because the OSBT is a product of a creole culture in the North American colonies, it didn't fully develop before sometime in first half of the seventeenth century. Moreover there are no sixteenth-century accounts of people outside of the colonial United States using similar barbecuing methods as the OSBT.

The evidence discovered by archeologists at the original Jamestown site of daily interaction between Powhatans and colonists suggests far more cultural exchange than is widely known. In fact, the historic Jamestown site contains the wealthiest repository of Powhatan artifacts in the Chesapeake region.[85] Before 1622, an eyewitness described

Powhatans and colonists living together "as one Nation," which strongly suggests an active cultural exchange. That exchange included smoking meats in a smokehouse (a.k.a. Virginia-smoked ham) and barbecuing meats on wooden hurdles set over pits.[86]

The unique conditions that existed in early seventeenth-century Virginia are the key to responding to the aforementioned 1895 *New York Sun* correspondent and explain why barbecuing was a "strictly Southern" tradition. Within 12 years after the arrival of English colonists on Virginia's shores in 1607, 3 important events had created the unique conditions that enabled the birth of southern barbecuing. By 1619, colonists had strong ties to several Native American nations created through trade and marriage. The first meeting of the Virginia House of Burgesses, the first elected legislature established in the American colonies, occurred on July 30, 1619. On August 19, 1619, the first enslaved Africans arrived in Virginia directly from Africa, not the Caribbean.[87] The Powhatan way of cooking whole carcasses while they rested for hours on wooden hurdles over a trench filled with hot coals combined with European livestock, salt, butter, vinegar, and red pepper, and African culinary expertise became the foundation on which African and African American cooks perfected southern-style barbecue. It didn't take long for Virginian politicians to learn that barbecues were very useful in their efforts to reach constituents.

CREOLE CAVALIERS

In the past, many southerners took pride in claiming to be descendants of Cavaliers, who were royalists during the English Civil War. That implied that their cultural roots were thoroughly English. Consequently the American aversion to being called Creole might be a factor in the origination of the COT. Because barbecuing is a cooking method associated with Creoles, the reasoning among some may have been that it couldn't have been born in the colonial United States because American colonists weren't Creoles. Creoles, according to American colonials, lived in the Caribbean, Latin America, Mexico, and South America.[88] Furthermore the erroneous etymology of the word barbecue that's based upon the French *de la barbe à la queue* may have also been a way of distancing Anglo-America from the stigma of being Creole.[89] After all, there would be less danger of being called Creole just because you hosted or attended a barbecue if the word had a European origin rather than Native American or creole origin. Perhaps the belief that Americans preserved their "Englishness" and passed it on to their posterity blinded them to the colonial American creole origins of southern barbecuing. Regardless of whether the aversion to being called Creole is what originally propelled the acceptance of the COT during the nineteenth century,

Charles W. Allen was referred to as a creole chef from Virginia. *The Boston Herald,* August 27, 1894.

northerners exhibited no hesitation when they referred to Virginians who attended barbecues as "the degenerate descendants of England's aristocracy" or to a celebrated, nineteenth-century, Virginian, mixed-race pitmaster named Charles W. Allen as a "Creole chef."[90]

The unique cuisine invented in colonial Virginia was familiar in some ways to Europeans and people from the New England colonies and unfamiliar in other ways. The New England politician and statesman Daniel Webster (1782–1852) noticed the creole nature of Virginian foods when he dined with Thomas Jefferson at Monticello in 1824. He described Jefferson's dinners as being "served in half Virginian, half French style."[91] Thomas Jefferson sent his enslaved cook James Hemings (1765–1801) to Paris to be trained in the art of French cooking. He returned to Virginia and taught those skills to his younger brother Peter (1770–18??) and other cooks at Monticello. When James and Peter added their Virginian touches to the techniques and recipes learned in Paris, they were contributing to Virginia's creole cuisine. In a similar way, the mixing of

"The Cook." The talent and hard work of enslaved cooks "changed the English palate into the Virginia palate." Notice the European-style gridiron in the lower right corner of the image. Strother, *Virginia Illustrated*.

cultures that took place in early colonial Virginia that gave rise to Virginia's barbecuing tradition and, eventually, what we know today as southern barbecue.

Regardless of how hard people in the North American colonies tried to deny their creole nature, the fact remains many did live in a Creole society with Creole cultures and creole cuisines.[92] Indeed, creolization in colonial Virginia "changed the English palate into the Virginia palate" and produced a new cuisine that became the basis for cuisine all over the southern United States.[93]

THE POWHATAN COOKING PIT

The culinary use of an open pit was something that the early English colonists in Virginia and Virginia's Powhatan societies had in common. The bottoms of Powhatan Indian pots were not flat, they were conical. The pointy-tipped bases made them perfect for resting in a deep layer of burning embers contained in a pit. The early twentieth-century American ethnologist Alanson Skinner (1886–1925) described how a Native American woman who lived around the Great Lakes set her "large, round, deep, pointed-bottomed kettle of brown earthen-ware" into a pit full of embers, "the base of which she screwed into the ashes by a quick, circular twist of the rim."[94] Charles De Wolf Brownell (1822–1909) was a landscape artist with an eye for details. In his 1853 book *The Indian Races of North and South America*, he described the fire pits used by Native Americans in their longhouses around the Columbia River in the Pacific Northwest as "a hole sunk in the [dirt] floor, to the depth of about twelve inches, under the aperture in the roof left for the escape of smoke."[95] Powhatans in Virginia did the same thing in their houses. They kept a fire burning at all times with a hatch in the roof above it to allow smoke to escape. The hot coals and ash in the pit acted as a stand to hold their pointy-bottomed pots upright while foods cooked.

Although Africans were cooking in earth ovens during the sixteenth and seventeenth centuries, evidence that they cooked over dug pits hasn't been found. Albeit there are accounts of Europeans in Africa cooking over dug pits. For example, James Bruce (1730–94) was a Scottish explorer who spent over 12 years during the 1760s and '70s searching for the source of the Nile River in North Africa. He recorded how he and his colleagues made cooking fires "by digging a hole and burning wood to charcoal in it for dressing our victuals." During the eighteenth and nineteenth centuries, cooks in the Norwegian army were taught to dig "cooking ditches" over which a long pipe was suspended to make a spit. The cooking ditches were to be dug "in the direction of the wind" so that smoke emitted from the cooking fires was blown toward an end of the trench rather than across it.[96]

COLONIAL VIRGINIA POLITICS

During the first half of the seventeenth century, aspiring politicians in Virginia figured out that the best way to attract voters who lived in a sparsely populated world without newspapers, radio, or the Internet was through social gatherings that featured speeches, alcohol, and barbecued meats. That way of politicking appealed to voters, especially the relatively poor planters that owned small tracts of land and who, as Lieutenant Governor Spotswood put it, had "an equal Vote with the Man of the best Estate in the Country."

During the seventeenth century, Virginia's main cash crop was tobacco. Because tobacco exhausts soil in only 3 to 4 years, planters were continually seeking new ground. The growing demand for new farmland was one factor behind Virginian's failure to concentrate populations around towns and cities as was done in New England and Pennsylvania.[97] The differences between settlement patterns in Virginia and New England influenced the differences in how political campaigns were conducted in each region. The American scholar James Hammond Trumbull contrasted Virginian politics and politics in New England: "What New Englanders managed by a caucus, the Virginians preferred to accomplish by *a barbecue*."[98] Colonials in New England and Virginia encouraged participation in politics with alcohol. Because populations were concentrated in and around towns in New England, politicians centered their outreach activities around taverns and town meetings. Eventually New England's contribution to American politics developed in the form of the political caucus, where influential men met to discuss strategy, set agendas for town meetings, and to select their preferred political candidates. Their way of politicking included town meetings, public meetings at taverns, and distributing pamphlets. All of that was accompanied by copious amounts of adult beverages served to potential voters.[99]

In Virginia, there were fewer cities and large towns with taverns to attract crowds. Therefore politicians there had to attract people to political meetings using barbecue and alcohol. The American playwright Robert Munford (1737–83) lampooned that practice among Virginia's eighteenth-century politicians in his comedy titled "*The Candidates; or, the Humours of a Virginia Election*" first published in 1770.[100] The differences in ways of politicking in the North and how it was done in the South were reflected in sentiments expressed by the Pennsylvania politician Samuel Breck (1771–1862). An entry in his diary mentioned that his host in Maryland "had given a barbecue to two hundred people the day before as an election feast—a vile and anti-republican custom still prevalent in this and the States to the southward."[101]

Nicholas Spencer (1633–1689) was a London merchant who arrived in Virginia in the 1650s. He became an influential planter and public servant. He wrote of life in

Powhatan Stew Pot with conical bottom. Photo by the author.

Virginia in 1680 through his Europe-born eyes as a "wild & Rambleing way of Living," which was a reference to the striking scarcity of towns in the colony.[102] The aforementioned Reverend John Clayton reported to the Royal Society of London in 1688 on the conditions in the Virginia colony at that time. He remarked, "Plantations run over vast Tracts of Ground . . . whereby the Country is thinly inhabited, their living is solitary and unsociable, tradeing confused, & dispersed; besides other inconviencys."[103] Those accounts of the dispersed population in colonial Virginia explain why politicians there couldn't just call a town meeting to reach voters, nor could they invite voters to a local tavern. Therefore they turned to hosting *entertainments* that featured barbecued meats washed down with copious amounts of alcoholic beverages accompanied by rough, English games.[104]

SOUTHERN BARBECUE'S ORIGINAL HABITAT

The desire among people in colonial Virginia to socialize and the desire among politicians to reach constituents sheds light on why barbecuing became a cultural trait of the South rather than the North. During the seventeenth century, entertainments were democratic events that were different than mere banquets and feasts. Banquets were attended with pomp and circumstance and were usually "confined to men of high estate." Feasts were traditionally held on holidays and were typically accompanied by public rejoicing. Even though entertainments might have included feasts, they were more personal than feasts and banquets. Hosts gave entertainments for the enjoyment of friends and equals, not subjects or people of lower standing than the host.[105] In that way, entertainments were a way of maintaining close social attachments with friends and family as well as between politicians and their constituents who were the politicians' equals—not their subjects. That also explains why Virginians called barbecues entertainments before they started calling them barbecues.[106]

Years before the Carolinas were established as colonies, barbecuing was already entrenched in colonial Virginian culture. Although there are no known detailed accounts of the OSBT written before the eighteenth century, wills and laws passed by Virginia's House of Burgesses show that seventeenth-century Virginians were hosting barbecues for summertime entertainments, weddings, and funerals. In 1645, mourners at John Smalcomb's funeral consumed a barbecued steer and a barrel of strong beer. They also used up "considerable [gun] powder" in shooting matches held during the barbecue. Before he died in 1647, Richard Leman arranged the purchase of an ox worth eight hundred pounds of tobacco to be barbecued for mourners at his funeral. In 1667, Daniel Boucher of Isle of Wight County left instructions in his will to provide "one loaf of bread to every destitute person" and a barbecued ox for the "whole number of poor residing there."In 1678, the colonial Virginia mourners of Mrs. Elizabeth (Worsham) Epes barbecued a steer and three sheep. The host served "five gallons of wine, two gallons of brandy, ten pounds of butter, and eight pounds of sugar" along with the barbecued meats. Strong drink was a prominent feature of many barbecues in Virginia until the start of the Prohibition period. That may explain why John Michael of Northampton specified that there should be "no immoderate drinking nor shooting at his funeral." In 1675, Edmund Watts of York County also forbade the serving of drinks at his funeral.[109]

Charles Lanman (1819–95) was aware of the unique conditions in early colonial Virginia that contributed to the development of southern barbecues. In addition to describing two types of Virginia barbecues—the social and the political—Lanman wrote: "It is quite certain that it [the practice of hosting barbecues] was first introduced into this country by the early settlers of Virginia; and though well known throughout all the Southern States, it is commonly looked upon as a 'pleasant invention' of the Old Dominion. The idea was evidently conceived by a rural population, and in a district where villages and the ordinary public buildings of the present time were few and far between. For purposes of business or pleasure, the people found it necessary, or advisable, to meet together in masses, at stated periods; and as these meetings were

SEVENTEENTH-CENTURY BARBECUES IN VIRGINIA

Several scholars have written about Virginia barbecues during the seventeenth century. Henry Cabot Lodge (1850–1924) wrote about the "rough, honest English sports" Virginians played at barbecues.[107] An account of seventeenth-century Virginia barbecues can also be found in Jennings C. Wise's (1861–1968) *Ye Kingdome of Accawmacke* published in 1911:

> A funeral at this time was a splendid, and for many of the attendants a highly enjoyable, occasion. The shadow of death had no place among those sunny spirits. Barbecues were given and rum liberally dispensed by the afflicted family, and a general spree was indulged in at the expense of the estate of the deceased. The more boisterous mourners usually carried their fowling pieces and fire-arms to the funeral, and after the feast and bowl had somewhat assuaged their sorrow and enlivened the solemn occasion, a barbaric celebration ensued.[108]

(continued from page 158)

made a kind of rural festival, and as the animals served upon such occasions were commonly roasted entire, it was not unnatural that the feast should eventually have become known as a barbecue."[110]

Twenty-five years before Lanman published his observations of barbecues in Virginia, a contributor to a New York newspaper wrote, "This sort of festival , however, is, we presume, as essential to any public celebration among the descendants of the Ancient Dominion [Virginia], which is its original *habitat*, as a sumptuous dinner is to a charity in England, or an inaugural address to the getting up of anything in literature or fine arts here ."[111]

CREOLIZATION IN ACTION

An ugly truth of the southern barbecue tradition is its roots in the suffering and exploitation of enslaved and oppressed people. Author Edmund S. Morgan called the institution of slavery "the central paradox of American history." It's also the paradox of the history of southern barbecuing. The men who risked everything for the words "All men are created equal" at the same time were either enslaving people or excusing those who did so while seemingly turning a blind eye to the paradox of celebrating Independence Day with a barbecue cooked and served by enslaved people. Edward Hooker (see Chapter 5, "Richard's Barbycu") could see that "incongruity" even though it was invisible to or ignored by his southern hosts at the 1806 Independence Day barbecue he attended in South Carolina.[112] Such uniquely American conditions like Hooker's incongruity set the stage for the southern barbecuing tradition to be born. According to scholars, creolization requires socioeconomic and politico-cultural conditions that result in forced inequality.[113] The conditions that existed in colonial Virginia alongside notions of liberty and freedom explain why the OSBT didn't develop and probably couldn't have developed anywhere else in the world.

When people with different cultures interact, culinary innovations often emerge. One example is the way Irish immigrants in the United States replaced pork with corned beef in their cabbage recipes. Another example is the way some chefs today combine Mexican and Korean recipes to make Korean tacos and Korean burritos. However, changes such as those creative and tasty culinary fusions represent the blending of cultural elements that make small changes to an existing culture. Unlike the results of creolization, they do not result in a new food culture that didn't exist before.

Although contributions from African Americans are what perfected southern barbecuing, the OSBT was not created by a single race or culture. More than a mash-up, it was a new culinary invention that didn't exist before it was created through the collective work of oppressed people of disparate cultures that shared similar culinary practices. In the case of southern barbecuing, those creators were both enslaved and free people of African descent, enslaved and free people of Native American descent, and indentured and free people of European descent.

During the first half of the seventeenth century, most Europeans in Virginia were poor, young, indentured, or formally indentured people and their children. Often indentured servants were cruelly treated and forced to live in primitive and unclean conditions. Even so, the treatment of indentured people was tempered by law and, as a result, wasn't as harsh as that of the enslaved. Further, unlike enslaved people who served for life, the indentured were freed from servitude after their period of indenture ended.

In addition to indentured Europeans, many Native Americans were enslaved or otherwise served people of European descent in Virginia. According to the latest estimates, as many as forty percent of all enslaved adults in some parts of seventeenth-century Virginia were Native Americans. So were as many as half of all enslaved children.[114]

There are also colonial-era reports of wealthy families who employed Native American women as cooks.[115] As late as 1833, Virginians were still employing Native American cooks who worked alongside African Americans. One contented diner praised the cooks' skills thusly, "After the fisherman comes the cook! And no matter what may be his color—an Indian or African sun may have shown [sic] upon him. He is yet more entitled to the 'highest consideration.'"[116]

According to a 1620 census of the colony, there were as many as 32 people of African descent residing in Virginia. By 1650, even though the population of Virginia had grown to about 15,000 to 19,000 people, only about 500 were of African descent. During Bacon's Rebellion in the 1670s, indentured men of European descent fought alongside as many as 10 percent of Virginia's African and African American men. The rebellion of so many indentured men frightened Virginia's Anglo planters, so they decided to move away from labor provided by mainly indentured people to labor provided by mainly enslaved people. Over the last three decades of the seventeenth century, the population of enslaved Africans in Virginia grew rapidly. For example, in 1670 there were approximately 2,000 Africans and African Americans in Virginia. By 1700 that number had grown to over 16,000.[117]

Although enslaved barbecue cooks were often celebrated for their skills at the pit, their lives were far from easy. Frederick Douglass wrote about the backbreaking labor, fatigue, floggings, hunger, and other tortures inflicted on those who were enslaved. He described how food was used to control enslaved people when he wrote of the "sorrow and hunger-smitten multitudes" who were encouraged to feast and drink on holidays with provisions provided by the plantation owner. Douglass explained the hangover from those events resulted in enslaved people "feeling, upon the whole, rather glad to go, from what our master had deceived us into a belief was freedom, back to the arms of slavery."[118]

There are no eyewitness accounts of how southern barbecuing was developed and there were no professional ethnographers around who could document it step by step. Further, the prejudices and superstitions of Europeans who wrote accounts of the early modern period Americas and the people of creole cultures influenced their conclusions. Therefore while we know creolization was at work, we must go beyond analyzing historical accounts and make some comparisons and inferences in regard to many of the details of its role in the development of southern barbecuing.

It's clear that contact between disparate groups—African, Native American, and European, free and enslaved—during the early modern period resulted in cultural exchange. When people of disparate cultures came into close proximity with one another on plantations in the Americas, they watched, smelled, tasted, asked questions, and commented on each other's culinary practices. Eventually new items like colonoware and new cuisines emerged organically all around the Americas. As a new culture slowly emerged, people weren't necessarily conscious of it.

When a comparison is made between how Jamaican jerk and Mexican barbacoa developed among creole populations, it's likely that the gradual development of the OSBT into a unique and new way of cooking occurred among people who were born in Virginia rather than those who were born in Europe or Africa. Therefore the OSBT could have started to emerge as early as the 1630s as that's about the time the first generation of Virginia-born colonials were entering adulthood.

The earliest detailed account of a barbecue pitmaster in action was written by John Lawson (1674–1711). While exploring the Carolinas in the first few years of the eighteenth century, he witnessed a Native American woman cooking "Barbakues" from "Morning till Night." Today, some consider barbecuing to be a man's job. However, the earliest detailed account of a barbecue cook is of a woman pitmaster. Lawson's early account of the female pitmaster bears witness to the strong influence Native Americans had on the development of southern barbecuing. Powhatan women used to cook outside over shallow, bowl-bottomed pits full of hot embers. Europeans also cooked outside over pits. Because both Europeans and Powhatans observed traditional gender roles, women would do the cooking using techniques and recipes they were taught by their mothers. Perhaps the southern barbecue pit was born when an indentured European who was a former sailor or soldier took a Powhatan wife and observed her cooking on a wooden grill over a shallow pit. In an attempt to be helpful, he suggested that she square up the walls of the pit to make it more efficient.

It's been documented that Powhatans didn't use salt or many other seasonings in their cooking. On the opposite end of the spectrum were Africans and people from England who were accustomed to eating salted meats seasoned with spices and herbs. Perhaps in an effort to make his wife's way of roasting and barbecuing meats more to his liking, a husband suggested a typical early modern European recipe that consisted of salt, vinegar, butter, and home-grown red pepper while cooks of African descent added spices, herbs, and expert finesse.

Occasionally indentured servants and enslaved people were allowed to hold entertainments, which were relatively large gatherings. Like Lawson's Carolina pitmaster, the Powhatan women would most likely choose to slow cook whole animal carcasses for such events. With the expertise of African Americans, European improvements to the cooking pit, and the addition of European seasonings combined with the Native

American way of cooking whole carcasses for long periods of time, southern barbecuing was beginning to take shape.

The population of Africans and African Americans in early seventeenth-century Virginia was small in relation to the population of people of European descent and Native Americans. Nevertheless there was cultural interaction between all three groups. According to Robert Beverly, indentured servants and enslaved people were "imployed [*sic*] together" and that implies those two groups collaborated.[119] According to the latest research, the majority of enslaved people brought to Virginia from the late 1670s to the early 1700s came directly from Africa rather than the Caribbean.[120] That played an important role in the development of southern barbecuing because sizable increases of enslaved people directly from Africa tended to perpetuate the process of creolization.[121] Therefore the influence that Africa-born people had on their children born in Virginia, and other Virginia-born people, was apparently a critical driver of creolization. As a result there were significant African influences on southern barbecuing, such as the use of vinegar to control browning, the artistic use of herbs and spices, and a refinement in the way whole animal carcass were cooked directly over coals so that they became tender and flavorful.

SPECULATIVE SCENARIO

The OSBT is a uniquely American way of cooking a whole, butterflied animal carcass while being basted with a salty liquid as it rests on a grill over an open pit filled with burning embers. There is no known credible evidence that it existed in any other part of the world before it existed in the colonial United States. The following is a speculative scenario for how creolization influenced the development of the OSBT.

At some point in the seventeenth century, a wealthy planter who was also a politician attended an entertainment held by indentured servants and enslaved people. He was offered some of their decidedly non-European barbecued meats and he liked it. He noticed how the carcasses were split down the backbone and cooked in one piece making it an inexpensive and convenient way to cook something tasty for a lot of people. That may have prompted him to make a request similar to "I'm holding an entertainment for my constituents next weekend and I'd like you to cook that (pointing to the barbecue) for my guests."

The guests at the politician's entertainment were impressed by the tasty, new-to-them barbecued meats. Soon other politicians and planters who were present adopted the practice, and after having their servants and enslaved people trained to cook barbecue, events featuring barbecued meats started to spread. Eventually the entertainments became known as barbecues and the southern barbecue tradition was born. Eventually it became a defining part of southern culture.

BARBECUE, RACISM, AND SLAVERY

Racism and the institution of slavery are reprehensible and altogether abhorrent, and the role they played in the origins of southern barbecuing doesn't in any way validate, justify, lesson, or otherwise excuse the vile evils associated with them. Rather, southern barbecuing is a tribute to the fortitude and perseverance of the enslaved and oppressed people who, in spite of the injustices and cruelty they endured, applied their talents, skills, and ingenuity to create a defining and iconic American culinary tradition that is still cherished today.

"Meat-Flavoring" BBQ Sauce

George Washington's preferred barbecue recipe has not been found. However, because he was a Virginian, we can look to recipes published in old cookbooks written by Virginians such as this recipe that's inspired by Marion Cabell Tyree's *Housekeeping in Old Virginia* for clues. This is an old recipe that was used by Virginian cooks long before it was published in 1878.

Use the sauce to season soups, stews, and roasted and barbecued fish and meats.

1 quart vinegar
2 onions, chopped
3 red pepper pods, chopped
2 tablespoons brown sugar
1 tablespoon celery seed
1 tablespoon ground mustard
1 teaspoon turmeric
1 teaspoon black pepper
1 teaspoon table salt

—

Put all ingredients in a saucepan, mix well, and bring to a simmer. Transfer the sauce to a clean, air-tight container and store in the refrigerator for up to 1 week.

SEVEN

JUBA'S 'CUE

The Original Southern Barbecue

What people call "barbecue" today can be made with everything from whole animal carcasses to hamburgers, hotdogs, and even European-style sausages. It can be cooked on a hot grill, over a pit, or with indirect heat in a smokey oven called a *barbecue smoker*. Regardless, there was a time in the United States when barbecuing meats for outdoor social events meant one thing: cooking butterflied whole animal carcasses resting on a grill situated over a dug pit full of hot embers while being basted with a salty liquid often made with a base of butter and vinegar. Understanding that fact is critical for understanding the history of southern barbecuing. This chapter describes the details of the original way southern barbecue was cooked and several of the unique characteristics of the southern barbecue tradition. Those details establish a baseline for comparing different outdoor cooking and food preservation techniques from the sixteenth century to modern times.

THE ORIGINAL SOUTHERN BARBECUING PERIOD

The Original Southern Barbecuing Period (OSBP) occurred approximately between the 1630s and the end of the Reconstruction period in the 1870s. During the OSBP, the original southern barbecuing technique (OSBT) was the predominant way of barbecuing known in the South. When new ways of "barbecuing" started to show up after the end of Reconstruction they gradually displaced the OSBT, and by the mid-twentieth century the OSBT was no longer the predominate barbecuing method used in the United States.

(continued on page 168)

LOUIS HUGHES'S FIRSTHAND ACCOUNT OF SOUTHERN BARBECUES

The following is a firsthand account of the OSBT as described by author and businessman Louis Hughes (1832–1913) who was born enslaved near Charlottesville, Virginia:

Portrait of Louis Hughes, ca. 1897. Hughes, *Thirty Years a Slave.*

> The slaves worked with all their might. The children who were large enough were engaged in bringing wood and bark to the spot where the barbecue was to take place. They worked eagerly, all day long;

(continued next page)

and, by the time the sun was setting, a huge pile of fuel was beside the trench, ready for use in the morning. At an early hour of the great day, the servants were up, and the men whom Boss had appointed to look after the killing of the hogs and sheep were quickly at their work, and, by the time they had the meat dressed and ready, most of the slaves had arrived at the center of attraction. They gathered in groups, talking, laughing, telling tales that they heard from their grandfather, or relating practical jokes that they had played or seen played on others. These tales were received with peals of laughter. But however much they seemed to enjoy those stories and social interchanges, they never lost sight of the trench or the spot where the sweetmeats were to be cooked. The method of cooking the meat was to dig a trench in the ground about six feet long and eighteen inches deep. This trench was filled with wood and bark which was set on fire, and, when it was burned to a great bed of coals, the hog was split through the back bone, and laid on the poles which had been placed across the trench. The sheep were treated in the same way, and both were turned from side to side as they cooked. During the process of roasting the cooks basted the carcasses with a preparation furnished from the great house, consisting of butter, pepper, salt and vinegar, and this was continued until the meat was ready to serve.[1]

(continued from page 167)

The following account from 1865 of the OSBT as done in Milledgeville, Georgia, reveals several details of the OSBT:

> The "carcasses," Lambs and Pigs, usually five or six of each, are already over the fire, and experienced hands are carefully attending to the work of doing them "up brown." The process of barbecuing is very simple, yet there are but few who can cook the meat and season it to that degree of perfection which the palate of an epicure demands. A hole is dug in the ground about three feet in width, one foot in depth, and regulated as to length, by the number of Lambs, Pigs and Chickens to be cooked. The whole carcasses are placed on small poles laid across the pit, and small sticks are run through the feet, to keep them from being burnt

> by a too close approach to the fire. A fire, built of large wood is made close by the pit, and the coals therefrom are carefully shoveled up and scattered under the meat. A seasoning *gravy* is prepared in a bowl; it is usually made of red pepper and vinegar, and sometimes tomato catsup is added. The *Barbecuer* ties a linen rag to the end of a small stick, which he keeps wet by frequent applications of the *gravy*, and with this stick he *slaps* the carcass while it is cooking. This keeps it moist, and thoroughly seasons the "whole hog."[2]

A person who experienced the OSBT firsthand described it as barbecuing "in its best form." A contributor to the *Daily News* declared, "A man hasn't got any part in the resurrection until he's eaten barbecued shote." The Canadian-born lawyer and journalist Alexander Edwin Sweet (1841–1901) praised the OSBP as a time when barbecuing was "the perfection of cookery, and that no meat tastes so sweet as that which is barbecued." Another boasted, "[T]here is no better eating to be got in any other way." The American poet Robert Francis Astrop (1814–65) captured the festive nature of barbecues in 1835, "Ye who love good eating, just go to a 'Cue— Ye'll find and enjoy it there, I warrant you."[3]

HARD WORK, LITTLE RECOGNITION

During the OSBP, one of the most efficient and economical ways of feeding a large group of people was with barbecued meats. Livestock was abundant and cheap, and enslaved people usually supplied labor. People who hosted barbecues served their guests outdoors, often on makeshift tables. Utensils were optional because guests ate the barbecue with their fingers. In rural areas, people often brought their own cup, knife, and spoon to such events.[4] The American missionary Hamilton Pierson (1817–88) commented in 1881 that barbecuing, "is the simplest possible manner of preparing a dinner for a large concourse of people. It requires neither building, stove, oven, range, nor baking-pans. It involves no house-cleaning after the feast. It soils and spoils no carpets or furniture. And in the mild, bountiful region where the ox and all that is eaten are raised with so little care, the cost of feeding hundreds, or even thousands, in this manner is merely nominal."[5] Those aspects of barbecuing were some of the factors that made barbecues frequent events in the South during the OSBP.

Although barbecues were convenient for the hosts and enjoyable for the guests, that wasn't the case for the enslaved people who had to do the hard work. Before the end of the Civil War, enslaved people had to slaughter the animals, chop the wood, dig the pit, and set up the cook site, which often included moving large and heavy iron pots in which they cooked Brunswick stew, burgoo, or barbecue hash. Enslaved people also did the hard work of building and arranging makeshift dining tables, baking large quantities of bread, making side dishes, transporting heavy barrels of water, beer, or whiskey, and oftentimes manually placing those heavy barrels of beverages in the waters of a nearby stream to keep them cool. During the meal, enslaved waiters remained busy serving and entertaining the guests. Enslaved pitmasters often stayed up all night barbecuing the animal carcasses to be ready at mealtime. After all that, the enslaved people who labored so hard from morning to night to create their barbecued masterpieces and make the event a success were often only allowed to enjoy the fruit of their labors if there were leftovers. After the barbecue, the tasks of cleaning up the mess left by the diners, putting out the cooking fires, returning all of the equipment to storage, cleaning up the kettles and utensils, and disposing of the refuse was left to them as well.[6]

Many historical accounts of barbecues refer to the cooks as "Negroes" or, in Virginia, also as those who "ruled the 'roasts,'" and most were enslaved.[7] Even so, some were mentioned by name in books, diaries, and newspapers. Recalling his life on a North Carolina plantation, confederate chaplain James Battle Avirett (1835–1912) recounted how an enslaved man referred to as Uncle Shadrac barbecued hogs and bullocks while basting them with a long-handled mop that he dipped into a pan of "vinegar, salt, and home-grown red pepper."[8] A reporter for an 1849 edition of the *Alexandria Gazette* mentioned an enslaved pitmaster in Chesterfield, Virginia, Uncle Ben Moody, and praised his skills at the barbecue pit and the Brunswick stew kettle.[9]

JUBA AND MANDY GARTH

In 1808, President Thomas Jefferson's (1743–1826) youngest sister, Anne Scott Jefferson (1755–1828), attended an Independence Day barbecue in Charlottesville, Virginia, in his stead.[10] The following details of the barbecue were reported in a local newspaper: "The citizens of Albemarle County convened in Charlottesville to celebrate the 4th. of July—the Declaration of American Independence was read to a large assembly in the CourtHouse.—At three o'clock the company animated by the presence of many of the most accomplished ladies in the vicinity, sat down to a handsome barbacue provided by Mr. Elijah Garth. After dinner, on the retiring of the ladies, the gentlemen drank the following toasts in the republican [spirit] of their own country."[11] The person who received credit for the barbecue didn't actually cook it. He was a wealthy man named Elijah Garth (1772–1812) of Albemarle County, Virginia.[12]

Ninety-eight years later, another member of the Garth family, William "Billy" Garth (1863–1934), was often referred to as "the prince of barbecuers."[13] A correspondent for

Depiction of an antebellum barbecue in Virginia, ca. 1859.

a 1906 edition of the *Washington Times* described Billy Garth as "fat, jolly, and speaks in a slow, soft Virginia drawl."[14] Accounts of his events printed in newspapers often failed to name the African Americans who did the hard work at the barbecues over which he presided. In 1905, a reporter for the *Times-Dispatch* wrote the following about one of Billy Garth's barbecues:

> A hundred feet from the stand was the long trench half filled with embers, over which were cooking two big porkers and three fat wethers [castrated rams], dressed whole. A dozen negroes superintended by "Billy" Garth, of Charlottesville, were kept busy turning the meat. Each carcass was fastened to two stout poles and then placed transversely over the trench where they were roasted to a turn. Some of the negroes were kept busy all the time dipping long handled swabs in buckets of vinegar sauce and smearing it over the cooking meat. The heat "drove the sauce in" as one old man explained. The result was meat flavored to suit the taste of the most fastidious gourmet.[15]

Juba (#31) and Mandy (#30) Garth, ca. 1870. Courtesy of Albert and Shirley Small, Special Collections Library, University of Virginia.

29
30

Barbecue pits at the Oklahoma State Fairgrounds in celebration of Governor Walton's inauguration, ca. 1922. It was reported that the combined length of the pits would reach at least one mile. Courtesy of Gateway to Oklahoma History, Oklahoma Historical Society.

Although newspapers failed to mention the names of the pitmasters who worked for the Garth family throughout the nineteenth century, there are some clues in the memoirs of Richard Thomas Walker Duke Jr. (1853–1926), who was a lawyer and politician born in Albemarle County, Virginia. Duke Jr., wrote his memoirs in 5 leather-bound books that cover the period from the start of the Civil War to the middle of the 1920s in which he mentioned a married couple named Juba and Mandy Garth. Juba and Mandy were pitmasters described as "old slaves of the Garth family."[16] It's

therefore possible that the enslaved people who barbecued the meats for Elijah Garth's 1808 barbecue in Charlottesville were ancestors of Juba and Mandy. Another African American pitmaster mentioned by Duke, Jr, was Caesar Young (1854–1935). Young garnered much fame cooking barbecue and Brunswick stew from the late nineteenth century to the first quarter of the twentieth.

By the time Duke Jr, penned his account of Juba and Mandy in 1924, they both had already passed away. Duke Jr. noticed the changes occurring to southern barbecuing after the end of the Reconstruction period. Referring to Juba, Mandy, and Caesar, he wrote, "With the death of these Negroes the art of 'barbe'cuing' has welnigh [*sic*] passed away, only Caesar Young—my servant—surviving to remember the art. He is one year younger than I am & when Caesar goes, as far as Albemarle is concerned the 'barbecue' will practically go out of existence—that is the barbecue in its best form."[17] Caesar Young died in 1935 on Christmas Eve at the age of 81.

THE SOUTHERN BARBECUE PIT

A prime example of how creolization among the three primary loaner cultures in colonial Virginia created a unique barbecue style is found in the barbecue pit used to contain hot embers under the grill. It is one of the most defining characteristics of the OSBT. Account after account of barbecuing in the South during the OSBP mentions the open barbecue pits dug into the ground. OSBP barbecue pits ranged from 12 inches to as much as 5 feet deep, 4 feet wide, and as long as was needed to hold the number of animal carcasses to be barbecued. In 1922 a Tulsa newspaper reported on the inauguration barbecue for the Oklahoma governor-elect J. C. Walton. That barbecue was attended by 50,000 or more people (reports vary from 50,000 to 100,000). According to one report, the combined length of the pits needed to barbecue all of the meats was one mile.[18] Although this event occurred well after the OSBP ended, in this case it was more economical to cook the barbecue over open pits rather than going to the expense of buying cookers made of iron or masonry to cook the huge amount of barbecued meats that was required.

Southern barbecue pits didn't have lids or covers during the OSBP. Barbecuing over an open pit produces a unique barbecue that can't be duplicated using any other method. Additionally, meats barbecued on open pits don't develop as strong of a smoky flavor as meats cooked in covered pits. Open barbecue pits also introduce a level of difficulty that doesn't exist when cooking in a modern barbecue cooker. One of the biggest challenges is balancing the embers' temperature with the strength of the wind, humidity, and the temperature of the air. Because wind can frequently change direction and intensity, it can pose significant problems when cooking over an open pit. Even moderate winds can significantly diminish the amount of heat that reaches the carcass. It takes skill, knowledge, and experience to maintain an adequate cooking temperature. Windy conditions also require the use of much more wood because of an increased need for hot coals. Compounding the difficulty is the fact that the only thermometers available to OSBP pitmasters were their hands.

The OSBT isn't necessarily a "low and slow" way of cooking. The coals often reached temperatures high enough to require the cook to repeatedly turn the carcass over. During the latter stages of the cook, the level of heat diminished. Even today some pitmasters barbecue pig carcasses at as much as 600°F at the beginning of the cooking

(continued on page 179)

INTERVIEW WITH WILL HILL

The following notes were made by Wilbur G. Kurtz I in 1938 during an interview with a nineteenth-century African American barbecue cook named Will Hill.

KURTZ: Will's recollections are of many years back, so no date can be put on them. The following details relate as to how barbecues were conducted as Will saw them at a very early age - and as he himself knew of them from active participation.

HILL: A trench was dug into the ground—twelve to fifteen feet long—four feet wide and two feet deep. Across this trench were laid iron rods or bars at rather close intervals—the ends resting on the rims of the pit. Usually, a blacksmith fabricated these bars into say six grills—each unit to take care of a hog—a sheep or a quarter of beef. These grills would look something like this—and being made in units, they would obviously be easier to handle and would be more practical than separate bars.

At one side of the pit—on the ground surface—a fire of oak or hickory sticks was made. When the fire had produced a quantity of glowing coals—the flames having disappeared—these coals were shoveled into the pit and spread along the bottom surface. Over this bed of glowing coals were placed the iron grills with spaces between them [like] this.

On these grills was laid the meat. Hogs were roasted whole—the head and hair removed and properly drawn, of course. The entrails fell to the lot of the slaves who made "chitlins" of them and they were considered a great delicacy when eaten hot from the skillet or used as a filler in cornbread—the "Shortenin' Bread" of the celebrated ballad. Sheep were similarly prepared and laid on the grill—and usually a quarter of beef was added for those who preferred it to either one of the other.

The basting of the meat was a continuous performance—as was the frequent turnings of the meat upon the grills. Two persons basted—another turned. The basting sauce was a cooked mixture of vinegar, mustard, pepper and sugar—with butter added for mutton basting. The basting fluid was contained in one or more pots—buckets or crocks. The swab for the basting was a stick about 3 feet long with a wad of white rags bound firmly to one

(continued next page)

end. This swab was dipped into the basting mixture and "dabbed" on the meat. When the top surfaces of the meat had been well covered, it was turned over to expose it to the heat from the live coals. This was, as aforesaid, a continuous performance, or the meat would burn.

The heat was regulated by the number of glowing coals placed on the floor of the pit—added according to temperature requirements. The oak or hickory fire alongside the pit kept up so as to have an abundant supply of live coals. The roasting usually began at midnight—and was kept up until nearly noon, at which time the heat was allowed to die away gradually.

Nearby was a huge iron pot over a fire in which Brunswick stew was slowly cooked. This is a mixture of chopped beef and pork—onions—tomato sauce and I don't know what all. It resembles a Scotch Haggis but has a higher spice content though not so peppery as is the genuine Mexican chili con carne. Indeed, the proper barbecued meat with the Brunswick stew is a rather highly seasoned concoction. And so tempting is it to some folks, they are likely to overeat of its succulent goodness. The Brunswick Stew was continuously stirred while cooking—no double boilers then. Six or eight persons were required to prepare and cook the meat and stew—if six or eight grills were in operation—which would supply food for two hundred guests. Alongside the pit was a long board table—built there—or cleated planks laid on wooden horses. Here the meats were cut up, thus making one so darn hungry. (I'll have to do something about it!)

When serving time arrived, the meats were cut up on the table—the dusky servers wielding huge butcher knives. If women, their heads were tied up with white headwraps—and they wore white aprons. The dresses were white of colored usually some dark material (not black) and sleeves rolled up. The men wore straw hats or were bare headed—sometimes the mere crown of an old hat—sans brim—and white aprons—white shirts—dark trousers—and of course—the sleeves were rolled up.

The meats were sliced—put on real plates— (no paper plates then) and from a steaming vessel of Brunswick Stew, a generous "helping was placed alongside the sliced meats. Pickles were added—(or chow-chow)—to the ensemble—the final touch being a couple slices of homemade white bread (something we know very little about these days).

Drinks—those days consisted of coffee and lemonade. Huge coffee pots alongside the fire that cooked the Brunswick stew—took care of this item. It was served in real cups and saucers with real spoons—(none of this paper stuff) and the lemonade was made just like it is made now. Spring water—or well water—was used. Probably little or no ice was used in large quantities—they saved that for the after-dinner juleps—if they had ice.

There was always plenty of black help at these Georgia barbecues. The dusky gentry who toiled in the silent watches of the night over the sizzling pits—the male and female slaves who did the cutting and serving of the plates—the troop of waiters who carried the plates and drinks to the long tables some distance away—[illegible] easily run the total up to twenty-five or thirty where 200 or more persons were to be served.

These long tables were of boards laid on horses, or more permanent units built and capable of removal. Alongside, were plank seats over which the hoop-skirted ladies had to climb if they chose to sit at a table—which many of them did not, for the greensward in the shade of the trees was more inviting.[20]

(continued from page 176)

process.[19] There were generally two ways of managing the embers in the pit during the OSBP. Deep pits were preferred by those who filled them with a tremendous quantity of hardwoods, such as white oak and hickory. After kindling the fire, flames could shoot up into the air as high as 25 feet, impressively lighting up the night sky. Those cooks let the wood burn down into a three to three and a half foot deep bed of live coals, after which they placed the meats on wooden sticks or iron bars that rested width-wise across the pit to create a grate. Using this method ensured there were enough coals in the pit to provide heat during the entire cook. Others preferred a *feeder fire*, a large fire in which hardwood was burned to create live coals used to replenish the embers in the pit during the long cook. The embers emitted very little visible smoke unless the basting liquid or juices from the meat dripped into them.

Numerous recipes for cooking southern-style barbecue were printed during the nineteenth century, and few fail to include the important step of digging the barbecue pit. In contrast no old British or West Indies cookbooks instruct the reader to dig a pit for coals under a grill before barbecuing an animal carcass. The fact that only American cookbooks instruct the reader to dig a pit to contain hot embers under meats as they are barbecued underscores the uniqueness of the OSBT, its barbecue baste recipe, its lack of a lid over the pit, the absence of dripping pans, and the way it required carcasses to be repeatedly flipped while being barbecued. That's strong evidence that the southern barbecue pit was born in the colonial United States and wasn't imported from the Caribbean.

THE ORIGINAL SOUTHERN BARBECUING TECHNIQUE

Although roasting meat outside beside a fire may be "caveman cooking," the OSBT is not a primitive cooking method. Neither is it merely cooking outdoors with fire, as some characterize it.[21] The OSBT requires extensive knowledge, experience, skill, and practice to master. It's as much an art as it is a science. It most certainly isn't the *earliest* and *easiest* form of cooking. It's a sophisticated technique that requires much expertise, which is a testament to the skill of those who invented and perfected it.

American author Martha McCulloch Williams (1848–1934) was an eyewitness to the OSBT and often attended barbecues when she was a little girl before the start of the Civil War. Here's Williams's description of barbecues during the OSBP:

> Of course, there was to be barbecue for dinner—the dancing crowd had given thirty pigs and lambs. These were brought to the ground at sundown the day beforehand, slaughtered, dressed, cut each in half and laid upon clean sticks over an earthen trench, two feet deep and as many wide, with a bed of hardwood coals glowing dusky red at the bottom. To cook it properly requires about twelve hours, so by one o'clock at the latest all must be over the fire. Eternal vigilance is the price of barbecue quite as much as of liberty. As the coals die out fresh ones are added from the log fire blazing at one side. About every ten minutes the meat is basted with salt water. In the last hour's cooking "dipney" takes its place—a wonderful compound of sweet lard, strong vinegar, and stronger pepper.[22]

She understood the skill and hard work required by the OSBT and commented, "All this sounds simple, dead-easy. Try it—it is really an art."[23] She was right. In 1911, a newspaper writer observed of the OSBT, "To barbecue a pig requires expert knowledge and long experience. Indeed, it is a science. . . . Some may bake a pig or roast one, but it [barbecuing] is a science that is attained only by inheritance."[24]

During the OSBP, cooks allowed hardwoods in the pit to burn down to live embers before placing animal carcasses on the grates skin-side up. No seasonings or rubs were applied to the meat before placing it on the grate. After the meat-side was adequately

Barbecue and stew being cooked using the original southern barbecue technique at a barbecue in Augusta, Georgia, ca. 1866. Sketch by Davis, *Harper's Weekly*.

seared, the carcass was flipped over so the skin side faced the coals. That's when the *basters* mopped, *sopped*, or *anointed* the meat side of the carcass.[25] After the skin side started browning, the carcass was flipped again. The skin side was not usually basted.

However, some cooks wiped the skin side down with a linen cloth from time to time to remove ash. The process of flipping and basting the meat side of the carcasses continued until they were "roasted to a turn." The "continuous performance" of flipping and basting means the jus wasn't saved and juices from the meats fell into the coals below. The resulting smoke and vapors that arose from them enhanced the flavor of the meat.[26]

Duke Jr. recorded the following firsthand account of Juba and Mandy Garth's OSBT. Even though he was far from a barbecuing expert, he was able to capture several important details:

> The process was as follows: A pit about ten feet long—five feet wide and about 3 feet deep, was dug in the ground & filled with kindling & green wood & set on fire about 5 o'clock in the morning & allowed to burn until it became a mass of glowing red hot coals. In the mean time [*sic*] pigs—quite young ones—& lambs—had been prepared & tied with green withes to two green poles about 6 or 7 feet longer than the pit was wide. They were then stretched over the coals & basted with melted butter in which some boiling water—salt & pepper were mixed. Two men were assigned to each animal, one on each side of the pit & turned the carcass over & over whilst a "baster" basted it with the melted butter.[27]

Although vinegar was a part of the baste recipe in the aforementioned account of Garth's 1808 barbecue, Duke Jr.'s account neglected to include it. Albeit he did notice the "baster" basting the meat with melted butter. During the OSBP, African American pitmasters also understood the importance of resting meats before serving. In 1844, a news writer observed, "When the roasting is completed the fire is allowed to die out, but the ox remains upon the spit . . . until it is time to cut up the meat for dinner."[28]

Unlike modern barbecue cooks who have many labor-saving gadgets and techniques, OSBP pitmasters didn't have injections, rubs, tinfoil, thermometers, or devices to manage the temperature of the pits. Being artistic experts at their craft, they used their training, experience, and senses to determine when the pit was at the right temperature, when the meat was ready to flip, and when it was ready to be served.

THE ORIGINAL SOUTHERN BARBECUE SAUCE

The basting liquid used during the OSBP was called *the seasoning* or *gravy* in Virginia.[29] In some parts of North Carolina, it was called *soption*.[30] In Tennessee, it was called *dipney*.[31] Cooks almost always made it using the primary ingredients of vinegar, salt, butter or lard, red pepper, and the addition of the pitmaster's secret herbs and spices.

Often those ingredients were made or grown at home. Red pepper was used in the original southern barbecue baste recipe as much from necessity as for flavor. Plantation owners allowed enslaved people to grow their own red pepper to avoid the expense of buying black pepper for them.[32]

The number of primary ingredients used in the basting sauce was dependent upon availability. When one or more weren't available, the basting liquid consisted of as many as were on hand or nothing more than salted water. Additional ingredients that had to be purchased, such as black pepper, were used only if the pitmasters or hosts could afford them. Personal touches to the baste recipe included herbs and "spicy condiments" like mustard, horseradish, mushroom ketchup, and so forth. By the 1840s, ingredients such as sugar, Worcestershire sauce, and tomatoes were added by some. The sauce was kept warm in kettles set over the hot coals and applied with clean linen attached to the ends of long sticks that Virginians called *long flexible wands* or long-handled ladles.[33] Illustrations and photographs of Virginians using their characteristic *wands* can be found from modern times to as far back as the 1850s.

An interesting aspect of the OSBT during the OSBP is its uniformity from one region of the South to another. Accounts of OSBP barbecues from all around the South mention the pit, the carcasses split down the backbone, the browning of the meat, and the vinegar- and/or butter-based basting liquid.

In 1918, the newspaper editor and author John Lewis Herring (1866–1923) shared a firsthand account of nineteenth-century barbecues in Georgia. He explained, "Barbecue in those days was seasoned in the cooking," which is a reference to the sauce that was used to "anoint" the animal carcasses.[35] Seasoning meat with a barbecue rub before barbecuing it wasn't a standard practice during the OSBP. That could be another practice that was contributed by Native Americans because it is well documented that seventeenth-century Powhatan cuisine avoided the use of seasonings.[36] Nevertheless at least one nineteenth-century account of a barbecue describes how meat was seasoned before going on the pit. Additionally, a few recipes found in nineteenth-century cookbooks call for seasoning meat before "barbecuing" it at the kitchen hearth or in an oven.[37] For example, American minister Rush Baynard Hall (1793–1863) wrote about a barbecue that he ostensibly attended during the 1820s in Indiana. He claimed that the carcasses were "peppered and salted" before being put on a "wooden gridiron" made of "strips of nice hickory" sitting over a pit of hot embers.[38]

The OSBP barbecue baste recipe was ubiquitous in the South and that reflected its origins in colonial Virginia. It has been estimated that between the years 1800 and 1809, sixty-six thousand enslaved people were traded between states. Of those, forty-one

(continued on page 186)

Top: Cooks basting barbecued pigs with "flexible wands" in Virginia, ca. 1859.

Bottom: Juba Garth basting barbecued pigs with a "flexible wand" in Virginia, ca. 1870.

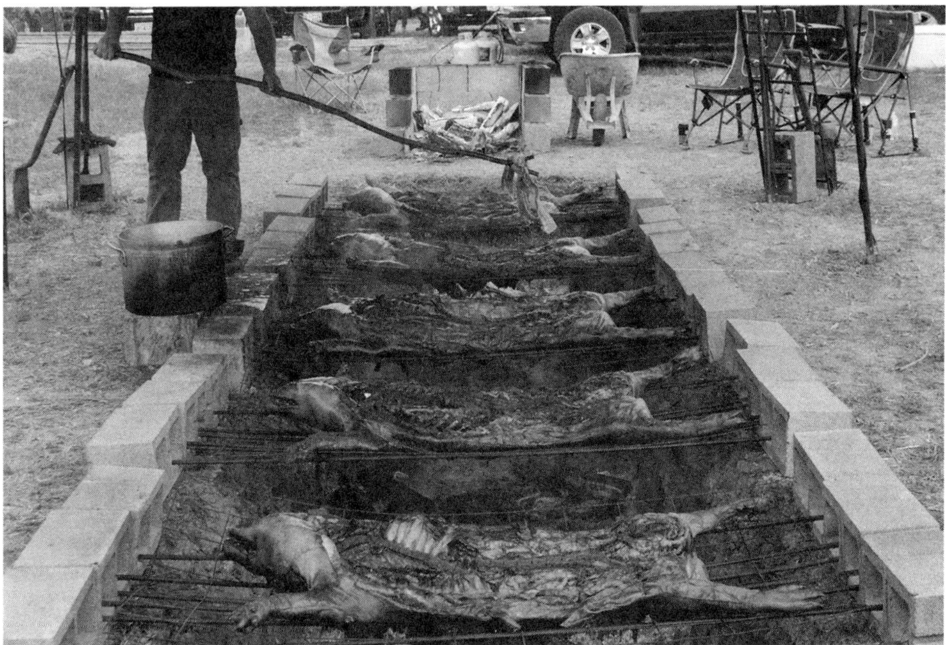

Top: A cook basting barbecue with a "flexible wand" at a barbecue in Charlottesville, Virginia, ca. 1920s. Holsinger Studio Collection. Courtesy of Special Collections, University of Virginia Library.

Bottom: Basting the pigs with a "flexible wand" in Woodstock, Virginia, ca. 2019. Photo by the author.

WESLEY JONES'S ACCOUNT OF SOUTHERN BARBECUES

Wesley Jones, born enslaved in 1840, was a South Carolinian pitmaster. In 1937, at the age of 97, he shared his barbecuing technique and recipe:

> Night befo' dem barbecues, I used to stay up all night a-cooking and basting de meats wid barbecue sass [sauce]. It made of vinegar, black and red pepper, salt, butter, a little sage, coriander, basil, onion, and garlic. Some folks drop a little sugar in it. On a long-pronged stick, I wraps a soft rag or cotton fer a swap, and all de night long I swabe dat meat 'till it drip into de fire. Dem drippings change de smoke into seasoned fumes dat smoke de meat. We turn de meat over and swab it dat way all night long 'till it ooze seasoning and bake all through.[34]

(continued from page 183)

thousand were from Virginia. From 1830 to 1860 alone, at least 300,000 enslaved people were trafficked from Virginia to the South and West.[39] Because most pitmasters in antebellum Virginia were African Americans, those forced migrations played a significant role in spreading Virginia's original barbecue recipe around the South.

The basting sauce used during the OSBP was initially inspired by European recipes for sauces meant to be served with roasted or broiled meat and fish.[40] As early as 1620, Virginians had imported Gervase Markham's (1568–1637) cookbook *The English Housewife*. Virginian cooks also had access to other cookbooks, such as *A Book of Cookrye* published in 1581, and *The Accomplish'd Lady's Delight* published in 1675. All of those books contain numerous recipes for sauces made of vinegar, butter, salt, pepper, and other spices meant to be served with roasted and grilled meats.[41]

During the OSBP, barbecued meats were only occasionally served with a sauce on the side. However, the sauce wasn't called *barbecue sauce*. It was just called *sauce*. Sometimes, it was merely a syrup made from honey or fruit. For example, at the 1806 wedding of Abraham Lincoln's parents, the hosts served honey and peach syrup in gourds to go with barbecued sheep. During an 1825 barbecue in Schuylkill, Pennsylvania, people enjoyed "a fine barbacue with spiced sauce." Others used liver, brains, and sweetmeats to make a sauce by boiling them until they were very tender.[42] They were then mashed and added to the basting liquid with red wine and breadcrumbs for thickening. Barbecue hash was used as a sauce for barbecued meats in Georgia and South Carolina.[43]

THE SECRET OF DIPNEY

Basting meats as they are being barbecued enhances flavor and helps prevent the surface of the meat from drying out. However, there was one other significant benefit. During the OSBP, African American pitmasters understood a secret known to few others even today. Martha McCulloch Williams wrote: "Then [in antebellum times] as now there were free barbecuers, mostly white—but somehow their handiwork lacked a little of perfection. For one thing, they never found out the exact secret of 'dipney,' the sauce that savored the meat when it was crisply tender, brown all over, but free from the least scorching."[44] It appears that one of those "free barbecuers" who didn't understand the secret of the dipney was "a red headed man" named Hubbard who lived in Courtland, Alabama. Hubbard's method called for cooking half-pig carcasses flesh-side down over a pit of coals without turning or basting them until the end of the cook. He let the meat cook until "the drying of the skin showed that they were nearly done, and then, when turned, the flesh was nicely browned and cracked open in deep fissures, so that when the hot gravy of sweet butter, vinegar and black pepper, was poured on, it penetrated to the bone—a far superior mode to frequently turning and basting."[45] Hubbard's method grew in popularity during the early twentieth century. Whether or not it is "far superior" to the OSBT is debatable.

Although they may not have understood the exact science behind it, African American pitmasters understood the value of basting meat with a vinegar-based liquid as it barbecued over direct heat. Alexander R. Boteler was impressed by how Virginian pitmasters basted lambs and hogs, and noted, "This part of the process was done with such earnest solemnity of manner, as to impress a beholder with the conviction that there was some important mystery meant by the particular ode in which the carcasses were so ceremoniously touched with the saturated cloths. During this operation, other attendants were busily engaged in turning over the huge roasts, one after another, so that all sides of each should be done equally alike."[46] Boteler's suspicion that there was an "important mystery" was correct.

The appetizing color of the bark on barbecued meats is the result of several things that occur during the cooking process. One is the Maillard reaction, a chemical reaction that imparts flavor to foods as they are browned by heat. Several things influence

Basting pigs with a butter and vinegar baste recipe that was used in antebellum Virginia. Courtesy of Joshua Fitzwater.

the reaction such as sugar, protein, heat, and the pH level on the meat's surface. That stands in contrast to how modern barbecue cooks often resort to adding sugar to create a faux bark on meats that are cooked "low and slow" in modern indirect-heat cookers.

The "secret of dipney" and "important mystery" is an understanding of how to manage the pH level of the surface of meat while it barbecues so that it creates a flavorful and delicious natural bark without scorching. When meat has an appropriate pH level for the temperature and the length of time it's barbecued coupled with the precise frequency of turning the meat, the bark (called "uncle Brown" in Virginia) comes out perfect every time. When the pH level of a food is low, the Maillard reaction slows, which means it will take longer to brown. When the pH level is high, the Maillard reaction speeds up. The pH level of vinegar is low, so vinegar-based basting liquids slow the browning of the meat and allows it to cook longer without scorching the surface. That's the important mystery and secret of dipney.

The combination of the constant turning of the carcasses and the application of the vinegary basting liquid was a secret employed by OSBP pitmasters for barbecuing meats to perfection, which resulted in, as was often remarked in those days, "just enough of the brown."[47] The Georgian pitmaster Will Hill witnessed southern barbecues from as far back as the 1860s. He well understood the vinegar-based dipney's secret. When he was interviewed by the historian Wilbur Kurtz (1882–1967) in 1938, he explained, "This swab was dipped into the basting mixture and 'dabbed' on the meat. When the top surfaces of the meat had been well covered, it was turned over to expose it to the heat from the live coals. This was, as aforesaid, a continuous performance, or the meat would burn."[48]

THE ATTACK

During the OSBP, observance of proper barbecue etiquette was often expected from all who attended barbecues and it varied depending on the type of barbecue being held. That's seen in several accounts such as this one from 1839 where a reporter called the moment the barbecued meats were served "the attack."[49]

> [The whole carcasses] are sopped or basted with a sort of preparation of vinegar, peppers, and other spicy condiments, every moment during the cooking until the attack. When the proper time arrives (and every estated gentleman prides himself on telling at a glance whether the thing is done right, "with just enough of the brown") the animals are laid whole upon boards, and the company assembled round to feast. It then becomes the duty of every gentleman to feed the ladies, that, to carve out those fat, spicy, rich and delicious morsels from the right places, and with ready tact.[50]

The first phase of "the attack" was a southern barbecue custom that started in Virginia, which required men to allow women to partake of the barbecued meats and other foods first. Those barbecues were called *Ladies Barbecues* in Virginia. Duke Jr. mentioned them in his *Recollections* and in 1883, Alexander Edwin Sweet left an account of a Ladies Barbecue held about ten miles outside of San Antonio, Texas. He noticed the OSBP custom of eating barbecued meats with fingers rather than forks and commented: "The dinner was free to all; and more than twenty thousand greasy fingers testified their owners' appreciation of the eatables, and gave at least one-third of the guests a reasonable excuse to get off that venerable truism about fingers being made before forks,—to get it off, too, as if it were a happy and original thought that had just then occurred to them." He also observed, "The ladies were admitted to the table first," and after all of them had dined, "the men were turned loose on the eatables."[51]

The most detailed account of Ladies Barbecues was left to us by the father of American fly fishing, Thaddeus Norris (1811–77). He described the Ladies Barbecue as an event where "matrons and maidens who danced were invited to attend."[52] Ladies Barbecues were fairly formal events where attendees were expected to wear their finest apparel. Norris commented that this "institution" descended to newer states, of which the Old Dominion may be called the mother; to Kentucky, to Tennessee, and other states where an institution of another sort [slavery] had been "wiped out." His description of Ladies Barbecues and of the way they spread from Virginia to other southern states brings to mind the Georgia barbecue depicted in the movie *Gone with the Wind*, where guests danced the Virginia reel and young men doted on Scarlet in a competition to see who would be the first to bring her the most delectable portions of the barbecued shotes.

When the aforementioned John M. Duncan was in Virginia in 1818, he attended a barbecue near Alexandria. He left the following account of how he violated etiquette by attempting to partake of the barbecued meats before the ladies were served:

> Seating their fair charge at one side, their partners lost no time in occupying the other, and as there was still some vacant space, those who happened to be nearest were pressed in to occupy it. Among others the invitation was extended to me, and though I observed that several declined it, I was too little acquainted with the tactics of a barbecue, and somewhat too well inclined to eat, to be very unrelenting in my refusal. I soon however discovered my false move. Few except those who wish to dance choose the first course; watchfulness to anticipate the wants of the ladies, prevent those who sit down with them from accomplishing much themselves.[53]

Another kind of barbecue was what Norris called "the little squirrel barbecue." It was a summertime barbecue held by a small company of friends after a morning of hunting. Hunting commenced at daybreak and continued until about 10 At that time, the small band of hunters would head to an appointed place near a cool stream or spring, which they used to chill foods and drinks. They constructed a wooden barbecue grill using sticks like the ones the Powhatan people first taught colonials to build in the early seventeenth century. They started a fire using hardwood and let it burn down into glowing coals. The young squirrels were cleaned, dressed, seasoned, and placed on the barbecue hurdle over the coals. The hunters barbecued the young squirrels slowly until they were tender and juicy. They took the "old squirrels" home and used them to make Virginia-style squirrel soup.[54]

Norris went on to describe what he called "the community barbecue," which was often accompanied by a fish fry. Many people from all around the community attended these barbecues. Everyone who could afford to do so lent a hand and donated labor, equipment, and food for the events. Large barbecue pits were dug, and wooden hurdles were placed over the pits to support the animal carcasses. The carcasses were positioned above the live coals as they barbecued. Muttons, shoats (young pigs), squirrels, and other meats were barbecued. Expert cooks prepared squirrel soup in large kettles seasoned with "onions and smoked middling," which is the original Virginia-style Brunswick stew recipe. The events were very festive with good food, fellowship, card playing, and horse racing.

Of these events, Norris considered the Ladies Barbecue to be "the most enjoyable of all." He wrote, "There were negro fiddlers, and negro cooks, and negro waiters, in all their 'pride, pomp and circumstance;' there were reels, and cotillions, and jigs; and most glorious of all, the pretty graceful girls. Can I ever forget them?" According to Norris, by 1875 few Ladies Barbecues were being hosted. Commenting on how grand southern barbecues were disappearing after the end of the Civil War, he wrote, "Are such gatherings still extant? I pray they have not entirely gone out with the 'institution' [slavery]. Why should they?"

BARBECUE STEWS

The only barbecue tradition in the world that has a corresponding barbecue stew tradition is southern barbecuing. Authentic barbecue stews aren't made with barbecued meats. Instead, they are stews that are traditionally served at barbecues. The three most famous barbecue stews are: Brunswick stew, barbecue hash, and burgoo. Two features shared by all of the barbecue stews are the long-simmering time and the constant stirring that prevents scorching.

Barbecue hash was very popular at barbecues because it provided a way to serve parts of the animal that weren't suitable for barbecuing. The meat scraps and offal were put into a large kettle with an equal number of onions (by weight) and simmered in water while being stirred continuously for hours until the meats dissolved into shreds. At the same time, the broth became thick and rich. Sometimes hash was thickened with breadcrumbs, and it was almost always seasoned with salt, peppers, and butter. Barbecue hash is still popular in South Carolina today.

Burgoo is a rich stew from Kentucky that's made with any combination of several kinds of meat with any variety of available vegetables. Some season it only with salt and pepper. Others add spices, herbs, cayenne, hard liquor, and even bitters. Like Brunswick stew, squirrel soup is an ancestor of burgoo. Unlike Brunswick stew, hash is not an ancestor of burgoo. Kentucky's greatest burgoo king Gustave "Gus" Jaubert (1838–1920) and his cooks take the credit for transforming burgoo from a soup into the thick, rich stew it is today.[55]

"How they Brew the Brunswick Stew." *Times Dispatch* (Richmond, VA), July 27, 1913.

Friends of Duke Jr., coined the phrase *barbecue stew* to refer to the Brunswick stew served at barbecues he and his father hosted.[56] Brunswick stew, which can claim barbecue hash as an ancestor, is a delicious, rich, and meaty stew made most often nowadays with chicken (sometimes a little beef is added). It was originally a squirrel stew or barbecue hash that was first cooked in Brunswick County, Virginia, during the 1820s by a man named Jimmy Mathews. Traditionally the stew is slowly simmered outdoors in large kettles with bacon or fatback, corn, butter beans, potatoes, onions, and tomatoes. It's seasoned with salt, black pepper, and red pepper with butter added just before

serving. It was said that without Brunswick stew "a Virginia barbecue would not be complete."[57] After the end of the Civil War, Georgians combined the basic barbecue hash recipe with Virginia's Brunswick stew recipe, and they created the Georgian version of Brunswick stew.[58]

BARBECUE CLUBS

Barbecue clubs were organizations of people who met on a regular basis for fellowship, entertainment, to build business relationships, and of course to enjoy barbecued meats. The earliest known barbecue club in the United States was the Buchanan's

Spring Barbecue Club officially formed by community members about a mile outside Richmond, Virginia, in 1788. Chief Justice John Marshall (1755–1835) was a founding member. It was said that the water from Buchanan's Spring "was pure, transparent, cool and delightful, embowered under old oaks." It was perfectly suited for barbecues during Virginia's hot summers "because of its fine water, magnificent shade, perfect quietude, and exemption from dust."[59] During the OSBP, a nearby water source was an essential feature of barbecues because they provided cool water to make drinks, such as lemonade and mint juleps, and to chill foods. The nearby water also helped keep diners cool as they enjoyed their meal.

Reports of the barbecued mutton served during meetings of the Buchanan's Spring Barbecue Club say that it was "cooked to a turn." Pork was "highly seasoned with mustard, cayenne pepper" and had a "slight flavoring of Worcester sauce."[60] The club continued to meet until the early months of the Civil War. By then the meeting place moved to an island in the James River. A report from 1862 tells us, "Respectable strangers, and especially foreigners, are always invited to the feast of the Barbacue," and club members were still enjoying Virginia barbecue, toddy, juleps, and quoits (a competition where people attempted to throw rings from a distance over or near a stake).[61] Clarke's Spring Barbecue Club was established in Richmond a few years after Buchanan's Spring Barbecue Club.[62]

In the 1870s, Duke Jr.'s father established the Cool Spring Barbecue Club in Albemarle County, Virginia. Duke Sr. was its first president. Club meetings convened at the "Barbecue Spring," located about half a mile away from Duke Sr.'s estate named Sunnyside. Its "exceedingly cold" waters made it a perfect location for hosting "old fashioned Virginia barbecues." Duke Jr. remarked that barbecues were held near the spring for longer than anyone could remember.[63]

Other notable barbecue clubs existed in the nineteenth and early twentieth centuries. An 1866 edition of the *Richmond Dispatch* mentioned the Monroe Ward Barbecue Club that met at Dr. Francis H. Deane's (1810–70) farm on the Mechanicsville turnpike near Richmond, Virginia. Club meetings featured speeches delivered by prominent members of the community, "'choice liquors,' and 'sumptuous viands' [a term for any item of food], and 'all the delicacies of the season.'" Unsurprisingly it was reported that after meetings members were "merry and happy."[64] The City Barbecue Club was established in Owensboro, Kentucky, in the early 1900s. It had about 30 members but, unlike other barbecue clubs, the members never adopted any bylaws nor a formal name for the club. For several years the club met annually to "get a good square meal of barbecued lamb and pork."[65] The El Paso Barbecue Club regularly held barbecues for several years during the early twentieth century. It was organized by the city's mayor and had a membership of about 100 people. Unlike other barbecue clubs, no speeches were allowed at club meetings. The mayor insisted that members meet "to get acquainted and talk among themselves."[66]

Barbecue clubs that focused on backyard barbecuing were established during the twentieth century. For example, in 1938 a travelling salesman from San Francisco named Maurice H. Auerbach organized the Buckaroo Barbecue Society. It was reported that Auerbach had a "national reputation as an authority on finely seasoned barbecued meats." Each member of the club had a nickname. Auerbach's was Old Smoky. The stated purpose of the society was "to encourage people to get outdoors and barbecue." The Buckaroo Barbecue Society celebrated grilling over hot coals, which was referred by the newspaper as "the California style of barbecue."[67] Today there are numerous regional, national, and international barbecue clubs and associations. There are no known records of eighteenth- or nineteenth-century barbecue clubs outside of the United States, making them another unique feature of the southern barbecue tradition.

THE END OF THE ORIGINAL SOUTHERN BARBECUING PERIOD

By the end of Reconstruction, the OSBT and the days of frequent large and free-to-the-public southern barbecues were coming to an end. Just as Duke Jr. and Norris predicted, as the generation that learned to barbecue before the end of Reconstruction passed away, eventually so did the OSBT. Over the course of about 70 years after the end of the Civil War, the OSBT was slowly set aside for less labor-intensive ways of "barbecuing," and "southern-style" barbecue was emerging all around the United States.

Many plantation owners who had become wealthy by enslaving people before the start of the Civil War were land-rich and cash-poor after it ended. Without the labor provided by enslaved people to slaughter the animals, chop the wood, dig the pits, formulate the baste recipes, and barbecue the carcasses, the days of frequently hosting large community and political barbecues in the South were over. In 1872 Mori Arinori (1847–89), the first Japanese ambassador to the United States, commented on the decline of southern barbecues:

> In the Southern States, certain festivals are common, but more so before the late war than now, which are known as "Barbecues." They are political, and sometimes bring together very large numbers of the planters and their families, and the time is generally devoted to speech-making, happily varied by eating

> and drinking the good things of the land. The principal food on these occasions, consists of beef or mutton, and the oxen or sheep are roasted entire, over a pit duly prepared and filled with burning coals. The cooks and caterers are generally negro men and women, and as they have the privilege of inviting their own friends, the groves where they assemble present a varied and fantastic scene.[68]

In 1876 a correspondent for the *Times-Picayune* wrote, "We speak of it [southern barbecuing] in the past tense, for we fear that 'Ichabod' is written upon its venerable forehead, and that since the rebellion its true glory is departed." He continued, "Pity if so good an institution has gone down, as we fear it has in its original simplicity, among the other wrecks of the war."[69] In 1887, a reporter for *Frank Leslie's Illustrated Newspaper* asserted with some exaggeration, "The day of the barbecue in [political] campaigns is over."[70]

After 1865, many newly freed African American pitmasters moved away from the South. They introduced southern barbecuing in the North and Midwest. For example, in 1879 a group of ten African American freedmen from Virginia moved to Cincinnati. They had steady work cooking old Virginia barbecue. On one highly publicized occasion, they barbecued two oxen and eight sheep. According to a press report, the barbecue "was a great success, and fully 5000 people partook" of the Virginia-style barbecue.[71] The western march of southern-style barbecuing was noticed by a correspondent for the *Chicago Herald* who wrote in 1892, "There is no state in the union so given to political barbecues as Indiana. In the old days of Jackson and Van Buren they used to give imposing barbecues in Virginia and Kentucky, but since the war Indiana has held the palm in the matter of political feasts."[72]

The end of the Reconstruction period marked the end of the OSBP and a slow transition to modern ways of barbecuing was just beginning. Consequently barbecuing in the United States was beginning to be fundamentally changed. The changes took several decades to occur, and by the turn of the twentieth century there were clear distinctions between barbecuing in 1800 and barbecuing in 1900. For example, in 1910 a newspaper correspondent noted, "The picturesqueness of the olden-time political meetings and the necessary barbecue passed away with the Civil War."[73]

BARBECUE GOES TO TOWN

As the Reconstruction period came to an end and the Progressive period (1878–1919) emerged, barbecuing in the United States began transitioning away from mainly community and political events to becoming big business. In 1893 an aged veteran of antebellum southern barbecues noted, "The barbecue of today bears little resemblance to the outdoor love feast of half a century ago."[74] Scott Ray (1848–97) was the editor of the Indiana newspaper the *Shelby Democrat*. In 1892 he was interviewed by a journalist with the *Chicago Herald*. He described how political barbecues declined after the end of the Reconstruction period because of commercialization. Speaking of a local barbecue held in Shelbyville shortly before the interview, he stated:

> One great fallacy ought to be dissipated and that is about these beeves. The farmers don't contribute 'em; they let on that they do, and that idea gets out, but they don't. The average farmer is not giving away beef cattle these days. No, we bought the whole of our 24 beeves, and paid an average price of $40 for them. Yes, and we had to hire men to slaughter them, men to prepare them for the fire, men to dig the trenches and haul the railroad iron on which to cook them. So, you see there was nothing done as a rural labor of love.[75]

Ray went on to describe how people in the town made a profit from the barbecue. He claimed that one saloon keeper cleared $1,000 (equivalent to more than $28,000 today) over the amount he contributed and including all of his other expenses.[76]

The proliferation of railroads, the demise of plantation agriculture, the advent of the automobile, and the proliferation of electrical power distribution systems all contributed to southern urbanization.[77] Because authentic regional cooking can't exist without thriving rural communities, according to American journalist and culinary expert Raymond Sokolov, urbanization in the South was a primary driver in the decline of the OSBT and the OSBP with its "rural entertainments," such as barbecues.[78] Southern urbanization, which started before the beginning of the Civil War, intensified after Reconstruction. In 1850, for example, 15.3 percent of the population of the entire United States was urban. It wasn't until 1900 that the percentage of the population in the South that lived in urban areas reached 15.2 percent. In 1860, a commentator for *De Bow's Review* complained about the changes he perceived in the South over the previous forty years: "The pursuits and amusements of our parents are not our pursuits and amusements." He claimed the changes were the result of "the country having become more and more dependent on the towns" and, as a result, "the barbecue, with its music and dance, is obsolete and almost forgotten."[79] Although that last statement was an exaggeration, it does indicate that the South was being impacted by urbanization. In 1870 the urban population nationally was at 25.7 percent. The South's urban population didn't reach that percentage until 1920. In 1891 the *Richmond Dispatch* reported that railroads had "almost revolutionized the Fourth of July . . . country folks rush to the towns and the city folks dash to the country. Thus, have excursion rates underdone the old-time 'celebrations.'"[80] Urbanization in the South slowed during the Great Depression but was stimulated again by World War II. For example, in 1930 5.5 million southerners were employed in agriculture. By 1950 that number was reduced to 3.2 million.[81] As southerners moved away from farms and into towns and cities, they became employed in better-paying industries—such as manufacturing—and service industries—such as transportation, entertainment, education, and finance.[82] Likewise when barbecuing moved from the country to the city, the expense associated with paying for whole carcasses and the highly skilled labor required to barbecue them rose. Rather than using home-grown pork, restaurateurs had to pay market prices for it.[83] In urban areas and cities, the market value of the labor needed to chop wood, dig a trench, blend the basting liquid, spend hours tending a pit along with the knowledge and experience needed to barbecue carcasses using the OSBT could cut deeply into a restaurateur's bottom line.[84]

In 1856 a northern newspaper author described the process of barbecuing a whole ox. He commented on the rude "contrivances in use for turning the carcass over" and added "doubtless our Yankee caterers will be able to invent a more convenient mode."[85] It turns out his prophecy came true.

The first known recorded account of a *more convenient* way of barbecuing an ox in *a vast oven* took place in the Harlem district of New York City in 1884. That first covered, indirect-heat barbecue "pit" made of iron is found in an 1884 edition of *Frank Leslie's Illustrated Newspaper*. Describing how the process of "barbecuing" a "fat ox" was changing during the Progressive period, the journalist wrote, "The primitive Southern method of performing this gigantic culinary feat was to suspend the carcass on a rude spit over a pit filled with live coals. But we live in an age of progress, and the art of barbecuing has not remained stationary." He went on to describe the details of how the ox was barbecued during the "age of progress":

> There is a vast oven of sheet-iron, not unlike the peanut roaster of the sunny Italian on the street-corner, only about 200 times as large as that interesting invention, being ten feet long, nine high, and four wide. Lengthwise through this oven runs an iron cylinder, upon which is secured, with skewers and chains, the dressed carcass of the ox. An animal which tips the beam at, say, 1,400 pounds in his clothes, weighs 800 pounds on the spit, and is calculated to satisfy the appetites of 3,000 beef-eaters. Whether he does or not, we are less positive. Four furnaces of glowing coals are placed on the ground at the four corners of the oven, and underneath the ox are large pans to catch the drippings. The delicious

The "vast oven" used to "barbecue" an ox in Harlem, ca. 1884. *Frank Leslie's Illustrated Newspaper*, October 18, 1884.

> contents of these pans are from time to time dipped out with a long ladle and poured over the Brobdingnagian roast by one of the sable chefs, while another slowly turns the spit by means of a gigantic crank.[86]

In a manner consistent with others during the Progressive period, the correspondent described this new way of barbecuing an ox in "a vast oven" as a "thoroughly scientific manner—cooked by machinery, as it were." The barbecue "machinery" cooked the ox using indirect heat provided by the "four furnaces of glowing coals" that were placed "at the four corners of the oven." The use of indirect heat rather than direct heat as is used in the OSBT meant the machine was more of a smoke-roasting oven than a southern barbecue pit. That's also indicated by the "large pans to catch the drippings" placed under the ox as it cooked. When barbecuing using the OSBT, drippings are not collected, they drip into the coals below.

Another late nineteenth-century "barbecuing innovation" includes barbecuing cuts of meat like ribs, roasts, and quarters rather than whole carcasses. That "innovation" was also encouraged by the proliferation of meat markets in towns and cities. Jessup

(continued on page 200)

COMMERCIALIZATION OF BARBECUE

Not only did the practice of serving sauce on the side begin to become widespread after Reconstruction, the practice of cooking in covered barbecue pits was also born. There are less than a handful of accounts of people barbecuing in covered pits before the 1870s. An early seventeenth-century story describes people at New-Dock in London barbecuing a pig and using a "dripping-pan" to cover it in order "to preserve it from Cooling."[87] In the 1750s, the Philadelphia shopkeeper Elizabeth Coates Paschall (1702–67) recorded a barbecued pig recipe in which she instructs the reader to "civer [cover] your Pig with a Large tin Driping pan" while it barbecues.[88] When friends and family gathered for a barbecue to celebrate the marriage of Abraham Lincoln's parents, Tom and Nancy Lincoln, the pitmaster "covered the meat with green boughs "to keep the juices in."[89] There is also a description of a southern barbecue in antebellum times where "pigs, chickens, pork, and such other matters as were to be cooked, were hung upon sticks laid across the trenches" and "tree boughs were laid over the whole."[90] However, those accounts describe the exception before the end of the Reconstruction period rather than the rule. The more profitable barbecuing became, the more formally trained chefs started trying their hand at it. Eventually baking techniques that employ indirect heat and lids on pits started to be called barbecuing in the United States.

(continued from page 199)

Whitehead (1833–89) was a chef, rancher, and cookbook author who specialized The in helping culinary professionals become more effective and efficient, thus ensuring greater profits. He gave the following advice in 1889, "It is commonly called roasting oxen or other animals whole; the word itself is French barb-a-que—from head to tail—but in practice so many disappointments occur through the meat coming from the bars [grill grates] burnt to a coal on the outside and too raw to be eaten on the inside, that those who have experience take care to roast only quarters or sides." Many cooks took Whitehead's advice to heart, apparently. By the 1890s, barbecue stands started to emerge in cities that sold barbecue made with inexpensive cuts of meat rather than whole carcasses. In an attempt to reduce the labor required to barbecue whole oxen, a few enterprising barbecue cooks employed steam engines for turning spits on which beef carcasses were attached. Because you can't sell alcohol or food to absent customers, organizers also introduced electric lights at barbecues in the 1890s. That extended the time for partying and selling alcohol late into the evening.[91]

The dramatic changes in how "barbecue" was being cooked during the Progressive Period were considered by some to be the results of progress and the increasing sophistication of American society. In 1887, a newspaper correspondent commented on the decline of political barbecues and speculated that if they could have survived anywhere, it should have been in Kentucky because "it is one of the most illiterate States in the Union, and lies somewhat aside from the current of progress." Perhaps the correspondent's opinion was shaped by Reverend John Dixon Long (1817–94) who complained in 1857, "There is not much difficulty in raising money in the South for a barbecue, or to procure pine and hickory poles and flags, or to buy whisky, for political purposes; but when funds are wanted for a library, to build a school-house, or to increase the salary of a school teacher—that is quite another question."[92]

Claims that barbecue cooked using postbellum techniques was inferior to barbecue cooked using the OSBT indicate differing opinions on whether the changes were progress or decline. For example, Kentuckians claimed there was only "imitation barbecue north of the Ohio."[93] In 1899 a *barbecue man* named Mr. Jackson expressed his opinion on what he called the *progression* of barbecuing:

> I was starring through the country then as a professional manager of barbecues. What days those were! You don't see such doings now. Your present-day endeavors to celebrate and have a good time make me laugh in derision. This is the season when barbecues ought to flourish in all their glory. Just the other day I read that there was going to be a big blow-out at some little town in New Jersey. The notice awakened many old memories, and I went down out of curiosity. And what did they have? Bah! A few thin slices of tough roast beef and a keg of pale cider! Just as if that constitutes a barbecue. It may be one of 1899 brand, but it wouldn't have passed muster in 1872.[94]

THE LEGACY OF OSBP PITMASTERS

The thousands of unnamed, enslaved individuals who made southern barbecuing an iconic, unique, and wholly American tradition deserve to be identified, recognized, and honored for their contributions to creating what is the most celebrated and authentic part of the original American cuisine. People everywhere grill foods. People all over the world cook meat in earth ovens. Europeans have been hot smoking meats for centuries. However, the OSBT was only practiced in the United States. Indeed the twentieth century practice of using the word barbecue to refer to grilling, roasting, hot smoking, and even griddling foods support the assertion that all other forms of "barbecuing" that exist in the United States today leverage the fame of the South's unique OSBT and those who perfected it.

Antebellum-Style Barbecue Baste

This delicious sauce recipe was inspired by accounts of nineteenth-century barbecues in Virginia. It works well as a basting sauce for meats both as they are barbecuing and as a table sauce to be served on the side.

1½ cup apple cider vinegar
¼ cup water
¼ cup distilled white vinegar, mixed with 2 teaspoons ground cayenne pepper. (You can substitute this with ¼ cup of vinegar- and/or cayenne-based hot sauce.)
8 tablespoons butter (if using as a basting sauce)
1 tablespoon paprika
1 tablespoon black pepper
1 tablespoon table salt
2 tablespoons prepared mustard

—

TABLE SAUCE: *Thoroughly mix all ingredients (except the butter; I use a blender). For best results put sauce in the refrigerator for 24 to 48 hours before serving.*

BASTING SAUCE: *Warm up the sauce (do not boil it). Add the butter by stirring it into the sauce as it melts. Keep warm while using it to baste foods as they cook.*

Antebellum barbecue cooks added their own secret ingredients to the basic baste recipe. So feel free to modify the recipe to make it your own.

EIGHT

NED'S BARBACUE

Transatlantic Misunderstandings

The Caribbean Origins Theory (COT) of southern barbecuing relies upon the assumption that people in Europe, the Caribbean, and North America shared the same understanding of barbecue and barbecuing during the Original Southern Barbecuing Period (OSBP). However, when primary sources from that period are carefully considered significant transatlantic differences become apparent. The COT's failure to account for those transatlantic differences has resulted in distortions and misinterpretations of the history of southern barbecuing. When the differences are understood and accounted for, barbecue history is more brightly illuminated in a way that exposes the fundamental flaw of the COT. A careful analysis of how barbecuing was understood by people in each region reveals compelling evidence in support of the assertion that the birthplace of the original southern barbecuing technique (OSBT) was the colonial United States. Accordingly, this chapter compares and contrasts the ways people in Europe, the Caribbean, and North America understood barbecue and barbecuing during the OSBP.

BRITISH-STYLE BARBECUE

Some southern-style barbecue enthusiasts argue that barbecue can only be made "from a gosh-darned pig."[1] In attempts to prove it, some quote passages written by eighteenth-century Britons that proclaim only pigs should be barbecued or "cooked after the West Indies manner," prompting them to demand, as was supposedly done in the days of old: "Send me, gods, a whole hog barbecued!" The problem with arguments like those is how they ignore the differences in how Americans, Europeans, and people in the Caribbean understood barbecuing during the OSBP.

During the OSBP, people in Jamaica understood barbecuing to be making jerked pork and cooking pig carcasses in earth ovens. People in the South (southern United States) understood barbecuing to be the processes of making jerky, smoking game meats or beef in smokehouses, and cooking whole animal carcasses on grills set over pits filled with live embers while basting them with a vinegary sauce. In the case of some upper-class American women, cooking whole shoats at the kitchen hearth or in an oven was a form of barbecuing. People in Britain understood barbecuing as roasting, broiling, baking, or braising whole, stuffed carcasses of young pigs peppered with cayenne and basted with Madeira wine. European sailors who visited the Americas during the seventeenth century understood barbecuing to be a process for preserving meat and fish. Understanding the differences of how barbecuing has been understood in different times by people in different parts of the world is critical for accurately interpreting the Barbecue History Body of Knowledge (BHBoK).

In 1771, a British barbecue enthusiast praised British-style "barbecued pig" that was "thoroughly impregnated with Madeira" for its "speedy digestion."[2] Still, even though some Britons dabbled with it during the eighteenth century, Britain didn't develop a long-held barbecuing tradition. During the OSBP many Britons had an unfavorable opinion of barbecuing and considered it to be a creole way of cooking fit only for people in the Americas. That might explain why the British interest in barbecuing was short-lived. By the turn of the twentieth century, it was all but forgotten.[3]

One of the earliest recipes for barbecuing a pig published in a British cookbook is "a Hog Barbicued whole, and grill'd" found in *The Compleat City and Country Cook*, which was published in London in 1736. It reads:

> You must have a Hog about six Stone [30 to 50 pounds[4]], and kill him and singe him, then open him just as you do a red Herring, split him quite through to the Skin, but do not cut the Skin; leave Head and all on, then truss his Legs double, and let him be skewer'd cross ways to keep him flat, and when cold and stiff, you must have a Frame made the Length of your Pig, and three or four Bars length ways, and lay your Hog on; then have in readiness two Sacks of Charcoal, and set it on fire; your Grilliron must be two Foot high, and your Charcoal spread the Breadth of your iron Frame, them broil it five Hours gently, and baist [*sic*] it with Madera [*sic*] Wine or Malmsey, and All-Spice and Carmel Butter; you must turn it but twice, so serve it away hot in an oval Dish made on purpose.[5]

The differences between that British recipe and the OSBT are glaring. Apparently young pigs were recommended in British cookbooks because it was easier to cook them at the kitchen hearth with the option of using an oven. As one cook put it, "Ovens won't stretch!"[6] Other recipes specify "a pig of ten weeks old," "a Hog of five or six Months old," and "a thick neck breed, about six weeks old."[7]

Even though at least one old British cookbook mentions "Pike Barbecued," though without giving the recipe, another offers a recipe for a "kid barbicued in quarters" and an article printed in a 1729 London newspaper facetiously mentioned "Shrimps Barbacu'd," in Britain the phrase "a barbecue" always referred to a barbecued pig, as previously discussed in Chapter 5, "Richard's Barbycu."[8] Therefore it shouldn't be surprising that the most common meat barbecued by people in England during the OSBP, on the rare occasion that they barbecued at all, was pork. Madeira wine and cayenne pepper were primary ingredients in many of their recipes.

There was little difference between recipes for roasting pigs and barbecuing pigs in eighteenth-century British cookbooks. Take, for example, the recipe titled "To Roast a Pig," from *The Ladies Handmaid: Or, a Compleat System of Cookery* published in London in 1758. The recipe calls for stuffing the pig with sage, butter, flour, pepper, and salt before sewing it up and spitting it beside a "good" fire. To save the jus, the author recommended the use of dripping pans. After the pig is done cooking, rub it "all over" with a coarse cloth until the skin is crisp. The sauce recipe includes butter, the jus, the pig's brains that have been finely mashed, and sage.[12] Elements in that recipe—such as stuffing the pig, sewing it up, and saving the gravy in a dripping pan—are also found in eighteenth-century British recipes for barbecued pigs. Some of those barbecuing recipes also call for "flouring the Back" of the pig while it's cooking, which was also common when roasting meats.[13]

The significant differences between how pigs were barbecued in England during the OSBP and how they were barbecued in the United States might be an attempt to "civilize" the cooking method. Several old English cookbooks allow for the whole barbecued pig to be cooked on a gridiron in the kitchen hearth, roasted on a spit "beside a large, brisk fire," braised, or baked in an oven.[14] Unlike the predominate OSBT recipe that called for seasonings and butter mixed with vinegar to be applied while the pig is being barbecued, British recipes called for seasoning the pig before cooking it. The OSBT doesn't include stuffing pig carcasses, applying spices, and sewing them up before placing the carcasses over a barbecue pit—or flouring their backs. Notably no old British recipes for barbecued pig instruct the reader to dig a pit and fill it with live embers. The use of Madeira wine to baste pigs in British barbecue recipes also sets them apart from the OSBT.

TO BARBICUE A PIG

An example of an eighteenth-century British barbecued pig recipe is "*To barbicue a Pig*" found in *The Lady's Assistant for Regulating and Supplying Her Table* published in London in 1777. The author instructs the reader to "make a stuffing" with sage, cayenne pepper, anchovies, the pig's liver, bread crumbs, and a little Madeira wine. Then, "beat them to a paste, and sew it up in the pig." The recipe doesn't call for barbecuing the pig on a gridiron. Instead the cooking instructions are to"lay it down, at a great distance, to a large brisk fire" and "baste it well [with Madeira wine] all the time it is roasting."[9] Other British cookbooks reprinted that recipe with only minor changes. Two authors replaced the Madeira with red wine along with the note, "It will take four hours roasting."[10] Some authors call for the unusual ingredients of veal or beef gravy in recipes for sauces served with barbecued, baked, and roasted pork. For example, a sauce recipe published in 1758 includes the ingredients of "half a pint of good beef gravy, and the gravy which comes out of the pig, with a piece of butter rolled in flour, two spoonfuls [*sic*] of catchup."[11]

(continued from page 206)

Unlike the OSBT, several English cookbooks published during the seventeenth to nineteenth centuries advise against basting meats while cooking them directly over coals. For example, the author of *The Compleat Housewife, Or, Accomplished Gentlewoman's Companion*, which was published in London in 1750, instructs the reader: "Observe never to baste any thing [*sic*] on the gridiron, for that causes it to be both smoaked [*sic*] and burnt."[15] Gervase Markham cautioned readers against allowing fat to drip into coals while broiling meat because it makes it "stink."[16] At any rate there is at least one credible account of Britons basting a pig with a linen mop dipped in vinegar as it was being "barbecued." The English playwright George Colman, the Younger (1762–1836) wrote of "barbecuing" a hog in England during the late eighteenth century:

> One day, among other dainties, we had a barbicued hog, a huge whole monster, which I thought very nasty;—but this might be partly fancy; for I took a prejudice against him while he was roasting: he was put down to a blazing fire

> in the field, where he was burn'd, scorch'd, and blacken'd, till he look'd like a fat Protestant at the stake, in the days of Bishop Bonnor: we all had a flap at him, with a rag dipp'd in vinegar, at the end of a stick, by way of a basting ladle, otherwise he would have been done to a cinder.[17]

Notice that Colman's "very nasty," "monster" hog was being "barbecued" with "a blazing fire." That mistake might explain the difficulty those British cooks had with preventing the hog from being scorched. Of course, Americans barbecued animal carcasses over live embers, not beside blazing fires.

One should not assume that Colman and his companions were barbecuing their monster hog in a way that was inspired by people in the Caribbean. As previously discussed, there are no credible records of anyone in the Caribbean *anointing* hogs as they were being barbecued. During the OSBP while Jamaicans were barbecuing pigs in earth ovens and Britons were barbecuing pigs by roasting, baking, or braising them, people in the American colonies were barbecuing pigs on wooden grills set over pits full of live embers while basting them with mops dipped in a vinegar-and-butter-based liquid. That strongly implies the way Colman took "a flap" at the hog "with a rag dipp'd in vinegar" was inspired by American pitmasters, not people in the Caribbean. After all, in 1724 the English reverend and mathematics professor Hugh Jones (1691–1760) wrote about the "whole Virginia Shoots [shoats, young pigs] being frequently barbacued in England."[18] At about the same time people in England were barbecuing Virginian shoats, recipes for barbecued pigs started showing up in British cookbooks. This includes the two earliest discovered thus far, which are "An Hog barbecued, or broil'd whole" published in 1732 in *The Country Housewife*, and "A Hog Barbicued" published in *The Compleat City and Country Cook* in 1736.[19] Those old recipes have more in common with the barbecuing style found in the colonial United States than the charqui, jerked pork, and pigs barbecued in earth ovens in the Caribbean. It's plausible that when people in England barbecued a Virginian hog, they would have attempted to barbecue it in a way that was similar how Virginians barbecued pigs.[20]

Elements of British barbecued pig recipes were incorporated into some American barbecue recipes during the eighteenth century. American women used to keep important information in their personal "book of receipts," and some contained recipes for barbecuing meats. Because the *receipts* were for feeding their families and entertaining guests at cozy indoor dinners, barbecue recipes in those books were often (not always) intended for meats cooked at the kitchen hearth rather than outside over a large pit dug into the ground. For example, the recipe "To Barbecue Shote," found in American author Mary Randolph's (1762–1828) cookbook, *The Virginia Housewife: or,*

Notice how the ox is roasted in front of the fire rather than directly over it, ca. 1789.

Methodical Cook, first published in 1824, exhibits apparent British influence. This recipe calls for a small pig (shoat) baked in an oven and braised in red wine after being stuffed with forcemeat (chopped and seasoned meat). Marion Cabell Tyree's *Housekeeping in Old Virginia* published in 1878 includes the recipe "To Barbecue Shoat," which calls for dredging a small pig in flour before baking it in an oven. Another example of British influence on American barbecue is found in the recipe "To barbecue a pig," recorded in 1765 in a book of receipts that calls for the southern way of basting a pig: using linen tied to a stick combined with the British ingredients of beef gravy and wine.[21] Apparently Jamaicans also eventually took up a British way of cooking pigs. In 1956, the *Evening Star* published a Jamaican cook's recipe for "Jamaican Roast," which included instructions for "the West Indian way" of roasting a suckling pig. The recipe exhibits strong British influence including selecting a "porker" that's "five to six weeks old," stuffing and sewing up the carcass, and baking it in an oven. Apparently the Jamaican addition to the recipe is the mango-rum sauce that was ladled over the pork before serving.[22]

NED WARD

Edward "Ned" Ward (1667–1731) was an early eighteenth-century English satirical writer that focused on political and social issues.[23] From 1699 and continuing to a few months before his death, Ward managed several alehouses and taverns that his readers frequented. In 1706, Ward was arrested and charged with seditious libel for his anti-government opinions. He was fined and forced to stand in the pillory.[24] Ward's reputation reached the British colonies in North America. In 1726, Cotton Mather (see Chapter 6, "George's Barbicue") warned his flock against "such pestilences, and indeed all those worse than Egyptian toads, [who were] the spawns of a Butler, & a Brown, and a Ward."[25]

Ward's writings are significant because he gave us the first claim that barbecuing is a "West-India Manner" of cooking, which is interpreted by adherents of the COT to mean that southern barbecuing was imported from the Caribbean.[26] All others after Ward who make the same claim are, knowingly or not, echoing him. Many assume Ward visited and was well acquainted with the West Indies because of an essay of his that was published in 1698 titled *A Trip to Jamaica: with a True Character of the People and Island*. However, that assumption is unfounded. There is no proof that Ward ever visited Jamaica.[27] Ward also published a pamphlet titled *A Trip to New England. With a Character of the Country and People* in 1699, but it's fairly well established that he never visited the American colonies.[28] As far as the satirist Ward was concerned, he didn't have to visit a place to write a detailed account of it.

In *Trip to Jamaica*, Ward expressed his Geohumoral beliefs when he portrayed England as a paradise on Earth and Jamaica as a criminal infested hell he called "The Receptacle of Vagabonds." He wrote that Jamaica is "the Dunghill of the Universe, the Refuse of the whole Creation, . . . a Close-stool for the Purges of our Prisons," a place where the Heavens "punish Mankind for their Offences," a place that's "as Sickly as an Hospital," and "as Dangerous as the Plague, as Hot as Hell, and as Wicked as the Devil." According to him, people in Jamaica lived in the universe's "dunghill."[29] None of those statements were based upon Ward's personal experiences. They were based upon his prejudices, things he heard, read, or his imagination.

By 1657 Port Royal was called "the wickedest city on Earth." The aforementioned John Taylor, who was in Jamaica in 1687, wrote of Port Royal that it was "verey [very] lose [loose] in itself, and, by reason of privateers and debauched wild blades which come hither. The city tis now more rude and anticque [grotesque] than 'ere was Sodom, fill'd with all manner of debauchery."[30] The earthquake that devastated Jamaica in 1692 was thought to be God's judgment. Shortly after the earthquake, Reverend

Portrait of Edward Ward. By Thomas Johnson, ca. 1714.

Dr. Emmanuel Heath, rector of St. Paul's Church in Port Royal, wrote that he had hoped "to keep up some shew of Religion among a most Ungodly Debauched People." However, in his estimation, Port Royal "had much the greatest share in this terrible Judgment of God."[31] It's probable that derogatory accounts of Jamaica such as those reinforced Ward's opinions of the island and the early modern belief that the Western Hemisphere's environment depraved the people who lived in the Americas.

Magnificent Roast Ox

The London-spy: The Vanities and Vices of the Town Exposed to View is a series of Ward's articles published monthly from 1698 to 1700 and in a single volume in 1703. The collection's main character is a London visitor called "the London spy" who is being introduced to the city by a friend who lived there. As the spy is taken on a tour of London at the turn of the eighteenth century, a baseline for understanding Ward's attitudes about the relationship between roasted beef and a "true Englishman," is revealed that can be juxtaposed with his perceived relationship between barbecued pigs and colonists. In chapter 8, Ward wrote about an ox feast in London with glowing terms such as "the wonderful piece of Beef—How it was Cooked—How it was Eaten."[32] The ox feast was held at "King's Head Tavern," where "the stateliest piece of beef in Christendom" was roasted outside beside an open fire. Though he made several witty comments about the cooks, he didn't denigrate those "professors of the noble art of cookery" or the act of roasting "such a magnificent piece of beef."[33] He praised the roast beef as a "treat" and as "excellent food" that was "as rich, fat, young, well fed, delicious meat, as ever was taken into the mouth, masticated between the teeth, and swallowed into the belly of a true Englishman."[34] Though "a generous plate" of beef was served to the London spy and his colleague, there was no accusation of gluttony and no admonition to observe moderation.[35]

Grunter on a Grid-Iron

Ward's *A Frolick to Horn-fair with a Walk from Cuckold's-point Thro' Deptford and Greenwich*, was published in 1700. The Horn Fair was an annual event in London held on October 18th.[36] It was a celebration of a story about King John's indiscretion with a married woman. As restitution, the king granted the woman's husband all the land he could see around him on the condition that he walk throughout it once a year wearing horns on his head while announcing that he is a cuckold (i.e., a man with an unfaithful wife). The vulgar tradition, as some called it, consisted of "a riotous mob" wearing horns on their heads who met at Cuckold's Point. From there, they marched through London to the district of Charlton, where the fair was held.[37] Daniel Defoe described Horn Fair as "The rudeness of which in a civilized, well-governed Nation, may well be said to be insufferable. The Mob at that time takes all liberties, and the Women are eminently impudent that Day."[38] Ward himself described Horn Fair as "an Annual Rendezvous for the Mob of London" that was "the Rudest Fair in England" where "the Rabble" make "the Church-Yard their Dunghill" and sell "Horn-Toys" used "to vex Cuckolds."[39]

"The Rudest Fair in England" is the context in which Ward wrote about his first encounter with a group of people barbecuing a pig. It took place at "New-Dock" in London:

> Having past [*sic*] by a great Number of these Condescending Mortals, we came to a Field which led to the Entrance of the Dock, about a Stones Cast on this side which, were a parcel of West-Indian-Creolians, lately come on Shore Cooking in the open Air, an English Porker after the Indian manner, which was attempted to be perform'd as follows: They drove Sticks in the Ground, and Fenc'd in a square place with Old Tarpaulins, leaving one side open for the Wind to Fan the Fire which was made in the middle with Charcoal, directly over which lay the Grunter on a Grid-Iron, made of Spits; which were laid Cross, from side to side; the part that lay uppermost, being cover'd with the Dripping-Pan, to preserve it from Cooling, and the Fat dropping into the Fire, cast up such savoury Fumes from the burning Grease, that the Nossel of foul Candlesticks thrust into a Kitchen-Fire by a Good House-Wife of a Cook, could not perfume her Sluttish-ships Territories with a more Obliging Odor; and about Six or Eight foot distance, from the main-Fire, was another Fire, to the Windward of the Pig, most Cunningly Contriv'd to Warm the Air, as it pass'd, lest its Coldness otherwise might be some Impediment to the Grilliading, or beastly Cooking of their ill favour'd Beast, whose Eyes were Roasted in his Head according to the Negroes Cookery, that he star'd like a Dead Pig; and that side that lay next to the Fire, with the Smoak of the Dripping was almost as black as the Charcoal beneath it; that I question not but by the Time it was Ready, it stunk like a piece of Cheshire-Cheese, Toasted in the Flame of a Candle, and look'd all over as black as the Rind of a Flitch of Bacon, that has hung Six months in a Country Chimney. We left them as busy about their Savage Piece of Cookery, as so many chosen Housewives dressing of a Weding [*sic*] Dinner.[40]

Ward wrote the above detailed, ostensibly firsthand account of people barbecuing a pig in London without mentioning the word barbecue. He also neglected to use the word in *Trip to Jamaica*. Apparently he may have been unfamiliar with the word at that time. In *Frolick*, the strange-to-him cooking technique was described as cooking "after the Indian [Native American] manner, . . . beastly Cooking . . . according to the Negroes Cookery," and a "Savage Piece of Cookery." It would be seven years after *Frolick* was published before Ward would write the word barbacue [*sic*] or make his now-famous proclamation that barbecuing is a "West-India" way of cooking.

Ward's ignorance of barbecuing wasn't limited to his late discovery of the word barbecue or his faulty assumption that it was only practiced in the West Indies. He revealed more of his ignorance when he wrote of the "fire, to the Windward of the

Pig" assuming that it was "most Cunningly Contriv'd to Warm the Air." A closer look would have revealed that the fire was a *feeder fire*, which was needed to replenish the embers under the pig as it cooked. Ward's claim that the barbecue cooks were "West-Indian-Creolians" also appears to be a display of his ignorance of barbecuing. The way the pig was barbecued at New-Dock resembles the way people in the British American colonies barbecued pigs, not the way people in the West Indies did it. Consequently the real value in Ward's account of people barbecuing a pig in London is not what it tells us about barbecuing; it's what it tells us about the things Ward associated with barbecuing.

Ward's contrasting accounts of the ox feast in *London-spy* and the pig feast in *Frolick* provide striking evidence of the fact that roasting meat outside on a spit beside a flaming fire is not a barbecuing technique. In Ward's world, roasting an ox was a civilized, orderly way to cook beef that was fit for a "true Englishman." Roasting beef reminded Ward of merry times similar to the "Ox Feast" the British general George Wade (1673–1748) provided his soldiers in 1731 to celebrate "his Majesty's Birth-day" with six oxen roasted whole and "liquor to drink the Healths of the King."[41] On the other hand Ward saw barbecuing a pig as a strange, uncivilized way of cooking that was "after the Indian manner" and "according to the Negroes Cookery" fit only for savages and uncouth Britons that have been depraved by the Caribbean's climate.

Ward's low regard for barbecuing is also seen in his description of "the Fat dropping into the Fire" that he believed produced a very unpleasant odor, which in his eyes was similar to "a piece of Cheshire-Cheese, Toasted in the Flame of a Candle." Apparently the aroma of fat from broiling meat dripping into hot coals was repugnant to people in early modern England. English cookbooks that were available to Ward issued warnings against it. Ward echoed those warnings when he sarcastically described the "savoury Fumes" of the "beastly Cooking."[42] Unlike the "professors of the noble art of cookery," who used a dripping pan to catch the delicious beef gravy at the London ox feast, the barbecue cooks near New-Dock used the dripping pan in what Ward considered to be an uncultured way. By placing it on top of the pig, the barbecue cooks wasted the jus by letting it drip into the coals, thus creating an unpleasant odor. At any rate, despite all that he got wrong about barbecuing, Ward is correct in his assertion that barbecuing is a mixture of African, Native American, and European cooking. That fact also explains why Ward, "a true Englishman," held it in such contempt.

The Barbacue Feast

Ward's *The Barbacue Feast: or, The Three Pigs of Peckham, Broil'd Under an Apple-Tree* was published in 1707. *Barbacue Feast* is the foundation on which rests the cornerstone of the COT and the erroneous claim that southern-style barbecuing was born in the Caribbean before being imported into the North American colonies. Nevertheless the pamphlet is too unreliable a source to be of value for understanding such a critical part of barbecuing history. Rather than a reliable early eighteenth-century account of people barbecuing a pig in Jamaica, *Barbacue Feast* is a litany of insults packaged in eighteenth-century slang directed at Native Americans, enslaved Africans, Jews, Scots, the Welsh, and a fictitious group of drunken sailors who were depicted as barbecuing three pigs under an apple tree. Apparently it was inspired by the account of people barbecuing a pig at New-Dock in *Frolick*. Furthermore the setting of the fictitious story in *Barbacue Feast* isn't Jamaica; it's Peckham, England.[43] That's yet another mistaken assumption that underpins the COT by propagating the myth that people in the early modern Caribbean barbecued pigs in a way that's similar to the OSBT.

The slang, innuendo, and fiction in *Barbacue Feast* makes it of very little value for an accurate understanding of the history of barbecuing. The early modern European opinions and beliefs about Creoles are vividly displayed throughout the pamphlet. Ward's use of crude, eighteenth-century slang expressions such as "Castor and Pollux," "Higgle de Pigglede Festival" and, "Wapping-Fireship," demonstrates that he probably never expected his work to be read in mixed company.[44] Just like *Frolick*, the real value of *Barbacue Feast* is how it assists us with understanding how Ward and his readers understood barbecuing or, more accurately, didn't understand it.

It appears that Ward's knowledge of barbecuing was gained by watching people in London barbecuing pigs, reading about it in cookbooks, other publications, and, possibly, from acquaintances who visited the Americas. That explains why Ward appears to be completely ignorant of the fact that people in Jamaica he called "West-Indian-Creolians" who "barbecued" pigs "after the Jamaica Fashion" actually did so in earth ovens or on grills when making jerked pork (see Chapter 2, "Herbert's Patta"). He also appears ignorant of the fact that people in the North American colonies barbecued pigs and other animals on wooden grills set over a pit full of coals while basting them with sauce. Apparently whenever Ward read or heard the word barbecue, he assumed it always referred to pigs cooked on grills.

The Hoggish Feast

Barbacue Feast begins with sailors in Peckham, England, drinking so much rum that nothing would satisfy "their English appetites so deprav'd," but a "litter of Pigs most nicely cook'd after the West-India Manner."[45] After some haggling with a hog drover, the sailors purchased 3 young pigs that Ward referred to as "shotes" and "Pig-hogs," explaining "for so I call 'em being between both."[46] Offering tickets for sale to as many

Hog drovers in Virginia. *Harper's New Monthly Magazine* 15 (October 1857).

as would join them in their "comical Celebration of their Swinish Festival," the newly formed Barbacue Society was composed of people of African, European, and Native American descent, or what Ward called "West-Indian-Creolians."[47] They decided to hold the pig feast under an apple tree simply because pigs enjoy eating apples.[48]

Along with a round of insults and a slang-laced description of an obscene image displayed on the tickets printed for the event, Ward turned to the cooks.[49] Dripping with sarcasm, he described the way the hogs' entrails were made into Hogs Puddings and distributed to the poor as "such charitable Entertainment" given by "bountiful good Christians."[50] The pigs were barbecued on a wooden grill built by "a dexterous Bull-Calf of a Carpenter."[51] The cook basted the pigs with a mixture of "green Virginia pepper, and Madeira wine" that was "plentifully daub'd on with a Fox's Tail ty'd to a long Stick."[52] Echoing Hickeringill's comments that associated barbecuing with cannibalism, Ward described the Peckham cooks as "a Gang of wild Cannibals."[53] Like the barbecue cooks mentioned in *Frolick,* the Peckham cooks also allowed fat from the meat to drip into the coals creating an "unsavory Gust" as the pigs were "smoak'd by the Fats falling into the Fire."[54] Eventually the pigs fell into the coals below. They were returned to their "primitive Uprightness" after "much Pains, and many Curses."[55]

When the cooking was finished, the pigs were crudely chopped up with an ax and served to "the ravenous Society" sitting at make-shift tables.[56] Ward's assumption that a barbecued pig needs to be "chopped up with an ax" again demonstrates that he knew little about barbecuing, because the only utensils required to serve meat from a pig that has been properly barbecued using the OSBT are human hands. As the meat was being served, a guest remarked, "As it is a Pig-Feast, the more Hoggishly we are serv'd, the more agreeable."[57] "Hoggishly" is not Ward's attempt at wordplay: it's eighteenth-century slang for rude, unmannerly, and filthy.[58] The "Pertakers" of this "Heathenish Feast" were serenaded by musicians who played "Squeak and Diddle."[59] "Like a parcel of ungodly Indians, without any Grace before Meat" the "three Barbacu'd Pigs, nicely cooked after the Indian Manner" were "greedily" devoured and washed down with buckets of punch spiked with rum.[60] In another throwback to *Frolick*, the "Tag, Rag, and Bob-tail" (slang for a mob of uncultured people) appeared as though they were preparing "to eat with the Devil" because of the long-handled ladles that were "bought at Charleton by some of the Cuckolds in the Company, upon last Horn-Fair-Day."[61] Ward also took the opportunity to introduce one of Hickeringill's barbecuing cannibals. A "Sea-Commander," dissatisfied with the music played by the "Land-lubbering tooting Dogs," angrily demanded of them, "unplay what you have play'd, or by the Dragon's Tail, we'll Barbacue you as we've done the Pigs."[62]

As the feasting abated, the drinking intensified to the point that everyone was so severely inebriated they "could neither stand nor go."[63] With his belly full, a merry guest stood up. Pulling "his broad-brim'd Hat into the puritanical Flip-flap," and contorting his face "to a very grave Pitch of Hypocrisy," he sternly lectured the "fiery-fac'd Brethren of the Porkheaded Congregation" on the virtue of moderation.[64] That hypocritical, sermon-like speech was Ward's way of associating barbecuing with gluttony.

A careful reading of *Barbacue Feast* indicates that seven years after *Frolick*, Ward still knew very little about barbecuing. The recipe and technique described in Ward's "Hoggish Feast" are similar in some ways to barbecuing as it was done in the North American colonies and as it was described in British cookbooks. Ward merely substituted "green Virginia pepper" (Virginia peppergrass seeds; a.k.a. poor man's pepper) for cayenne pepper, as was prescribed in the prevailing British recipes. Moreover the cooking method bears no resemblance to any known firsthand accounts of barbecuing in Jamaica or anywhere else in the West Indies during the eighteenth century.

The barbecue cook's use of a fox's tail attached to a stick to baste the barbecuing pigs is another fanciful detail concocted to mock "Creolians." As the cook was vigorously basting the pigs, he looked "like a Smithfield Cook, with a Fly-Flap in his hand, banging away at the Flesh-flies." Ward was portraying the "Creolian" cook as being so careless, incompetent, and unclean that he used a filthy fly swatter to baste the "savage" barbecue.

Describing the barbecued pigs as being "fit for the Table of a Sagamoor," Ward demonstrated again that he recognized the Native American role in the origins of barbecuing. *Sagamoor* (*Sagamore*, a Native American ruler) comes from the Algonquian language found in the eastern United States, but not the West Indies. Ward also used an eastern Algonquian word, *Squaw*, to demean Native American women. If Ward was making the case that barbecuing is exclusively a "West-India" way of cooking, his use of Algonquian words is out of place. Words spoken by Native Americans in the Caribbean would be more appropriate. If he was insinuating that the "Creolians" in Peckham, England, referred to Indian women as squaws, that would be evidence that they were from the American colonies, not the Caribbean.

Ward's disapproval of the way Africans, Europeans, and Native Americans in the Americas mingled their food cultures is obvious. In *Barbacue Feast*, Ward associated barbecuing with Native Americans at least three times. He wrote that the pigs were cooked "after the Indian Manner" once, and twice he noted that the pigs were "barbecued according to the Indian Fashion." He also referred to barbecuing as "Negroes Cookery." Yet those facts are ignored by people who write about barbecue history. Even though the phrase "after the West-India Manner" garners all of the attention from people who write about barbecue history, Ward only associated barbecuing with the Caribbean twice; once as cooking "after the Jamaica Fashion," and another as cooking "after the West-India Manner." However, if Ward meant barbecuing was born in the West Indies, we must also interpret Ward to mean that Jamaica is the specific place in the West Indies where it was born. However, apologists for the COT ignore Ward's statement referring to barbecuing as cooking "after the Jamaica fashion," and declare that Haiti gave us barbecuing. However, if Ward's assertion about Jamaica is ignored, his supposed declaration that barbecuing is cooking after the "West-India Manner" must be ignored, too. Therefore when correctly interpreted in full context, none of Ward's statements need to be rejected or ignored. When all of his statements are considered, it's clear that Ward was saying that barbecuing is a "savage Piece of Cookery" that originated among Native Americans, Africans, Europeans, and their creole descendants

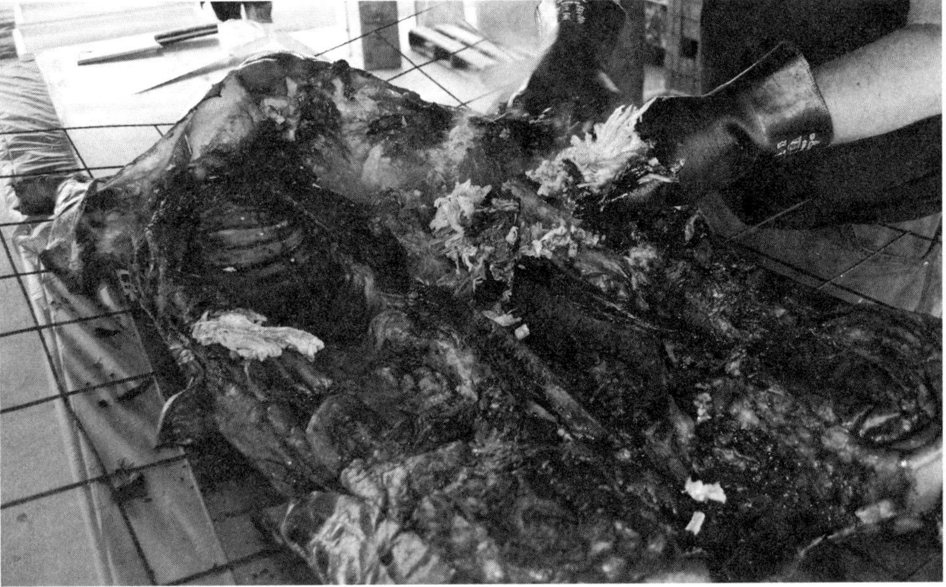

Properly barbecued pork can be pulled with bare hands; no axes necessary. Photo by the author.

in the Americas. Instead of revealing the *birthplace* of barbecue, Ward was correlating the *act* of barbecuing with what in his mind were Creoles and unrefined Europeans. Just as he did in *Frolick*, he did so in *Barbacue Feast*. He linked the act of barbecuing to people he pejoratively believed to be English "rabble" that he believed were "depraved" by their close interactions with enslaved Africans and enslaved Native Americans.

A phrase written by a man who knew just enough about barbecuing to substantiate his prejudiced views does not make for a convincing argument in support of the notion that southern barbecuing was imported from the Caribbean. When the COT is considered in the full context of Ward's world view and the phrases "after the West-India Manner" and "after the Jamaica Fashion," his meaning becomes clear. Ward mistakenly believed that people in Jamaica barbecued pigs in the same way as the people he ostensibly witnessed barbecuing at New-Dock. However, according to reliable records, that is not the case. By referring to barbecuing as a "West-India Manner" of cooking, "savage," and "heathenish," Ward was contrasting what he perceived to be the superiority of "true Englishmen" with what he called "Creolians."[65] Rather than giving us a history lesson on the origins of southern-style barbecuing, he was essentially making the pejorative statement: "Barbecuing is how *those* people [Creoles] cook, not how respectable Anglos cook."

(continued on page 220)

DICTIONARIES ARE LIKE WATCHES

Pope's questionable knowledge of barbecuing has been quoted in dictionaries for centuries. Although dictionaries are valuable tools, they aren't meant to be history books. Samuel Johnson, the compiler of *A Dictionary of the English Language*, understood the limitations of dictionaries. He once wrote to a friend, "Dictionaries are like watches; the worst is better than none, and the best cannot be expected to go quite true."[70] In the preface of the 1773 edition of his dictionary he commented, "I applied myself to the perusal of our writers; and noting whatever might be of use to ascertain or illustrate any word or phrase."[71] Those statements reveal that literary quotes found in dictionaries are not necessarily there to make an authoritative historical statement. Rather they demonstrate the usage of the word being defined. When interpreting the BHBoK, it's essential to identify when quotes used by dictionary compilers to illustrate the meaning of the word barbecue are historical fact or fiction. In the case of Pope, they are satirical fiction.

(continued from page 219)

The assertion that barbecuing had a one-time birth in the Caribbean ultimately rests on a single phrase: "cook'd after the West-India Manner," written in a work of satire that has been repeatedly misinterpreted and far removed out of its context. When it comes to Ward's supposed knowledge of the history of barbecuing, we should take him at his word. He wrote in *Trip to Jamaica*, "I only Entertain you with what I intend for your Diversion, not Instruction."

ALEXANDER POPE

Alexander Pope (1688–1744) was an early eighteenth-century English satirist and poet who some consider to be the greatest poet of his time.[66] He didn't have a high regard for the lowbrow literature published by Ward.[67] He suggested that some of Ward's essays were so worthless they could hardly be traded for second-rate tobacco even in the colonies where tobacco was cheap. He even mocked Ward by claiming that people threw eggs at him as he stood in the pillory for seditious libel.[68]

POPE'S GLUTTON NAMED OLDFIELD

Pope associated a barbecued pig with a man named Oldfield. Some believe Oldfield was an English politician named Richard Oldfield, but no direct evidence for that assertion has been discovered.[72] Interestingly a Richard Oldfield owned an estate in Jamaica, Wards dunghill of the universe, during the first half of the eighteenth century.[73] When Pope characterized the phrase "a Hog barbecu'd" as a "West-Indian Term of Gluttony," he associated Oldfield (who may have had interests in Jamaica) with the stern lecture on moderation delivered with a "very grave Pitch of Hypocrisy" to the gluttonous "Porkheaded Congregation" in Ward's *Barbacue Feast.*

According to Pope, a glutton named Oldfield demanded a barbecued hog (see box, "Pope's Barbecue Legacy"). If Oldfield were a better man in Pope's eyes, no doubt he would have demanded a "wonderful piece of Beef" instead. What better way for Pope to insult Oldfield than to associate him with Ward's well-publicized description of what to him was a repulsive, gluttony-inducing way of cooking practiced by "ungodly Debauched People" who degenerated because they spent too much time in "the Refuse of the whole Creation"? Pope was expressing the belief among some Britons of his day that people in English colonies were gluttons who barbecued pigs like "uncivilized Indians" and enslaved Africans. In their minds, the "West-Indian" aspect of it only added to the insult.

(continued from page 220)

The passage that made Pope famous among barbecue enthusiasts is: "Oldfield, with more than Harpy throat endu'd, Cries, send me, Gods! A whole Hogbarbecu'd!" Pope's other famous barbecue-related passage arose from his realization that most of his European readers wouldn't know what a "hog barbecu'd" was. Therefore he added a footnote explaining his British understanding of barbecuing, "Hog barbecu'd, etc. A West-Indian Term of Gluttony; a Hog roasted whole, stuff'd with Spice, and basted with Madeira Wine."[69] Pope's British beliefs about barbecuing stand in contrast to the beliefs of people in the southern United States who have never considered stuffing a pig with spice to be a necessary step before barbecuing it outside over a barbecue pit.

Based on what he wrote, it's safe to assume that Pope didn't know any more about barbecuing than Ward. Both were only familiar with British-style barbecued pig recipes. Pope's addition of "West-Indian Term of Gluttony," is a reverberation of Ward, not an authoritative statement of fact. Southerners are as fond of barbecued pigs as Ward was of roasted oxen, and Ward's and Pope's beliefs that barbecuing and gluttony go hand in hand has never been held by people in the South.

Additional evidence that Pope shared Ward's low opinion of people in the colonies can be found in his derogatory description of New England. In his 1728 mock-heroic poem, titled *The Dunciad*, Pope referred to the English colonies that Ward wrote about as "ape-and-monkey lands."[74] Obviously Pope was as confused as Ward when it came to the differences between the North American British colonies where there were no monkeys or apes, and colonies in South America where there are monkeys, but no apes.

Both Ward and Pope were constrained by what they were told, read, and observed in England. Accordingly, they always referred to a barbecued pig as "a barbecue," not an outdoor event. The fact that eighteenth-century British authors like Andrew Burnaby, John Duncan, and Isaac Weld mentioned in Chapter 5, "Richard's Barbycu," felt the need to explain barbecuing to readers in Europe, suggests that Ward—like many other eighteenth-century Britons—very well may have been ignorant of the fact that barbecuing on wooden grills set over hot coals in a dug pit was common in the North American colonies.

Pope is no more of an authoritative source for factual barbecuing history than Ward. Those two associated people with barbecuing as a way to ridicule them. The value in Pope's notions of barbecuing is the same as the value in Ward's: it merely sheds light on the beliefs held about barbecuing among eighteenth-century Britons. Therefore Ward's and Pope's writings about barbecuing are not a solid foundation for a credible accounting of the history of southern barbecuing.

WARD'S PIG FEAST THAT FEATURED POPE'S HOG ROASTED WHOLE

Some interpret Ward's use of the phrase "the Barbacue Feast" to mean an outdoor social event, just like Americans have used it for centuries. However, based upon the eighteenth-century British understanding of barbecuing exhibited by Pope and others, that's not true. Ward was not using the word barbacue to refer to an event. He used it to refer to the three pigs. Because a barbecue to Ward was a barbecued pig rather than an event, the proper interpretation of his phrase "the Barbacue Feast" as he meant it, must be "the barbecued pig feast" or "the pig feast." Ward himself verifies this. One of the "pertakers" in *Barbacue Feast* referred to the event as a "Pig-Feast," which is a play on the old English phrase *ox feast*. Ward did a similar thing when he called the pertakers of the feast a "Barbacue Society." The phrase Barbacue Society is a play on Beefsteak Society, which was the name of a respected London club during Ward's time. He had much regard for its members who regularly met to enjoy a hearty meal of old English roast beef.[75] That wordplay was Ward's way of contrasting what in his mind was the civilized with the uncivilized; a roast ox feast versus a barbecued pig feast. Instead of holding an honorable and proper ox feast like "true Englishmen," those "West-Indian Creolians" in Peckham, England, held what Ward considered to be a creole-style feast with pigs cooked using a mixture of "Indian" and "Negroes" cooking.

Unfortunately, Ward's and Pope's satire and questionable knowledge of barbecuing have been recited as fact over and over by proponents of the COT and often with embellishment. The appeal of Ward's often-cited phrase "litter of Pigs most nicely cook'd after the West-India Manner" from a pamphlet full of satire and ridicule lies in its simple explanation for a very complicated subject. It's perfect for short soundbites on television and callouts in magazine articles. Nevertheless when interpreting things Ward and Pope wrote about barbecuing, one must be mindful that those authors wrote about it from the uninformed viewpoint that existed in England during the eighteenth century. When Pope referred to barbecuing as West Indian, he was just paraphrasing Ward. When Barclay's 1774 dictionary called barbecuing "a hog dressed whole after the West Indian manner," it was referring to what was written by Ward and to Pope's paraphrasing of him, not to an independent verification or serious investigation into the history of barbecuing.

Charles Lanman wrote in *Haw-ho-noo: or, Records of a Tourist* published in 1850, "By some, this species of entertainment [American barbecue festivals] is thought to have originated in the West India Islands." There are several glaring problems with Lanman's statement: Although people in the Caribbean held feasts and outdoor social events during the early modern period, they didn't hold or attend events they called barbecues. That usage of the word barbecue is uniquely and distinctively American, and, as previously discussed, people in other countries that call such events barbecues nowadays learned that practice from Americans. During the OSBP, "a barbecue" in the United States, before and after the War for Independence, was a very specialized outdoor event that was hosted for celebrations, entertainment, and politics. Lanman embellished what Ward and Pope wrote by incorrectly reading his understanding of the word barbecue into historical passages. Lanman didn't point out that the "some" he referred to all rely on Ward's assumption that barbecuing is a West India way of cooking.

(continued on page 224)

WILLIAM BECKFORD: THE "CREOLEAN" LORD MAYOR

Ward's prejudice against people he called "Creolians," "Sagamoors," "Squaws," and "Negroes" who preferred a pig feast over an ox feast was also found in newspapers and periodicals.[76] It was demonstrated in opinions held by some Britons of the Jamaican-born Lord Mayor William Beckford (1709–90). Beckford's father was a wealthy plantation owner in Jamaica. As a boy Beckford's father sent him to England to be educated in the hopes it would make up for his Jamaican "otherness" and ensure his ability to be assimilated into British society. Apparently his efforts were successful—to a point. Beckford first gained prominence in England as an outspoken supporter of parliamentary reform and eventually ascended to the office of lord mayor of London twice.[77] His British-born countrymen named him the "Creolian Lord Mayor." In a sarcastic commentary on "the lord mayor's feast" held in honor of Beckford in 1762, a critic ridiculed his Jamaican birth: "We hear that at the lord mayor's feast, the company was regaled with one hundred hogs barbecued, and that the negroes who now fill all the city offices in his lordship's gift, made a very fine shew."[78] Lamenting the evils of sugar, which some believed to be the source of "all disorders," an outspoken critic associated Beckford with it stating, "the vilest of all compositions, filled with all the noxious particles of all the elements, and only capable of giving inspiration to a Creolian Lord Mayor."[79] Denigrating Beckford's Jamaican roots, a concerned Briton commented that there were "so many creoles" in Parliament he feared the sugar cane might "triumph over the hop-pole, and the barbecued hog over the roast-beef of the English."[80] Those opinions should not be taken as proof that people in Jamaica were barbecuing hogs using a technique that was similar to the OSBT or the one prescribed in British cookbooks. Beckford's critics may have been, and probably were, as misinformed about barbecuing as Ward.

(continued from page 223)

Consequently Lanman misinterpreted Ward's and Pope's spurious barbecuing history claims. A careful reading of what Ward and Pope stated about barbecuing clarifies that they didn't claim entertainments called barbecues originated in the West Indies. Ward made the one-time statement that barbecuing is a West India way of cooking. He did not claim that barbecues (a.k.a., outdoor social events) originated in the West Indies.

When Samuel Johnson printed his British definition of the word barbecue in 1785 as "a term used in the West Indies for dressing a hog whole; which being split to the backbone, is laid flat upon a gridiron, raised about two foot above a charcoal fire," he was relying on Ward and Pope. However, accounts left by eyewitnesses who were actually in early modern Jamaica tell a very different story about barbecuing there. They describe pork that was jerked on pattas and barbecued in earth ovens. No eyewitnesses described people mopping pigs with fox tails dipped in a basting liquid made with Madeira wine while they were being cooked on a wooden grill. Indeed there are no known credible records of anyone in the West Indies barbecuing a whole hog during the OSBP in the way Ward described in *Barbacue Feast*.

The way Ward's unreliable account of barbecuing has been repeated as fact over and over in dictionaries, barbecue history books, and the mass media has created the impression that there are far more witnesses to the claim that southern barbecuing was imported from the West Indies than there really are. In truth there isn't a multitude of witnesses to the supposed Caribbean origins of southern barbecuing. There is only one unreliable witness: Ned Ward.

Apple-Vinegar BBQ Sauce

Although Ward's barbecue knowledge was suspect, it appears he would agree that apples are a delicious compliment to pork. This barbecue sauce recipe was inspired by Virginia barbecue recipes from the past and is my tribute to the multitude of apple orchards found all around the Old Dominion. The sauce is also inspired by my father who built a barbecue pit in our backyard that was beside a tall apple tree.

1½ cup apple cider vinegar
1½ cup apple cider
3 tablespoons white sugar, or to taste
1½ tablespoons tomato ketchup
1 tablespoon lemon juice
½ tablespoon table salt
1 teaspoon Worcestershire sauce
1 teaspoon black pepper
½ teaspoon ground cayenne, to taste
½ teaspoon ground sage
Water, as needed

—

Heat the apple cider to boiling in a 2-quart saucepan; reduce heat. Simmer uncovered until to ½ cup remains. Add all of the other ingredients (except the water), and bring back to a simmer over medium heat, stirring often. Immediately remove the sauce from the heat source and let it cool. If too acidic, add water using 1 tablespoon at a time until it suits your taste. For best results, refrigerate overnight in a sealed container before serving.

NINE

SAM'S BARBECUE

Uncle Sam's Barbecue Tradition

Over the centuries Uncle Sam's barbecue (a.k.a., American barbecue) has been a defining part of American culture. Americans have enjoyed barbecued foods at family meals, political rallies, community feasts, on holidays, birthdays, and sporting events. American barbecue has even been carried into space. In the 1960s, Apollo space program engineers developed a spacecraft maneuver called the "barbecue roll," which is still used to prevent spacecrafts from overheating. Astronaut Sonny Carter took barbecued ribs with him on a space shuttle mission in 1989. In 2011, astronauts on the International Space Station enjoyed barbecued brisket. Unique events such as those set American barbecue traditions apart from every other barbecue culture in the world.

BARBECUING IN THE TWENTIETH CENTURY

American barbecuing has undergone much change since it's multicultural birth among people of African, European, and Native American descent. After those groups combined their culinary practices, the process of creolization went to work to help them create a new way of cooking that eventually came to be known in the colonial United States as barbecuing. Over time, as one barbecue era slowly came to an end, another emerged. A few decades after the end of the Civil War, the word barbecue started to apply to just about any kind of outdoor cooking. Nevertheless the many forms of barbecuing that emerged in the United States have remained entrenched in American

The important notice posted at Paulie's Pigout in Afton, Virginia. Photo by the author.

culture. By the turn of the twentieth century, barbecuing in the United States was undergoing more change than it had in any other time in its history. By the mid-twentieth century, barbecuing whole- or half-animal carcasses over open, uncovered pits while basting them with a butter- and vinegar-based sauce had become the exception rather than the rule as the "Hubbard method" (see Chapter 7, "Juba's 'Cue") started growing in popularity. As will be discussed, there are many reasons for the changes. Among them was the rising cost of skilled labor. As food journalist Kathleen Purvis observed, "It's tough to make a living off a $4 chopped-pork sandwich, especially if you have to chop down a tree to cook it."[1]

After John Sinclair's 1906 novel *The Jungle* exposed the unsanitary conditions in Chicago meatpacking plants, the government started regulating the food industry. As a result, health department regulations also became a driver behind significant changes in barbecuing techniques. One exasperated pitmaster quipped, "Anyone with a lick of sense knows you can't make a good barbecue and comply with a health code."[2] Because in-ground pits were frowned upon by Progressive period health and cleanliness reformers, pitmasters had to find alternatives if they wanted to stay in business.

The oven used in Harlem to barbecue an ox in 1884 (see Chapter 7, "Juba's 'Cue") marked one of the most significant changes in what Americans believed to be barbecuing. By the 1920's the slow transition from barbecuing animal carcasses using the Original

ELECTRIC GRILLS

By the start of the twentieth century, electric grills were available to home cooks. In 1890, a journalist for the *Pittsburg Dispatch* described a novel dinner held in Melbourne, Pennsylvania, where the guests were served steaks cooked on an electric grill.[4] The Olean Electric & Power Company in New York encouraged customers to buy electric grills with the sales pitch, "Try it and you will be convinced that the ELECTRIC WAY is the BEST WAY."[5] In 1924, 5,000 Americans dined on what a newspaper reporter called "Electric Barbecue": "Four steers weighing about 2,000 pounds each were roasted in an electrically heated pit in the West recently, the meat being served to 5,000 persons. With the temperature automatically controlled, it required 24 hours to cook the beef thoroughly. The improvised oven was 32 feet long, 4 feet wide and 6 feet deep."[6]

(continued from page 228)

Southern Barbecuing Technique (OSBT) to barbecuing them by roasting and baking them in smoky ovens was becoming widespread. In 1922, a columnist for *The Flint Daily Journal* described the changes as "improvements of the ages," which is a phrase straight out of the Progressive period. She wrote:

> In the old days in the South, it was quite a feat of cooking to provide a barbecue. There they suspended the carcass of the ox on a spit over a bed of live coals. The modern barbecue, however, has acquired some of the improvements of the ages, and when you attend one of these feasts nowadays you find the ox has been roasted in a great oven built on the same principle as a peanut roast, but some two hundred times as large. Inside this oven is an iron cylinder on which the carcass is placed and held to it with skewers and chains. The beds of live coals are put in the four corners of the oven and the cylinder with the ox upon it is slowly revolved. Underneath the ox roast are large dripping pans to catch the drippings, which are from time to time dipped out with a ladle and poured over the roast. In from six to eight hours, according to the size of the ox, the roast is done, and it is then carried according to the usual custom to the banquet table, where it is served to the hungry guests.[3]

An electric grill advertisement from the *Topeka State Journal,* February 7, 1913.

The turn of the twentieth century saw the advent of the gas-fueled barbecue cooker. In 1916 a large gas-fueled "oven" was built to cook beef and lamb for 5,000 people at a barbecue in Ogden, Utah. A newspaper correspondent reported, "To supply the demands of the menu previously announced, two whole beeves were roasted in the big oven which was built expressly for that purpose. This oven is 17 feet long, 13 feet wide and 8 feet high. . . . The plan of construction of the oven afforded ample room for two slaughtered lambs, which were roasted while the gas fire was removing rawness from the beef. . . . The ovens and also a large tank in which 4800 ears of corn were roasted, required 3000 feet of gas to keep them hot during the cooking process. The seasoning of the meat was declared perfect."[7]

Fireless cookers were another invention that emerged around the turn of the twentieth century. A fireless cooker was essentially an insulated container (similar to our modern coolers and thermoses) in which foods were cooked. The food to be cooked was placed in pots and heated using a conventional stove. The heated pots were then sealed and placed in the fireless cooker that was also sealed with a tight lid. The hot foods were cooked by the residual heat that was preserved in the insulated chamber.[8] Fireless cookers were billed as energy-efficient stoves because they didn't need any added fuel while operating. In 1919 Armour & Company shipped 2,500 pounds of fresh, hot barbecued beef in "sixteen especially built fireless cookers" nearly 500 miles away from their Chicago plant for an event held for employees of the Carnegie Steel Company in Sharon, Pennsylvania. Company executives asserted the superiority of their new "barbequing" process "over the old tiring and bothersome methods of barbequing meats over a smoky fire." Armour marketers boasted, "The new system results in the juices of the beef being basted right back into it so that none of the flavor is lost, making it twice as wholesome." It appears that Armour & Company described their new way of barbequing as more Progressive period progress and improvement:

> This process eliminates considerable waste and the bothersome methods used years ago when it was necessary to spend hours cooking a steer on the spit, burning the outside to a crisp and leaving the inside undone. Previously this was done at barbeques with a searing of faces and losing of tempers over a hot smoky fire. Now, however, in these days of wireless telegraphy, cross Atlantic nonstop flights, etc., it is not necessary to do this to have barbequed beef or meats of any kind at large picnics or barbeques, for Armour and Company have made a special study of barbequing meats and with the aid of the especially built fireless cookers can handle the largest of orders, having prepared the meat for an order which fed 1200 people at one time.[9]

Rather than progress, fireless barbecue cookers, indirect-heat cookers, and gas-fueled ovens represented the commercialization of barbecuing and a way to make barbecuing cheaper and easier for restaurateurs and caterers.

The turn of the twentieth century also saw the practice of serving barbecue sauce on the side become widespread; even in Texas where we are told barbecue doesn't need sauce because there is "nothing to hide." In 1909 "all kinds of barbecue sauces" were served on the side with the barbecued meats at a barbecue held by the people of Bryan and Brazos counties in Texas.[10] In California, Mexican barbacoa was becoming

A "fireless cooker," ca. 1912.

accepted as a new form of American barbecue. Californians started hosting "Spanish barbecues" where meats were "barbecued in true Spanish style." One such barbecue was held in 1909 in Whittier, California, at El Ranchito—the former home of the first Mexican governor of California, Pío de Jesús Pico (1801–94)—that featured a "whole ox barbecued a la Mexicana." As a Spanish barbecue held "especially for eastern visitors," it was apparently meant to introduce easterners to California's style of barbecue. The famous California-barbecue man Joe Romero (1852–1932) barbecued a 550-pound ox in an earth oven. The bill of fare included delicious sides such as Spanish beans, chili, enchiladas, and tamales.[11]

Another development from around the turn of the twentieth century is "barbecue gravy," which started showing up on restaurant menus as early as 1910.[12] In 1918, a restaurant in Ada, Oklahoma, advertised "Barbecue at 85 cents and 40 cents a pound. Bring your bucket and get plenty of gravy."[13] Writing under the penname Jane Eddington, Caroline Maddocks Beard (food writer for the *Chicago Tribune* from 1910 to 1930)

Joe Romero, ca. 1910. James, *The 1910 Trip of the H.M.M.B.A. to California and the Pacific Coast.*

described barbecue gravy that was "served on all our highways in so many places up and down the land" as "watery meat gravies, either with tabasco sauce, or pepper sauce, or cayenne, or something of that type to make the eater forget to savor any combination for any other thing than the discomfort which he seems to enjoy."[14] Of course, the use of jus implies the meats used to make the "barbecue" gravy were either roasted or baked, not barbecued using the OSBT. Barbecue gravy is still served by some nowadays. It's often made with a typical brown gravy mixed with a small amount of barbecue sauce. It's also common practice for competition barbecue cooks to add barbecue sauce to the jus from their competition-style briskets and pork butts. Although it received the name "barbecue gravy" sometime around the turn of the twentieth century, the concept of adding barbecue sauce ingredients to jus from baked and roasted meat goes back to at least *The Virginia Housewife*. That book instructs the reader to add typical seventeenth- and eighteenth-century Virginia barbecue baste ingredients to the jus from a "barbecued" shoat that has been baked in an oven.[15]

BARBECUING AND WORLD WAR I

Unlike during the Civil War, World War I didn't stop people from hosting large barbecues. In 1915, the Boston lawyer James Jackson Storrow II (1864–1926) hosted a barbecue at his home in Lincoln, Massachusetts, to aid the National Allied War Relief Fund. Cooks prepared two beeves "roasted whole, after the manner of English feudal times." Three thousand people attended.[16] In 1915, North Carolinians hosted "an old fashioned North Carolina barbecue and old Virginia Brunswick stew" in Raleigh for their Virginian guests from Richmond, Norfolk, and Williamsburg. They wanted to show Virginians "how connoisseurs of the trenches prepare the stuff here without the liquid accompaniment that must always attend a Virginia barbecue."[17]

A large Democratic barbecue held in October of 1915 in Maysville, Kentucky, was captured on film and turned into a movie that was featured for several nights at the local theater.[18] Advertisements for at least three barbecues held in July of 1916 in Edgefield, South Carolina, appear on a single page of the July 26, 1916 edition of the *Edgefield Advertiser*.

Although barbecues were being held all around the country during World War I, there were concerns that they were contributing to food shortages, not in the United States but in Europe. The *Richmond Times-Dispatch* reported under the headline "May Forbid Barbecues" in 1917, "County and municipal officials in various parts of North Carolina have under consideration plans to prohibit barbecues as a step toward the conservation of pork and an increase in hog production." The rationale for the proposal was based on the fact that shoats (young pigs) were often barbecued, and it was believed slaughtering them "prohibited a marked increase in production."[19]

In 1918 the Texas-state food administrator urged the locals in El Paso to stop holding barbecues because "barbecues waste meat and bread."[20] That same year, barbecue-stand operators in Arizona petitioned the Food Administration to allow them to serve barbecued goat on Tuesdays, which was one of the wartime's "meatless days."[21] However, there wasn't a food shortage in the United States. American farmers produced a record amount of beef and pork in 1918.[22] Americans were sacrificing meat and wheat so those foods could be sent to Europe to feed the millions of people impacted by World War I.

BARBECUING AND PROHIBITION

Richard Thomas Walker Duke Jr. (first mentioned in chapter 7, "Juba's 'Cue") complained about the "iniquitous, hypocritical, tyrannical & fanatical Legislation known as the 18th Amendment." He grumbled, "a Barbecue without something to drink was . . . a d-mn dreary place." He gave Prohibition partial blame for the decline of old-fashioned Virginia barbecues writing, "But prohibition has killed it [barbecues] anyway as it has destroyed the old fashioned delightful conviviality of men & women & the dinner party is now a thing of "gobble, gabble, git" & in some respects a funeral is more

BARBECUE BOB

Even though Prohibition dealt a blow to southern barbecuing, it remained an important part of American culture. That fact is testified to by Robert Hicks (1902–31). In the 1920s, Hicks worked as a cook at Tidwell's Barbecue located near Atlanta. He was also a musician, and in 1927 he recorded his first record titled "Barbecue Blues." The record soon became a best-seller, and from that time forward, Hicks became to be known as "Barbecue Bob."

(continued from page 234)

cheerful."[23] Duke Jr. wasn't the only one who felt that way. Before the start of the famous "Walton Barbecue" held in Oklahoma in 1923, officials warned attendees, "Leave your corn liquor at home when you come to Oklahoma City for Jack Walton's barbecue and square dance!"[24] Of course, with between 50,000 to 100,000 attendees (reports differ) at that barbecue, you can bet not everyone complied with the rules.

BARBECUING AND THE GREAT DEPRESSION

Many barbecue cooks struggled during the Great Depression. One example is the experience of J. B. M. Goldsmith (Goldie). In 1929, Goldie invested his life savings of $500.00 to open a barbecue stand at 1154 East Washington Street in Phoenix, Arizona. $500.00 in 1929 would be about $7000.00 today. He not only invested his money, but he also invested his hard work and his expert knowledge of cooking barbecue. On October 1, 1929, at 7:00, Goldie celebrated the grand opening of GOLDIE'S VIRGINIA BARBECUE. However, the day didn't go as Goldie had planned. By 1:30, Goldie's barbecue stand was in ruins. The entire operation burned to the ground due to defective wiring. The business was a total loss, and Goldie carried no insurance. There were no follow up reports to indicate if Goldie and his business ever recovered from the loss.[25]

By the end of the 1930s, many African Americans who had learned to barbecue whole carcasses over open pits in antebellum and Reconstruction times had died, and their knowledge and skill passed on with them. Of course, the influences of commercialization (costs versus profit) continued to make an ever-growing impact on barbecuing that included the use of roasting, baking, and grilling as well as tomato and sugar in barbecue recipes. That prompted scoffs from purists who railed against tomato in barbecue sauces and the notion that barbecue could be cooked with a stove.[26] Nevertheless, despite all the changes, the original southern barbecuing technique still wasn't completely abandoned.

BACKYARD BARBECUING

In the 1920s, Henry Ford (1843–1947) fueled the backyard barbecue trend when he started selling charcoal (made with sawdust leftover from manufacturing cars) and charcoal grills with his automobiles. Ford's grills were so popular some dealerships were devoting as much as half of their retail space to grilling supplies.[27] *Sunset's Barbecue Book*, first published in 1938, provided Americans with a comprehensive handbook for all kinds of outdoor cooking. Sweet, tomato-based barbecue sauce recipes were being printed in newspapers, so were recipes for cooking "barbecue" using the kitchen stove, and charcoal grills were being mass produced and sold for as little as $1.25.[28]

Backyard barbecues were first popularized in California as far back as 1919 before spreading to other regions in the United States. That's when a columnist mentioned "a novel 'backyard barbecue'" that was hosted by a prominent family in San Diego, California. By 1928 a columnist claimed that backyard barbecuing was becoming so popular in California "it threatens to rival the movies." A few months after the start of World War II, a newspaper reported that Americans were "seeking simpler means of entertainment because of wartime requirements." They found those simpler means in backyard barbecues. In 1942 a correspondent wrote under the heading "America Goes Backyardish" that "the charcoal grill craze has become epidemic." In 1943 it was reported, "Californians, [are] particularly addicted to backyard barbecues." In 1945 a columnist wrote that "barbecue suppers and backyard picnics are a favorite western sport."[29] After the end of World War II, the mass media popularized the practice of calling cookouts backyard barbecues all around the United States.

Many people all over the South refuse to call outdoor events where steaks, hamburgers, hotdogs, and other sausages that are cooked on a charcoal or gas grill a barbecue. To southerners, such outdoor events are *cookouts* because foods of all kinds are merely cooked outdoors on grills, or in pots and pans over fires, and don't necessarily require meats to actually be barbecued. The author of the book *Barbecue Chef*, published in 1950, explained, "By the time World War II had arrived, most of the countryside and roads had become overrun with people and cars and opportunities for outdoor festivity narrowed. But soon the desire for escape from the tensions and congestion of post war stimulated the development of the backyard or so-called patio barbecue party. This patio party does not as a rule accommodate the larger crowds of bygone years and is often 'tainted' by a few modern conveniences." He went on to dedicate the book to occasions when "savory foods are prepared outdoors or on open fires with informal entertainment and relaxation the general idea." By admitting that backyard barbecues were "tainted," the author acknowledged that the term "backyard barbecue" was just a new name for what he called a "patio party," where foods are cooked with "open fires."[30]

"SMOKED" BARBECUE

The notion that hot-smoking meats is a form of barbecuing was born in the twentieth century. Traditionally, southerners cold smoked hams and bacon in smokehouses and barbecued whole or half animal carcasses over barbecue pits. Accordingly, before the twentieth century, no one confused the two terms barbecued and smoked. The way people today conflate hot smoking and barbecuing stems from how the mass media promotes smoke-roasted briskets and sausages served in central Texas as being "barbecued." The affordable, easy-to-use, electronically controlled, charcoal-powered, and pellet-powered ovens that are popular among backyard cooks have also played a role in convincing the world that the act of hot smoking meats is barbecuing.

Interestingly, many southerners sneer at the notion of barbecuing a hot dog, which is a sausage, while never questioning Texans when they "barbecue" sausages. Nevertheless, although sausages can be cooked or grilled over OSBP-style pits in the southern barbecuing tradition, they can't be barbecued over them any more than hamburgers or hot dogs can be barbecued. That's merely an observation, not a criticism of central Texas-style barbecue.

Unlike southern barbecuing, which has its roots in a blending of African, Native American, and European cooking, central Texas-style barbecuing was introduced at around the turn of the twentieth century after meat market operators started cooking meat in an attempt to increase its shelf life. The meat market operators, some of whom had German and Czech ancestry, used a German and eastern European smoke-roasting technique to cook sausages, beef, and pork.[31] Like central Texas's hot smoked brisket, the pastrami and corned beef that's served in Jewish delis have roots in eastern Europe.[32] The family resemblance isn't hard to recognize. Pastrami is traditionally hot smoked with the added step of being boiled or steamed before it's served. Some delis even serve sliced pastrami or corned beef complete with pickled vegetables on the side just like hot smoked brisket is served with pickled vegetables on the side in central Texas.

One of the earliest mentions of barbecued brisket is listed on the menu for a Christmas dinner held in 1904 in Arizola, Arizona, that included "Barbecued Brisket

(continued on page 239)

COMPETITION BARBECUE

Barbecue competitions have become a cultural phenomenon in the United States and around the globe. Entering and competing in an American barbecue competition can be an expensive and time-consuming venture. Just about any wood or charcoal-powered barbecue pit can be used in most contests. Barbecue teams face a variety of weather conditions. High winds, drenching rains, cold and extreme heat can be expected. To help deal with the unpredictable conditions, many teams invest in professional-quality cookers. Professional barbecue cookers are usually insulated, which helps reduce the negative effects of unpredictable weather. Generally, they are also much heavier than a typical backyard-style cooker.

Many competition cooks use grades of meat that are far too expensive for the typical barbecue restaurant to serve. Add to that the cost of wood, charcoal, rubs, sauces, pans, utensils, fire extinguishers (which are required by sanctioning bodies), shelter (tents, trailers, RVs, hotel, etc.), gasoline for vehicles, entry fees for contests, time off from work, and the other miscellaneous costs, it can run upwards of $2,500 to compete in a single event. Then there is the time preparing for the contest, blending injections, practicing techniques, and so on. That makes competition barbecue an expensive hobby for some and a profession for others.

The ingredients and cooking techniques used to produce competition barbecue are often far outside the realm of the OSBT. For example, just about all competition barbecue cooks inject meats with a flavorful liquid. Competition barbecue also requires copious amounts of sugar. Some competition barbecue judges have stated that competition barbecue is too rich to eat for an entire meal and one or two bites is enough.

Competition barbecue is often braised as much as it is barbecued. Braising is a cooking method whereby meat is simmered in a small amount of liquid. For example, many competition-barbecue cooks place ribs in the cooker uncovered for about two hours until they acquire a pleasing color. Then, they wrap the ribs in foil with ingredients that might include, butter, sugar, and barbecue rub. Those ingredients make a braising liquid in which the ribs are cooked for about another two hours until they are tender. A similar technique is used for chicken, pork shoulders, and beef briskets.

The brisket cooker at Snow's BBQ in Lexington, Texas. Photo by the author.

(continued from page 237)

of Veal."[33] By 1918, people in the western United States were referring to their smoke-roasted meats as being barbecued. The June 1918 edition of *Popular Science Monthly* includes an article with plans to build a barbecue, which had by that time "become a popular feature with many of the more luxurious dwellings of the West." The barbecue was meant to be used for "smoking and grilling fresh meats."[34] By the end of the 1920s, barbecued brisket was appearing on menus in Texas. The Sunken Garden restaurant in Houston served barbecued brisket in 1929.[35] In a few decades, people in the West were able to convince the rest of the country that their smoke-roasted meats and sausages were barbecued, much like Californians convinced a large part of the United States that grilled steaks are barbecued. By the 1930s, the "Texas smoked barbecue" parlance was in full swing, as seen in a 1934 edition of the *Houston Chronicle* where a grocery store advertised its "Genuine Pit Smoked Barbecue."[36] In 1939, a fellow named Fred Brown of Beaumont, Texas, reported the theft of a barbecued chicken and eight pounds of barbecued brisket. The police chief admitted, "Here is one robbery where we won't recover any [of the loot]."[37] By 1940 barbecued brisket was being served in Kansas City, Missouri.[38] By 1941 barbecued brisket was showing up on menus in Oklahoma.[39] By the 1950s barbecued brisket was showing up on menus published in newspapers all around the country.

CITY MEAT MARKET.

Hy. Bozka & Son, Proprietors

DEALERS IN

Meats of all kinds—the very best. Sausage and Barbecue. Highest prices paid for Hides.

Early twentieth-century advertisement that appears to make a distinction between sausages and barbecued meats in Shiner, Texas. *Shiner Gazette,* June 15, 1911.

Originally meat markets in central Texas were not restaurants; they were butcher shops. As such meat market proprietors were just interested in selling meats for people to take home. Because meat market operators were cooking the meats rather than specifically barbecuing them, they didn't serve a barbecue sauce. Customers purchased the meats, and the counterperson wrapped them in butcher paper so they could be taken home. At some point in the twentieth century, someone started referring to those smoke-roasted meats as being barbecued. Because of that people starting to request barbecue sauce. Although some meat markets in Lockhart, Texas, fought the trend, barbecue sauce is now served by every prominent place in central Texas that serves Texas-style barbecued brisket. Those restaurants also offer forks, chopped barbecue sandwiches, and a wide variety of side dishes.

AMERICAN BARBECUE AROUND THE WORLD

Some immigrants in the United States learned about the American love of barbecue and took advantage of it. For example, Bulgogi, which is marinated meat cooked on griddles, didn't become popular in the United States until after proprietors of Korean restaurants started calling it "Korean barbecue" in the 1950s.[40] Today, however, the lure of the word barbecue is no longer confined to people in the United States. The mass media has done much to spread the word barbecue, which it defines as grilling or cooking with fire, far and wide. For example, an Italian publication has stated that the

Slicing barbecue at a lunch stand at the 1939 Gonzales County Fair in Gonzales, Texas. By Russel Lee. The Miriam and Ira D. Wallach Division of Art, Prints and Photographs. Photography Collection, New York Public Library.

English term barbecue "is a cooking method as old as the discovery of fire" and "in all the languages of the world has the same meaning: cooking food on the grill over burning embers" (author's translation).[41] That definition was picked up from Americans most likely through the mass media. However, such modern definitions of the word barbecue and of barbecuing are very different than the definitions that existed before the turn of the twentieth century.

Enabled by the advent of the World Wide Web in 1989, Americans created barbecue discussion sites that allowed people from all over the world to share outdoor cooking techniques that were being referred to as barbecuing. The barbecue editor for *Texas Monthly*, refers to some of the web-inspired changes as "Big City Barbecue" and commented, "The new [barbecue] region is the Internet."[42] Modern notions of barbecued tofu, barbecued jack fruit, and barbecued watermelon appear to support that assertion.

Today some Europeans hold outdoor social events that feature grilled foods that they call barbecues, and the internet was a significant force behind that practice. Moreover the style of barbecuing that's most widespread in Europe is what people in the

During the HOLIDAYS call on

PERRY

For your——

BARBECUED MEATS,
O'POSSUM,
GROUND HOG, COON,
BEEF, PORK, and
MUTTON.

Wholesale and retail.
The best in the city.

HENRY PERRY,
THE BARBECUE KING,
1514 E. 19th St.

Top: Juke joint and gas station in Melrose, Louisiana. By Marion Post Wolcott, 1940. Library of Congress.

Bottom: Henry Perry "the Father of Kansas City Barbecue." *Kansas City Sun*, December 8, 1917.

southern United States call grilling. Texas-style smoke roasting has grown in popularity in Germany, England, and Australia since the advent of the World Wide Web.[43] Even so, there is no evidence that the OSBT is popular in Europe or Australia.

American manufacturers of outdoor cooking products have also helped spread American barbecue across the globe. For example, in 2010 an American grill manufacturer executed a successful campaign to popularize outdoor grilling in India even though many people there don't eat beef or pork. The next year, the *Times of India* published an article with the headline "License to Grill: India Takes to the Barbecue." Today India has a thriving backyard grilling culture.[44]

THE FUTURE OF AMERICAN BARBECUE

Many famous southern barbecue restaurants that first opened their doors in the early to mid-twentieth century served barbecue that was rooted in local tradition. Often relatively simple family recipes were served and locals loved the results. Today barbecue restaurants all around the country are now offering what they call "North Carolina pork," "Texas brisket," "Memphis ribs," and "Kansas City burnt ends," which has become a sort of modern barbecue sales gimmick. Some restaurants in Texas are even serving burnt ends although they neglect to add the "Kansas City" tag, even though that's where they originated. From a business standpoint, labeling barbecue after well-publicized regions makes sense because of the free marketing provided by the mass media and its way of almost completely ignoring local barbecue styles that aren't part of their modern notions of barbecue. Not everyone thinks the modern trends in American barbecue are good things. Some still prefer to eat barbecue that has a connection with the people who live in the region in which it's cooked. One barbecue scholar explained it this way: "NYC's Texas barbecue is like Houston's New York pizza."[45] The point is well taken. The homogenization of barbecue in the United States might be endangering traditional and delicious local barbecue styles. That might also be a factor in why many old-school family-owned barbecue restaurants are shuttering for good. Yet whether or not Michelin-starred chefs, newspaper editors, and television producers can maintain barbecue's fame far into the future is yet to be seen.

Although American barbecue traditions have undergone many tangible changes through the centuries, there is one intangible that has never changed: the way barbecues reinforce a sense of community and belonging. From the first entertainments in the seventeenth century centered around barbecued venison to backyard barbecues today centered around hamburgers and hotdogs, American barbecues have always been about much more than the mere act of eating. They reinforce the intangibles that come from eating together with loved ones and friends.[46] As it has in the past, American barbecue's immutable and intangible characteristics will continue to sustain its popularity well into the future. Indeed it's worthy of the tribute paid in 1923: "The barbecue then is entitled to great respect and homage. Long may it wave, and may the art of properly preparing the 'cue never be lost!"[47]

Spotsy Dip

This recipe is representative of a modern, backyard barbecue offering. It's quick and easy to make with ingredients that are staples in American's pantries.

Spotsy Dip was created several decades ago in Spotsylvania, Virginia. It's a delicious example of a regional twentieth-century sauce and local delicacy. A delicious version of the sauce has since become a favorite at a national chicken restaurant chain. It's a welcome accompaniment to barbecued meats, chicken wings, and even French fries. Here's how locals make a delicious version of it using a sweet barbecue sauce they buy at local grocery stores.

¼ cup of a sweet, hickory-smoked barbecue sauce
½ cup mayonnaise
1 tablespoon sugar
2 tablespoons yellow mustard
cayenne pepper, to taste

—

Mix all ingredients well and serve.

ACKNOWLEDGMENTS

This book is a labor of love with extra emphasis on *labor*. It was a mammoth endeavor that I couldn't have completed without the help of many people over the course of many years. Unfortunately, I can't remember everyone's name and, regrettably, I'm sure I will forget to mention several who deserve thanks. The many helpful people who assisted me in finding resources in libraries and historical societies were indispensable. The proprietors of barbecue restaurants, stands, food trucks and barbecue cooks like Matthew and Julie Schaffer, Matthew and Alicia Keeler, John Vest, George McIntyre, Floyd Thomas, Forrest Warren, Howard Conyers, Barry Saunders, Ruben Showalter, Luke Darnell, and Zardrell McKnight that freely shared their cooking processes and wonderful stories about their way of barbecuing were bright spots in the long journey of writing this book. I owe a debt of gratitude to all of the unsuspecting souls who patiently listened when our conversation invariably drifted into the subject of the history of barbecuing. They will never know how important they were in helping me tease out and refine the narrative of this book.

I want to extend my gratitude to Roberto Perez and Robert Grattan for their invaluable assistance with translating Spanish and French resources. Thanks to Professor Andrew Warnes for assisting me with accessing resources that I couldn't have reviewed without his help. I am grateful for the insights shared by Al McNeill on many important and critical social issues that surround southern barbecue. I am deeply appreciative of the wonderful people at the University of South Carolina Press, especially Aurora Bell and her team. Their assistance, advice, support, and professionalism were instrumental in improving this book.

Last, but not least, I want to thank my wife, Gail, for the hours of traveling with me to barbecue restaurants, events, and competitions while listening to me expound on barbecue, barbecue history, barbecue facts, barbecue myths, barbecue cooks, barbecue restaurants, barbecue sauce, barbecue competitions, barbecue recipes, barbecue traditions, barbecue books, barbecue TV shows, barbecue magazines, barbecue web sites, barbecue culture, barbecue pitts, . . . well, you get the point. Without my wife's love and support this book would not have been possible.

NOTES

INTRODUCTION

1. "2022 State of the Barbecue Industry," hpba.org. March 25, 2022, accessed March 30, 2022, https://www.hpba.org/Resources/PressRoom/ID/2140/.
2. "Kansas City Barbecue Society Events." kcbs.us. accessed March 20, 2021, https://www.kcbs.us/explore_events.php. The Kansas City Barbecue Society is just one of many barbecue organizations in the Unites States that sanctions barbecue cooking contests.
3. Thomas Lethbridge, "Kansas Barbecue Joint is Serving Barbecue from a Vending Machine," twistedfood.co.uk, May 16, 2020, accessed July 19, 2020, https://twistedfood.co.uk/.
4. *Times Picayune* (New Orleans, LA), "A Barbecue," October 12, 1844.
5. For one of the most complete accounts of the Caribbean Origins Theory, see Natasha Geiling's "The Evolution of American Barbecue," smithsonianmag.com, July 18, 2013, accessed December 1, 2019, https://www.smithsonianmag.com/arts-culture/. In *Holy Smoke* (University of North Carolina Press, 2008), 27, John Shelton Reed and Dale Volberg Reed appear to embrace the speculation that asserts barbecue was imported from the Caribbean into Virginia and the Carolina colony where citrus juice was replaced with vinegar. Reed, *On Barbecue*, 5–6, claims the original southern barbecue baste descends from a Caribbean barbecue baste made with lime juice. It was brought to the United States in the nineteenth century when the lime juice was replaced with vinegar. In *The Barbecue Bible* (New York: 2011), 2, Steven Raichlen asserts, "Born in the Caribbean, true barbecue is primarily practiced in the United States—especially Texas, Kansas City, Memphis, and the South." Scott Jones (a nationally recognized writer and the former Executive Editor of *Southern Living*), wrote in "Defining Barbecue," *Costco Connection*, July 2021, "Barbecue's origin can be traced to the Indigenous people of the West Indies and Native Americans using indirect heat to cook whole animals. Spanish explorers called this new method *barbacoa*, which eventually took hold as the English word barbecue. The techniques and flavors expanded throughout the South, primarily influenced by African slaves and European immigrants, before heading west to Texas and up the Mississippi to Memphis, Tennessee." Cynthia Clampitt's *Pigs, Pork, and*

Heartland Hogs: From Wild Boar to Baconfest (Lanham, 2018), 99–101, provides a detailed description of the COT.

6. James R. Veteto and Edward M. Maclin, "Smoked Meat and the Anthropology of Food: An Introduction," in *The Slaw and the Slow Cooked* (Nashville: Vanderbilt University Press, 2011), 13.
7. Robert F. Moss, *Barbecue: The History of an American Institution, Revised and Expanded Second Edition* (Tuscaloosa: University of Alabama Press, 2020).
8. Jim Auchmutey, *Smoke Lore: A Short History of Barbecue in America* (Athens: University of Georgia, 2019), 210.
9. Ken Albala, *Food: A Cultural Culinary History Course Guidebook* (Chantilly, 2013), 10, 101. Cooking over a pit filled with burning embers during prehistoric times was "the original way to barbecue." Chicken that has been browned on a grill is referred to as "barbecued." Meathead Goldwyn, "What is Barbecue?" amazingribs.com, accessed April 4, 2020, https://amazingribs.com/. Asserts that smoke is what makes barbecuing unique. Barbecuing includes everything from cooking in earth ovens to Indian tandoori to grilling steaks. Meathead Goldwyn, "Barbecue History," amazingribs.com, accessed April 4, 2020, https://amazingribs.com/. Argues that barbecuing has existed in Greece, Japan, China, India, Europe, and the Middle East for at least as long as it has in the Americas. Describes "spit roasting" as a "major barbecue cooking method" that goes back to ancient times, and that Europeans have been painting depictions of barbecues "since pig hair bristles were first wrapped around a stick to make a brush." Reed, *On Barbecue*, 101. States that "real" barbecue is meat cooked with smoke and heat from burning hardwood.
10. Raichlen, *The Barbecue Bible*, 2. The "truest form" of barbecuing was "born in the Caribbean." Geiling, "The Evolution of American Barbecue," is an often-cited article that claims, "The Caribbean barbecuing technique" was originally brought to what is today the Southern United States by Hernando de Soto after barbacoa, "the original barbecue," was witnessed in the Caribbean.
11. Warnes, *Savage Barbecue*, 4, 7, 9, 30. Based upon the similarity between the words barbecue and barbaric, Warnes postulates that the word barbecue retains remnants of sixteenth- to eighteenth-century European notions of savagery, and are still reflected, to some degree, in American barbecue culture today.
12. Moss, *Barbecue*, 142. Asserts the "birthplace of barbecue" was Virginia. Reed and Reed, *Holy Smoke*, 46. "In the late 1700s, the barbecue heartland was found in Tidewater Virginia."
13. Adrian Miller, *Black Smoke: African Americans and the United States of Barbecue* (Chapel Hill: University of North Carolina Press, 2021), 28.
14. Joseph R. Haynes, *Virginia Barbecue: A History* (Charleston, SC: The History Press, 2016).
15. Thomas Andrews and Flannery Burke, "What Does It Mean to Think Historically?" Historians.org, January 1, 2007, accessed Dec. 21, 2019, https://www.historians.org/.
16. Bryan, *The Kentucky Housewife*, 91.
17. *[Bolivar, TN] Bolivar Bulletin*, August 24, 1871.
18. Hill, *Mrs. Hill's Southern Practical Cookery*, 171.

19. Robb Walsh, *Legends of Texas Barbecue Cookbook: Recipes and Recollections from the Pit Bosses* (San Francisco, 2002), 33–34.
20. Watson, *Physicians and Surgeons of America*, 398.
21. Charles Loftus Grant Anderson, *Life and Letters of Vasco Núñez de Balboa* (New York, 1941), 247.
22. James Boswell, *The Life of Samuel Johnson, LL.D.: Including A Journal of His Tour to the Hebrides*, vol. 5 (Harper & Brothers, 1831), 438.
23. Thornton, *American Glossary*, vol. 1, 41.
24. "The letter from Syria . . . ," *Aurora [Philadelphia, PA] General Advertiser*, March 11, 1799.
25. Paul Gaffarel, *Nuñez de Balboa: La Première Traversée de L'isthme Américain (Nuñez de Balboa, the first crossing of the American isthmus)* (Paris, 1882). 45; Loftus Grant Anderson, *Life and Letters of Vasco Núñez de Balboa* (New York, 1941), 131.
26. Helps, Spanish Conquest, vol. 2, 293.
27. del Castillo, *Historia verdadera*, 294–95. A barbican is a defensive structure used in medieval times to fortify the entrances to towns, castles, and forts. The original passage was recorded in 1576 in *Historia verdadera de la conquista de la Nueva España* (*The True History of the Conquest of New Spain*).
28. James Burney, *History of the Buccaneers of America*, 42.
29. Exquemelin (1686), "Jean-Baptiste's Boucan."
30. Charles Loftus Grant Anderson, *Old Panama and Castilla Del Oro* (Boston, 1914), 84–85.
31. de Mailly, et al., *Histoire de la Révolution*, vol. 10, 112.
32. "Origine du mot Boucan et de ses dérivés," in *L'Intermédiaire des Chercheurs et Curieux*, no. 322 (Paris, October 10, 1881), 630–31.
33. *Dictionnaire Universel François et Latin*, vol. 1 (Paris, 1721), 1136; *Dictionnaire Universel François et Latin: Vulgairement Appelé Dictionnaire de Trévoux*, Abbé Brillant, ed. (Paris, 1771), 981.
34. Malachy Postlethwayt, "Spanish Buccaneers," in *The Universal Dictionary of Trade and Commerce* (London, 1766).
35. Larwood and Hotten, *History of Signboards*, 499.
36. Timbs, *English Eccentrics*, 528.
37. Mona Baker, *In Other Words*, 3rd edition (London and New York, 2018), 18. Christa Hauenschild and Susanne Heizmann, eds., *Machine Translation and Translation Theory* (New York, 1997), 37–48, 52–54.
38. Goodrich, *Universal Traveller*.
39. Jean de Léry, *History of a Voyage to the Land of Brazil*, Janet Whatley, trans. (Berkeley, 1993), 127.
40. Reed and Reed, *Holy Smoke*, 15; Betty McKay Fraine, et al., *Archibald McKay, 1720-1797, Scotland to Cumberland County, North Carolina: descendants and related families* (Tulsa, 1979), 95; Jim Auchmutey, "The Cradle," in *Smoke Lore* (Athens, 2019), 22.
41. James D. McKenzie, *History of Barbecue Church* (1965), 40–41.
42. Timbs, *English Eccentrics*, 528.

CHAPTER 1: HERNANDO'S BARBACOA

1. For an example, see Rufus Ward, "Ask Rufus: Brutality and barbecue 475 years ago," *cdispatch.com*, December 14, 2015, accessed February 1, 2020, https://cdispatch.com/.
2. Lawrence A. Clayton, Edward C. Moore, Vernon James Knight, *The De Soto Chronicles Vol 1 & 2* (Tuscaloosa, 1993), 498–99.
3. Edward Gaylord Bourne, *Narratives of the career of Hernando de Soto*, vol. 1 (New York, 1904), 102; Rufus Ward, "Ask Rufus: Brutality and barbecue 475 years ago," *cdispatch.com*, December 14, 2015, accessed February 1, 2020, https://cdispatch.com/. Doyle, *Faulkner's County*, 27; Kirksey-Owen, "Barbecue," devingreaney.wordpress.com, November 27, 2009, accessed January 20, 2020, https://devingreaney.wordpress.com/. Geiling, "The Evolution of American Barbecue."
4. Lawrence A. Clayton, Edward C. Moore, Vernon James Knight, *The De Soto Chronicles Vol 1 & 2* (Tuscaloosa, 1993), 104, 106, 126, 146, 152.
5. For examples of Spain's desire to convert Indigenous people in the Americas, see Hernan Cortes, *Hernán Cortés: Letters from Mexico*, Anthony Pagden, ed. (New Haven: Yale University Press, 2001), 12, 18, 23, 106–7, 332–33, 340, 346, 351–52, 442–43.
6. Juan C. Zamora, "Indigenismos en la Lengua de los Conquistadores," in *Hesperia: Anuario de Filología Hispánica*, no. 5, 2002, 195–209.
7. Ibid.
8. Willem F. H. Adelaar, *The Languages of the Andes* (Cambridge, 2004), 179. Quechua is an Indigenous language family spoken by the Quechua people in South America. It is called Quechua in Peru and Bolivia, and Quichua in Ecuador and Argentina.
9. Walter William Skeat, "The Language of Mexico; and the Words of West-Indian Origin [Read at a Meeting of the Philological Society, November 2, 1888.]," in *Transactions of the Philological Society, 1888–1890* (London, 1891), 136–49.
10. Martyr, *De Orbe Novo*, vol. 1, 96.
11. Gaffarel, *Histoire du Bresil*, 58.
12. Oviedo y Valdés, *Sumario de la natural historia De Las Indias* (Mexico City: Fondo de Cultura Económica, 1950), 118.
13. Carrillo, "'Historia General,'" 321–344.
14. Gentleman of Elvas, *Discovery and Conquest*, x.
15. Bourne, *Narratives of the career*, vols. 1 & 2, x.
16. "Garcilaso de la Vega," *Encyclopedia Britannica*.
17. Garcilaso de la Vega, *La Florida del Inca*, vol. 1 (The Royal Office: Madrid, 1723), 221.
18. Bourne, *Narratives of the career*, vol. 2, 86.
19. Winship, *Coronado Expedition*, 457; Vacandard, et al., *Original Narratives*, 276. The exact dates of Pedro de Castañeda's birth and death are not known. Scholars estimate that he was born between 1510 and 1518. His wife filed a claim with the Spanish government in 1554 requesting payment for her husband's service to the king, which implies he had died by that time.
20. "Q", *Good Eats*, Food Network, June 11, 2003.

21. Rufus Ward, "Ask Rufus: Brutality and barbecue 475 years ago," cdispatch.com, December 14, 2015, accessed February 1, 2020, https://cdispatch.com/.
22. Raichlen, *BBQ USA*, 14.
23. Rufus Ward, "Pirates, Pigs and 470 Years of Barbecue," in *Columbus Chronicles: Tales from East Mississippi* (Charleston, 2012), para. 2.
24. Geiling, "The Evolution of American Barbecue."
25. Doyle, *Faulkner's County*, 27.
26. Daniel G. Brinton, *The Arawack Language of Guiana in Its Linguistic and Ethnological Relations* (Philadelphia, 1871), 11.
27. Tylor, "Fire, Cooking, and Vessels," 261.
28. Constantine Samuel Rafinesque, "Comparative Taíno Vocabulary of Hayti," in *The American Nations, or, Outlines of Their General History, Ancient and Modern* (Philadelphia, 1836), 232.
29. Stevens, *New Dictionary*.
30. Birkenmaier and Whitfield, "Building a Barbacoa," 63.
31. Macías, *Diccionario Cubano*, 139–40.
32. Gonzalo Fernández de Oviedo y Valdés, *Historia general y natural de las Indias*, vol. 1 (Madrid, 1851), 556.
33. Abbot, *Hernando Cortez*, 32.
34. For examples of claims that Oviedo was the first to pen the noun *barbacoa*, see Alexander Lee, "The History of the Barbecue," historytoday.com, August 8, 2019, accessed April 4, 2020, https://www.historytoday.com/; Elizabeth S. D. Engelhardt, *Republic of Barbecue Stories beyond the Brisket* (Austin, 2009), 88; Raichlen, *Planet Barbecue!*, xv.
35. Navarrete, *Colección de los viages*, vol. 3, x. "Dicen que los tienen todos aquellos Caciques en las barbacoas como maiz, porque es tanto el oro que tienen que no lo quieren tener en cestas." Translation: It is said that all of those Caciques have so much gold that they have to store it in barbacoas, like corn, instead of in baskets.
36. Edward Gaylord Bourne, *Narratives of the Career of Hernando de Soto in the Conquest of Florida*, vol. 2 (New York: Allerton Book Company, 1922), 110. "When the soldiers as they were used to do began to climb upon the barbacoas in an instant the Indians began to take up clubs and seize their bows and arrows and to go to the open square." Edward Gaylord Bourne, *Narratives of the Career of Hernando de Soto in the Conquest of Florida*, vol. 1 (New York: Allerton Book Company, 1922), 44. "Another got up with a lance into a maize crib made of cane called by Indians barbacoa and defended the entrance with the uproar of ten men."
37. Edward Gaylord Bourne, *Narratives of the career of Hernando de Soto*, vol. 1 (New York, 1904), 100–101. "They found some bodies of dead men fastened on a barbacoa. The breasts, belly, necks, and arms and legs full of pearls." "They took away from there some two hundred pounds of pearls."
38. Pacheco, et al., ed., *Colección de documentos*, vol. 2, 277.
39. Fray Domingo de Santo Tomás, *Lexicon o Vocabulario de la lengua general del Peru* (By Francisco Fernandez de Cordoua, 1560), 99. Both charqui and charquini appear as far back as 1560.

40. Eells, *South America's Story* (New York, 1935).
41. Deagan and Cruxent, *Columbus's Outpost,* 66, 135.
42. Joseph de Acosta, *The Natural & Moral History of the Indies*, vol. 1 (London, 1880, [1604]), 290.
43. Wright, *New and Comprehensive Gazetteer*, vol. 4, 419. "The principal occupations of the inhabitants [of Rio Grande, Brazil] are the breeding of cattle, for which the pasture land is well adapted; the dyeing and preparing of hides, and making charque, or what is called jug beef, which is beef salted and dried in a peculiar manner. This constitutes the general food for sailors." Hill, *Lights and Shadows*, 130; Rees, "Rio de Janeiro," *Cyclopaedia*, vol. 30. When Drake arrived at Jamaica in the 1590s, he acquired "forty bundles of dried beef," Mancall, ed., *Atlantic World,* 374.
44. Thales A. Zamberlan Pereira, "Was it Uruguay or coffee? The causes of the beef jerky industry's decline in southern Brazil (1850–1889)," *Nova econ.*, Jan-Apr 2016, 7–42; "The Preservation of Food," *The Farmer's Magazine*, March 1865; Holguín, *Vocabulario en la lengua*; Hall, *Extracts from a Journal,* vol. 1, 169–71. "The jerked beef of commerce."
45. Comp, *Collecção de vocabulos*, 10.
46. G. M., "The Saladeros, Corrals, and Gaucho of the Pampas," in *The Mirror*, vol. 1, no. 9, February 26, 1842, 130–32; Wright, *New and Comprehensive Gazetteer*, vol. 4, 419; "Jerked Beef," *Public Ledger*, November 17, 1842; Thales A. Zamberlan Pereira, "Was it Uruguay or coffee? The causes of the beef jerky industry's decline in southern Brazil (1850–1889)," *Nova econ.*, Jan-Apr 2016, 7–42; "The Pastoral Wealth of the South American States," in *Country Gentleman's Magazine* (London, 1876), 436–44.
47. Clayton, Moore, and Knight, *De Soto Chronicles Vol 1 & 2*, 498–99.
48. Gentleman of Elvas, *Virginia richly valued*, 115.
49. Breton, *Dictionaire Français-Caraibe*, 196, 349; Lovén and Curet, *Origins of the Tainan Culture*, 439; Duna Troiani, *El caribe insular del siglo XVII. Tratado sobre la lengua y la cultura de los Callínago. Traducción al español del Dictionnaire caraïbe-français* (1665), de R. Breton. LINCOM, 2015, Languages of the World/Dictionaries, hal-01202673, pages 22, 43.
50. Pierre Grenand and François Grenand, "Le Boucanage de la Viande et du Poisson," in *La viande: un aliment, des exican*, F. Aubaile, M. Bernard, P. Pasquet, eds., (Edisud, 2004), 69–83; Steven N. Dworkin, *A History of the Spanish Lexicon: A Linguistic Perspective* (Oxford, 2012), 95; Asado o Barbacoa, *forum.wordreference.com*, February 2019, accessed March 8, 2020, https://forum.wordreference.com/.
51. "A Guide to the Argentine Asado," *pickupthefork.com*, October 11, 2016, accessed February 1, 2020, https://pickupthefork.com/.
52. Julián Pérez Porto and Ana Gardey, *Definición de Barbacoa, definicion.de*, 2017, accessed December 31, 2019, https://definicion.de/barbacoa/; Rivas, *Cocina prehispánica mexicana*, 75.
53. Asado o Barbacoa, *forum.wordreference.com*, February 2019, accessed March 8, 2020, https://forum.wordreference.com/.
54. Baretti, *Dictionary, Spanish and English.*
55. Editorial Club de la Prensa, *Anglicismos en El Idioma*, 95.

56. Dworkin, *History of the Spanish Lexicon*, 95.
57. Görlach, ed., *Dictionary of European Anglicisms*, 15–16. The term barbecue became popular in Europe after 1945. There it refers to "a meal grilled out of doors on a metal appliance" and "a party at which such a meal is eaten."
58. Pati Jinich, "Finding the Soul of Sonora in Carne Asada," *nytimes.com*, August 11, 2020, accessed December 27, 2021, https://www.nytimes.com/.
59. "Carne Asada with La Familia," *Pati's Mexican Table*, PBS, October 2, 2020.
60. Oriol Rodríguez, *Esta es la historia de la barbacoa, tapasmagazine.es*, April 18, 2019, accessed 31 Dec. 2019, https://tapasmagazine.es/.
61. Thomas E. Weil, et al., *Area Handbook for Argentina* (American University, 1974), 135.
62. James Lumpkin Taylor's *Portuguese-English Dictionary* defines *jerra* as "an outdoor barbecue or picnic," 373.
63. Sarah Bak-Geller Corona, "Culinary Myths of the Mexican Nation," in *Cooking Cultures: Convergent Histories of Food and Feeling*, Ishita Banerjee-Dube, ed. (Delhi, 2016), 227.
64. Tylor, *Anahuac*, 95.
65. Mariano Velázquez De La Cadena, *A New Pronouncing Dictionary of the Spanish and English Languages* (New York: D Appleton and Company, 1900), 79.
66. Tylor, *Researches into the Early History*, 228.
67. Dnews, "Hawaii's Feral Pig Ancestors Predate Captain Cook," Seeker.com, 15 Sept. 2016, accessed February 1, 2020, https://seeker.com/.
68. Lewis, *Journal of a West-India Proprietor*, 151; Gosse and Hill, *Naturalist's Sojourn*, 395.
69. Labat, *Nouveau Voyage*, vol. 3, 65–69. A description of boucan de tortuë. Labat, *Nouveau voyage*, vol. 8, 287–88. A description of a sheep cooked in an earth oven.
70. Williams, *Dictionary of the New Zealand Language*, 21; "Hāngī," Traditional Māori Foods, newzealand.com, 2005, accessed January 12, 2020, https://www.newzealand.com/us/feature/.
71. Ortiz, "Introduction," *Book of Latin American Cooking*, para. 41.
72. Williams, *The islands and their inhabitants*, vol. 1, 147.
73. Walter W. Froggatt, "Australian Termitid.e, Part I," in *The Proceedings of the Linnean Society of New South Wales*, Second Series, vol. 10, Part the Third (Sydney, January 1, 1896), 432; Peter Sutton, "Material Culture Traditions of the Wik People, Cape York Peninsula," in *Records of South Australia Museum*, vol. 27, no. 1, May 1993, 31–52.
74. Le Vaillant and Helme, *Travels from the Cape*, 255.
75. Rivera, *Diccionario de cocina*, 67–68.
76. Emmons and Laguna, *Tlingit Indians*, 140.
77. Helen C. Rountree, "Subsistence," *The Powhatan Indians of Virginia: Their Traditional Culture* (Norman: University of Oklahoma Press, 1989), 52–53.
78. Barrueto Mejía Ramón, et al., *Astronomía De México en la Época Colonial: Platillos Principales y su Evolución Actual* (Instituto Politécnico Nacional Escuela Superior De Turismo, April 23, 2010), 125.

79. Matthew Lewis, *Journal of a West-India Proprietor* (London, 1834), 151; Philip Henry Gosse and Richard Hill, *A Naturalist's Sojourn in Jamaica* (London, 1851), 395.
80. Markham, *Peruvian Bark*, 250.
81. In *Diccionario de Mejicanismos* Féliz Ramos y Duarte, et al., defines *barbacoa* as "Meat cooked in a hole that's been heated like an oven," 82 (author's translation).
82. Busto, *Diccionario enciclopédico-mejicano*, 303.
83. Rivera, *Diccionario de Cocina*, 67.
84. High, "Barbeque in the Beginning," *History of South Carolina Barbecue*.
85. Webster, *Noah Webster's First Edition*.
86. Mayer and Brisbin, *Wild Pigs*, 36.
87. Izard, letter to Alice Izard, May 28, 1801.

CHAPTER 2: HERBERT'S PATTA

1. Hickeringill, *Jamaica Viewed*, 51; Angela Bartens, "Creole Languages," in *Contact Languages: A Comprehensive Guide*, Peter Bakker, Yaron Matras, eds. (Boston, 2013), 67; P. Hirbec, F. Hannequart, J. Taillardat, *Histoire et Traditions Forestières*, no. 28 (Paris: Les Dossiers Forestiers, l'Office national des forêts, 2015), 63.
2. Phillippo, *Jamaica*, 59.
3. Delle, *Colonial Caribbean*, 34.
4. Cundall and Pietersz, "The Abbot of Jamaica to the King of Spain July 1611," in *Jamaica Under the Spaniards*, 34–35.
5. Poyntz, *Present Prospect*, 13–14. *Engin* is an archaic word of French origin that means skill or cleverness; "Jerk, and dry salt it": some authors interpreted "Jerk" literally and apparently assumed it meant "to stretch." However, in Poyntz's account, it could have just referred to the process of drying meat in the air without the use of salt. See Stafford, *Early Inhabitants*, 143: "They cut into thin strips and stretched, or jerked, and dried in the sun." Fitzpatrick, *This is New Mexico*, 241: Strips of deer meat, jerked and dried, are pounded to a powder that is stored away. The meat is cut into strips, and then each strip is taken by its two ends and actually stretched, or "jerked," after which the strip is hung to dry in the sun.
6. "Baabi" is a Jamaican abbreviation for barbecue. It refers to a platform attached to a tree that is stood upon while it is being trimmed. Cassidy, et al., ed., "baabi," *Dictionary of Jamaican English*, 15.
7. Brassey, *In the Trades,* 32. "A barbecue is the name given, in Jamaica, to the house which contains the threshing-floor and apparatus for drying coffee." Whiteley, *Three months*, 7: "This punishment took place one evening on the barbecue, where pimento is dried"; Phillippo, *Jamaica*, 40. "After having undergone the process of pulping, it [coffee] is dried on terraces called barbecues, and is then fit for local use or exportation." Pullen-Burry, *Ethiopia in Exile,* 21. "The barbecue, a cemented platform where coffee, pimento, and other crops are dried."
8. Thistlewood, *In Miserable Slavery*, 26.
9. Thomas, *Untrodden Jamaica*, 87.

10. Thomas, *Story of a West Indian*, 280–81.
11. Carey, *Maroon Story*, 73.
12. Cassidy, et al., ed., "pata," *Dictionary of Jamaican English*, 341.
13. Taylor, *Jamaica in 1687*, 135.
14. Sloane, *Voyage to the Islands*, vol. 1, xvi.
15. Gaunt, *Where the Twain Meet*, 188.
16. Brice, *Grand Gazetter*, 661.
17. "The Captain's Story: or Adventures in Jamaica Thirty years Ago," in *The Leisure Hour, Volumes 367-418* (London, 1859), 722. Appeared in the November 17, 1839 edition.
18. Beckford, *Descriptive Account of the Island of Jamaica*, 330.
19. Dallas, *History of the Maroons*, 63.
20. Reid, *Maroon*, 107.
21. Scott, *To Jamaica*, 105.
22. Johnson, *Dictionary of the English Language.*
23. Carter, *Compleat City*, 194–95.
24. Retired Military Officer, *Jamaica, as it Was*, 70. Scholars believe the author is the Briton Bernard Martin Senior (ca. 1788–ca. 1860).
25. Nugent, *Lady Nugent's Journal*, 204, 95.
26. Lewis, *Journal of a West-India Proprietor*, 151.; Gosse and Hill, *Naturalist's Sojourn*, 395. "The 'barbecued pig' in Jamaica that was prepared "in the forest, roasted in a rude oven of heated stones."
27. Senior, *Encyclopedia of Jamaican Heritage*, 254–56; "Fiery Foods in Jamaica," *Man Fire Food*, Season 2, Episode 13, 2013. Jamaicans called pork that was cooked by being wrapped in leaves and buried in a pit with hot rocks "jerked pork." *Dictionary of Jamaican English*, F. G. Cassidy and R. B. Le Page, eds. (University of the West Indies, 2002), 245. Describes "jork puok" as pork that's cut in pieces, boiled in a pot with butter, herbs, spices and "country pepper." That might be a modern way of cooking that emulates cooking meats in a covered pit.
28. Moreton, *West India Customs*, 41.
29. Long, *History of Jamaica*, 866.
30. Walton, *Present State*, vol. 1, 120; An Association of Heads of Families and Men of Science, *The Household Encyclopædia*, vol. 1 (London, 1858), 152. Brawn is "the pickled flesh of the boar."
31. Stewart, *View of the Past*, 74; Stewart, *An Account of Jamaica*, 179.
32. Carey, *Maroon Story*, 70–71; Jessica B. Harris, "Caribbean Connection," in *Cornbread Nation 2: The United States of Barbecue*, Lolis Eric Elie, ed. (Chapel Hill: University of North Carolina Press, 2004), 16–18.
33. Fray Domingo de Santo Tomás, *Lexicon o Vocabulario de la lengua general del Peru* (By Francisco Fernandez de Cordoua, 1560), 99; A. O. Exquemelin, *The History of the Bucaniers of America . . . Written in several languages* (Boston: Benjamin B. Mussey & Co., 1853), 41–42. French planters started settling Tortuga in 1598. Those who couldn't succeed in farming turned to hunting or piracy.
34. Christaller, *Dictionary of the Asante*, 364; Farquharson, *African Lexis*, 309–10.

35. Brice, *Grand Gazetter*, 661.
36. Burney, *History of the Buccaneers*, 43.
37. Walton, et al., *Present State*, vol. 1, 120; Chapter 3, "Jean-Baptiste's Boucan."
38. William Ellis, *The Country Housewife's Family Companion* (London, 1750), 23. "Scald or burn off the Hair." Charles Carter, "A Hog Barbicued whole, and grill'd," in *The Compleat City and Country Cook* (London, 1736), 194; Claude d'Abbeville, *Histoire De La Mission Des Peres Capucins en l'Isle de Maragnan et terres* (Paris, 1614), 294. Claude ddAbbeville (d. 1632) was a French missionary who served in Brazil among the Tupinamba people at the beginning of the seventeenth century. In his *Histoire De La Mission Des Peres Capucins en l'Isle de Maragnan et terres* published in Paris in 1614, he recorded the gruesome details of how Tupinamba women buccaned the dead bodies of their enemies. Similar to how Maroons singed the hair off wild pig carcasses, the Tupinamba women put the dead bodies into a fire "until all of the hair is burned off" afterwhich they removed the entrails and buccaned the flesh. Zora Neale Hurston, "Cudjo's Own Story of the Last African Slaver," *The Journal of Negro History*, vol. 12, no. 4, Association for the Study of African American Life and History, Inc., 1927, 648–63. Made the claim, "Hogs are prepared by taking brown sage and burning off the hair, then washing the skin thoroughly."
39. Livingstone, *Last Journals*, vol. 1, 58.
40. Park and Rennell, *Travels in the Interior Districts*, vol. 2, x.
41. Hennepin, "Jean-Baptiste's Boucan."
42. Livingstone, *Last Journals*, vol. 2, 61; Dampier, *New Voyage*, vol. 1, 86.
43. Burton, *Lake Region*, vol. 2, 282.
44. Révoil and Heudebert, *Vers les grands lacs*, 248.
45. Livingstone, *The Last Journals*, 60.
46. Hall, "Account of the Gunnar Peak Camp," 35–36; Baker, *Nile Tributaries*, 551–52.
47. Kingsley, *Travels in West Africa*, 210.
48. Mohammad U. H. Joardder, Mahadi Hasan Masud, *Food Preservation in Developing Countries: Challenges and Solutions* (Cham, Switzerland: Springer, 2019), 83, 168.
49. Q. B. Olatunji Anthonio, "Notes on Some Important Livestock of West Africa," in *General Agriculture of West Africa* (London: Routledge, 2019), from section "6.5 Fish.".
50. O'Connell, Hawkes, and Jones, "Hadza Hunting," x; Pierre Grenand & François Grenand, "Le Boucanage de la Viande et du Poisson," in *La viande: un aliment, des symboles*, F. Aubaile, M. Bernard, P. Pasquet, eds. (Edisud, 2004), 69–83.
51. Ethnographic analogy is an anthropological technique based on the premise that two or more cultures that have some basic similarities, especially ecological and economic ones, may likely have other similarities in related areas of life. That supports the notion that people all over Africa shared similar food preservation techniques.
52. Christaller, *Dictionary of the Asante*, 364; Farquharson, *African Lexis,* 309–10.
53. Zora Neale Hurston, *Tell My Horse: Voodoo and Life in Haiti and Jamaica*, Henry Lewis Gates Jr., ed. (New York, 1990), 36.
54. Thomas, *Story of a West Indian*, 295.

55. Scott, *To Jamaica and Back*, 177. "Importations of American bacon have driven out of the market the "jerked hog" of the Maroon." Philip Henry Gosse and Richard Hill, *A Naturalist's Sojourn in Jamaica* (London, 1851), 397. "American bacon in the provision shops have driven out of the market the jerked hog of the Maroon."
56. "Tourism Development in Jamaica- A Synopsis," *jtbonline.org*, accessed March 28, 2020, www.jtbonline.org/tourism-in-jamaica/brief-history/.
57. Harris, *Island Barbecue*, 11.
58. "Eating Moves Outdoors with Spicy Barbecue a Favorite," *Richmond [VA] Times-Dispatch*, June 13, 1954.
59. Harris, *Island Barbecue*, 11.
60. DeWitt, *Hot & Spicy Caribbean*, 10. "The method has evolved, however, and the pork is no longer overcooked," meaning the pork is no longer cooked long enough to make pork jerky.
61. Senior, *Encyclopedia of Jamaican Heritage*, 254–56.
62. "The Barbecue at Sandy Point," (Fredericksburg, VA) *Free Lance Star*, January 5, 1901. There is an account of a barbecue in Westmoreland County, Virginia, where cooks barbecued a deboned ox carcass. However, that occurred in the year 1901, which is after the OSBP ended.
63. Gosse, *Naturalist's Sojourn*, 396. "Trafficking in jerked pork" and "a side of jerked hog, which he sold passing along, in measured slices, to ready customers, as an especial delicacy for the breakfast table."
64. Haynes, *Brunswick Stew*, 69.

CHAPTER 3: JEAN-BAPTISTE'S BOUCAN

1. Margry, *Exploration des affluents*, 107, 282, 286, 289, 295, 299, 371, 380. Many mentions of boucanage. Explorers buccaned meats during expeditions in order to preserve them.; La Chapelle, *Modern Cook*, vol. 2, 268. "Hog's Boucane," "When we come into Countries afar off [The New World], we kill some Hogs: the Legs are salted, the rest is cut into Slices, the length of one or two fingers; they let them lie in Salt two or three Days. Then they are laid upon a Fishplate, and afterwards smoak'd; they use them for Breakfast broil'd; they are served up with a Dash of Vinegar and Shalots."
2. Charles Bigarne, *Patois et Locutions Du Pays De Beaune* (Beaune, 1891), 33-34. Speculates that the word *boucan* originally referred to the loud noises made by workers in forges and foundries that used to be in Bouconville, France. William A. Read, *Louisiana Place Names of Indian Origin: A Collection of Words* (Tuscaloosa: University of Alabama Press, 2008), 98.
3. Le poulet boucané, histoire et origine de ce plat caribéen, vivelasoupe.com, December 14, 2018, accessed May 16, 2020, https://vivelasoupe.com/, April 8, 2014, accessed May 16, 2020, http://les-voyages-de-gridelle.over-blog.com/.
4. Thomas Walsh, "How to Cook without a Stove," *Maclean's*, July 9, 1955; Charles Boberg, *The English Language in Canada: Status, History and Comparative Analysis*, (New York: Cambridge University Press, 2010), 31–3, 112.
5. "Conservation de la viande," *wikiwand.com*, accessed February 1, 2020, http://www.wikiwand.com/fr/.

6. J. N. Brierley, *Trinidad: then and now* (Trinidad, 1912), 25–26; George Francis Dow, John Henry Edmonds, *The Pirates of the New England Coast, 1630-1730* (Salem, 1923), 11; Burney, *History of the Buccaneers of America*, 43–50.
7. P. Bach, "Les Origines De Saverne," in *Revue Catholique d'Alsace*, vol. 6 (Strasbourg, 1864), 375.
8. Grenand and Grenand, "Le Boucanage," 69–83; Mathieu, "Relaciones Del Taíno," 233–54.
9. de Laudonnière, *L'histoire notable,* 12. Laudonnière (1529–1574) was a French Huguenot explorer and the founder of the French colony of Fort Caroline in what is now Jacksonville, Florida. de Laudonnière, *History of the First Attempt,* 12.
10. de Laon, *Relation du voyage,* 157.
11. Roorda, Derby, and Gonzalez, eds., "Pirates, Governors, and Slaves," in *Dominican Republic Reader,* para. 2.
12. Anne-Gabriel Meusnier de Querlon, *Abrégé de l'histoire générale des voyages*, vol. 13 (Paris, 1820), 283–84. "Quique la Chasse du Boeuf sut leur principale occupation, ils se saisoient quelquefois un amusement de celle du Porc." Translated: "Although cattle hunting was their [buccaneers] main occupation, they occasionally hunted wild pigs for sport."
13. John Latimer, *Buccaneers of the Caribbean: How Piracy Forged an Empire* (Cambridge, 2009), 75.
14. Hickeringill, *Jamaica Viewed*, 51–52.
15. Ibid.
16. Coles, *English Dictionary.*
17. Alexander Oliver Exquemelin, *The Buccaneers of America*, William Swan Stallybrass, ed., (London, 1924 [1684]), 44.
18. Barbour, "Privateers and Pirates," 529–66; Stevens, *Buccaneers and Their Reign,* 185; Haring, *Buccaneers in the West Indies,* 269–272; James Burney, *History of the Buccaneers of America* (London, 1816), 375–82.
19. Du Tertre, *Histoire generale*, vol. 3, 141.
20. Anne-Gabriel Meusnier de Querlon, *Abrégé de l'histoire générale des voyages*, vol. 13 (Paris, 1820), 283–84.
21. Alexander O. Exquemelin, "Introduction," in *The Buccaneers of America*, trans. Alexis Brown, (London, 1972), para. 44. Argues that Exquemelin was born in Harfluer, France, but settled in Holland possibly because he was a Huguenot.
22. Exquemelin, *De Americaensche Zee-Roovers* (Amsterdam, 1678). Some scholars believe Exquemelin was French but settled in Holland after his buccaneering days.
23. Alexander Olivier Exquemelin, *De Americaensche zee-roovers*, (t'Amsterdam: Jan ten Hoorn, boekverkooper, 1931), 44; Clarence Henry Haring, *The Buccaneers in the West Indies in the XVII Century* (New York: E. P. Dutton and Company, 1910), 62, 68; A. O. Exquemelin, *The History of the Bucaniers of America . . . Written in several languages* (Boston: Benjamin B. Mussey & Co., 1853), 40–41.
24. Alexandre Olivier Exquemelin, *The Buccaneers of America*, Alexis Brown, trans. (New York, Dover Publications, 2000), 58–59.
25. Haring, *Buccaneers in the West Indies*, 281–82.

26. H. L. Sayler, "A Buccaneer History," *The Lamp*, September, 1903; Thornbury, *Monarchs of the Main*, vi.
27. Exquemelin, *Histoire des avanturiers*, 107.
28. Basil A. Reid, "Myth 7: The Island-Caribs Were Cannibals," in *Myths and Realities of Caribbean History* (Tuscaloosa, 2009), 88–99. The Island Caribs were a group of Indigenous people of who inhabited the Caribbean.
29. Robert Beverly, "Of Their Cookery and Food," in *History and Present State of Virginia* (London: printed for R. Parker, 1705), book 3, chap. 4, 12.
30. Pénicaut, "Relation de Pénicaut," 390.
31. William A. Read, *Louisiana Place Names of Indian Origin: A Collection of Words* (Tuscaloosa: University of Alabama Press, 2008), 98.
32. de Charlevoix, *Histoire de l'Isle*, 6.
33. William Dampier, *A New Voyage Round the World*, vol. 1 (London, 1699), 20.
34. Ibid., 86
35. Hennepin, Joliet, and Marquette, *New Discovery*, 342–43.
36. Dampier, *New Voyage Round the World*, vol. 3, 141.
37. Ayers, et al., *Voyages and adventures*, 22.
38. Dampier, *New Voyage Round the World*, vol. 3, 93.
39. Lionel Wafer, *A New Voyage and Description of the Isthmus of America* (London, 1699), 176.
40. Ibid., 105.
41. Ibid., 224.
42. Donnelly and Diehl, *Pirates of Virginia*, 39–41.
43. Jean Baptiste Labat, *Nouveau voyage aux isles de l'Amérique*, vol. 5 (Paris, 1722), 61–62.
44. "Les Colonies Fançaises," *L'Exposition de Paris*, 266; de La Cornillère, *La Martinique en 1842*, 124.
45. Toczyski, "Jean-Baptiste Labat," 61–69.
46. Fitz-Adam, *The World*, vol. 2, 281–86.
47. John Eaden, *Memoirs of Pere Labat*, 148.
48. Burney, *History of the Buccaneers*, 48.
49. Labat, *Nouveau voyage*, vol. 5, 130.
50. Brooke-Knight, *Captain's Story*, 722.
51. Jean Baptiste Labat, *Nouveau voyage aux isles de l'Amérique*, vol. 5 (Paris, 1722), 130.
52. Jean Baptiste Labat, *Nouveau voyage aux isles de l'Amerique*, vol. 4 (Paris, 1722), 214–23.
53. John Eaden, *Memoirs of Père Labat*, 52.
54. Toczyski, "Jean-Baptiste Labat," 61–69.
55. Jean Baptiste Labat, *Nouveau voyage aux isles de l'Amerique*, vol. 4 (Paris, 1722), 221.
56. Ibid., 542; Jean Baptiste Labat, *Nouveau voyage aux isles de l'Amérique*, vol. 6 (Paris, 1742), 489.
57. Littré, *Dictionnaire de la langue*, 2580.
58. Jean Baptiste Labat, *Nouveau voyage aux isles de l'Amerique*, vol. 4 (Paris, 1722), 214–23.
59. Two examples of the phrase in Labat's times occur in *Amsterdam: avec privilege de nos seigneurs, les états de Hollande et de West-Frise*, March 2, 1731, and October 30, 1731.

60. Reed and Reed, *Holy Smoke*, 27.
61. Esquemelin, *Buccaneers of America*, 216.
62. Reed and Reed, *Holy Smoke*, 27. "Labat observed that they used a mop of lemon juice, salt, [and] chile peppers."
63. Swift & Company, *Kitchen Encyclopedia,* 14. "Braising is a method much used in France, and is a cross between boiling and baking."
64. Jean Baptiste Labat, *Nouveau voyage aux isles de l'Amerique*, vol. 4 (Paris, 1722), 218.
65. Labat, *Nouveau voyage*, vol. 8 (Paris, 1742), 287.
66. Apicius, *Cooking and Dining in Imperial Rome*, 194 gutenberg.org, August 19, 2009, accessed November 15, 2020, https://www.gutenberg.org/ebooks/29728.
67. Bradley, *The Country Housewife*, 165–66.
68. Reed and Reed, *Holy Smoke*, 27. "Since lemon juice in quantity was hard to find in the Carolinas and Virginia, it was often replaced by vinegar, and—voila!"
69. Scora, "On the History," 369–75.
70. Robert May, The Accomplisht Cook (London, 1671), 37, 144.
71. Robina Napier, *A Noble Boke off Cookry*; Thomas Gloning et al., *Ouverture de Cuisine*; Gervase Markham, *The English Housewife*; John Nott, *The Cook's and Confectioner's Dictionary*; François Pierre de La Varenne, *The French Cook*; Martino de Rossi, *The Art of Cooking: The First Modern Cookery Book*; Redon, et al., *The Medieval Kitchen: Recipes from France and Italy*; *The Harleian Cookbook, 1450*.
72. Frances Sergeant Childs, *French refugee life in the United States, 1790-1800; an American chapter of the French revolution* (Baltimore, 1940), 33–35; Dubois, *Avengers of the New World,* 8–9.
73. *Nouvelle Biographie Générale*, vol. 24, 498; *Dictionaire Historique*, vol. 102, 546.
74. Moreau de Saint-Méry, "Norfolk, Portsmouth," in *The Virginia Magazine of History and Biography*, 48(3) (Richmond, 1940), 253–64.
75. Médéric Louis Elie Moreau de Saint-Méry, *Description topographique, physique, civile, politique et historique de la partie française de l'île Saint-Dominge*, vol. 3 (Paris, 1876), 443–44.
76. Kamen-Kaye, "Ichthyotoxic Plants," 71–90; "Mullein Leaf," mountainroseherbs.com, accessed October 24, 2020, https://mountainroseherbs.com/.
77. Price, *De la réhabilitation* 417; Felix, *Understanding Haitian Voodoo*, x.
78. *Haiti Sun*, February 28, 1960.
79. Paul, *Measuring Christian-Voodoo Syncretism,* 21.
80. Felix, *Understanding Haitian Voodoo*, 63.
81. Macaulay, *Haiti ou renseignemens,* 90–91.

CHAPTER 4: BEAUCHAMP'S BARBECADO

1. Martyr, *De Orbe Novo*, 124.
2. Staden, "How They Cook Their Food," in *Captivity of Hans Stade*, 132–33.
3. José Ignacio Roquete, *Nouveau dictionnaire portugais-français* (Paris, 1841), 812. Moquém is "a boucan; the grid used to smoke meat" (author's translation). Moqueár is a verb that means "to dry and smoke the meat on the moquém" (author's translation).

4. Nicolás del Castillo Mathieu, "Relaciones del Taíno con el Caribe Insular," *Thesaurus: Boletín del Instituto Caro y Cuervo*, May–August 1982, vol. 37, no. 2, 233–54.
5. Patrícia Merlo, "Repensando a tradição: a moqueca capixaba e a construção da identidade local," *Interseções*, June 2011, vol. 13, no. 1, 26–39; Nicolás Del Castillo Mathieu, "Relaciones Del Taíno Con El Caribe Insular (Relationships of the Taíno with the Insular Caribbean)," in *Thesaurus Boletín of Del instituto Caro Y Cuervo*, May–August 1982, 233–54.
6. Hakluyt, *Principal Navigations,* 519–20, 546. The archaic spelling of several words in the quotation have been modernized.
7. Jean de Léry, *Histoire d'un voyage faict en la terre du Brésil* (Geneve: Pour Antoine Chuppin, 1580), 219.
8. P. Morgan, Morgan Library & Museum, "Folios 108v–109r," in *Histoire Naturelle Des Indes: The Drake Manuscript in the Pierpont Morgan Library* (New York, 1996), 219. The original French caption is, "Les yndiens font ung grand feu et voiant que le bois est consomé en charbon prengnent quatre fourchettes de bois et les fichent en terre et mettent plusieurs batons de travers dessus lesdictes fourchettes de hauteur du feu d'un pied et demy appres ce estendent leur poisson et chair et quand il sent la challeur du feu la fumee de la graisse qui tombe dans le feu faict boucaner ou rotir ladicte chair et poisson et est ung bon menger et le tourne souvent de peur quil ne brusle et estant ladicte chair et poisson cuite et rotie a la coulleur de harenc sor."
9. Thomas Harriot, "XIIII, The Broiling of their Fish Over the Flame," in *A Briefe and True Report of the New Found Land of Virginia*, W. Harry Rylands, ed. (The Holbein Society, 1888). Quotation updated with modern spelling.
10. Réné Goulaine de Laudonnière, *History of the First Attempt of the French to Colonize the Newly Discovered Country of Florida*, Richard Hakluyt, trans (1869; originally published in 1565), 172, 174–75. "They carry, also, sometimes fish, which they cause to be dressed in the smoke." "They eat all their meat broiled on the coals, and dressed in the smoke, which, in their language, they call boucanet."
11. Cundall and Pietersz, "The Abbot of Jamaica to the King of Spain July 1611," in *Jamaica Under the Spaniards,* 34–35.
12. Smith, *Generall Historie*, vol. 1, 60.
13. Etymology of jerky (n.d.), *etymology.com*, accessed February 1, 2020, https://etymologeek.com/eng/; Skeat, *Notes on English*, 343. The digraph "qu" before the vowel "i" (as in "qui") in *charquini* is the Spanish way of indicating the sound "ki."
14. Neill, "Sir Edmund Plowden" in *The Pennsylvania Magazine of History and Biography*, 206–216; Penington, *Examination of Beauchamp Plantagenet's Description,* 163–67; Hall, "New York Commercial Tercentenary," 471.
15. Plantagenet, *Description of the Province of New Albion*, 25.
16. Hickeringill, *Jamaica Viewed,* 59.
17. Ibid., 65.
18. Michel Pag, "Boucaner La Viande Et Le Poisson Dans La Forêt – Guyane," *Parc Amazonien de Guyane*, accessed May 10, 2020, https://parc-amazonien.wmaker.tv/.

19. Jean de Léry, *Histoire d'un voyage faict en la terre du Brésil* (Geneve: Pour Antoine Chuppin, 1580), 219.
20. Pierre Grenand and François Grenand, "Le Boucanage de la Viande et du Poisson," in *La viande: un aliment, des symboles*, F. Aubaile, M. Bernard, P. Pasquet, eds. (Edisud, 2004), 69–83.
21. Catlin, *Illustrations of the Manners*, 124–25. "Their mode of curing and preserving the buffalo meat is somewhat curious."
22. Beverly, *History and Present,* book 3, chap. 4, 12; Randolph, "Historical Notes and Commentaries on Mary Randolph's *The Virginia House-wife*," in *The Virginia Housewife*, ed. Karen Hess, xxxviii.
23. Robert Beverley, *The History of Virginia: In Four Parts* (Richmond, 1855), 138. "They [Powhatans] accustom themselves to no set Meals, but eat night and day."
24. Rodway and Watt, *Chronological History,* 171.
25. Fitzpatrick, ed., *Writings of George Washington*, vol. 2, 270.
26. Bob Drury and Tom Clavin, *Valley Forge* (New York: Simon & Schuster Paperbacks, 2018), 86; *Pennsylvania Gazette*, October 15, 1760. Although Washington may have objected to jerked beef, in 1760 three hundred South Carolina soldiers were provisioned with "a large quantity of jerked beef."
27. Rappaport, "Seeds of War," in *Stability and Change in Revolutionary Pennsylvania: Banking, Politics, and Social Structure*, 175. "Agricola" was the penname of the Irish-born Pennsylvania statesman George Bryan.
28. Agricola, *Dunlap's Maryland Gazette*, January 27, 1778.
29. Catlin, *Illustrations of the Manners,* 124–25.
30. Ewers, *The Blackfeet,* 76. When hunting on the open plains, Native Americans used buffalo dung as fuel for fires.
31. Bryan, *Kentucky Housewife*, 91.
32. *New English Dictionary,* 665.
33. E. W. Mellor, "Jamaica: The Crown of Our West Indian Possessions," in *Journal of the Manchester Geographical Society*, vol. 22, Manchester, July–December 1906, 123.
34. R. J. Massey, "When Wild Animals Swarmed in Georgia," *The [Atlanta, GA] Sunny South*, July 19, 1902.
35. Clayton, "A Letter from the Rev. Mr. John Clayton," 328–36. Clayton, "Letter from the Rev. Mr. John Clayton . . . CE 1687," in *Philosophical Transactions of the Royal Society of London* (London, 1809), 328–36.
36. Beverly, *History and Present,* book 3, chap. 4, 12; Henry Norwood, *Voyage to Virginia* (Washington, DC: W.Q. Force, 1844), 38. In the mid-1600s, Colonel Norwood (1615–89) dined with a Powhatan chief in Virginia. Thinking he had to cook venison himself using what he guessed was the Powhatan way, he dropped a venison steak onto the coals of a fire. The chief laughed and showed him how to make a skewer that was thrust into the ground beside the fire on which he placed the steak.
37. Duncan, *Travels through Part*, vol. 1, 296–300.

38. Edmund Berkeley Jr., "Quoits, the Sport of Gentlemen," in *Virginia Cavalcade Magazine*, Summer, 1965.
39. Jerky and Food Safety, usda.gov, accessed December 4, 2021, https://www.fsis.usda.gov/food-safety/.

CHAPTER 5: RICHARD'S BARBYCU

1. Adriaan Berkel, *The Voyages of Adriaan Van Berkel to Guiana Amerindian-Dutch Relationships in 17th-Century Guyana*, Martijn Bel, et al., ed. (Havertown, 2014), 88–89, 103; Thurn, *Among the Indians,* 14, 47; Berkel, *Amerikaansche voyagien*, vol. 1, 47; G. W. van der Meiden, "Barbecue en barbakot," in *Onze Taal, Maandblad van het Genootschap Onze Taal,* Jaargang 73, januari, 2004, 12–13, 81.
2. William C. Spengemann, "John Smith's True Relation," in *A New World of Words: Redefining Early American Literature* (New Haven, CT: Yale University Press, 1994), 58–59.
3. Clayton, "A Letter from the Rev. Mr. John Clayton," 328–36; Duke of Richmond, "Part of a Letter from His Grace," 685; "Corona Turns out in Honor of Fourth," *Riverside [CA] Independent Enterprise*, July 5, 1919; "Eats and Votes," *Ironwood [MI] Daily Globe*, September 7, 1938; "Bank Employees Study Group is Organized Here," *The [Lumberton, NC] Robesonian*, September 12, 1947; "Barbecuted Bear and Beef for Cherokee," *Council Bluffs [IA] Nonpareil*, November 4, 1949.
4. M'Quin, *Bill of Fare*, 51.
5. John L. Boswell, *Supplement to the Courant*, vol. 21, no. 22, September 13, 1856, 173.
6. Worgul, *Grand Barbecue*, 4.
7. Pierre Grenand and François Grenand, "Le Boucanage de la Viande et du Poisson," in *La viande: un aliment, des ymbols*, F. Aubaile, M. Bernard, P. Pasquet, eds., (Edisud, 2004), 69–83.
8. Tylor, "Fire, Cooking, and Vessels," in *Researches into the Early History*, 261.
9. U. K. Singh, K. N. Sudarshan, *Language Education* (New Delhi, 2006), 128. "Only a few words, if any, are fully equivalent in meaning in any two languages."
10. J. d'W. M., *Diccionario Militar*, 109.
11. Ligon, *A True and Exact History,* 89.
12. Karen Hess, "Historical Notes on the Work and Its Author, Amelia Simmons, An American Orphan," in *American Cookery* (Bedford, 1996), x.
13. Patricia Penn Hilden, "Hunting North American Indians in Barbados," in *Issues in Caribbean Amerindian Studies*, vol. 6, no. 2, indigenouscaribbean.files.wordpress.com, Aug. 2004–Aug. 2005, 1–7, accessed October 19, 2019, https://indigenouscaribbean.files.wordpress.com/.
14. Arends, et al., ed., *Pidgins and Creoles*, 3.
15. Lewis, *Journal of a West-India Proprietor*, 395.
16. For boucan see Turnbull, *Narrative of the Revolt,* 65; *Illustrated London News*, March 28, 1857; Thurn, ed., *Timehri*, Issue 1, 277–78.
17. Andrew Warnes, *Savage Barbecue: Race, Culture, and the Invention of America's First Food* (Athens, 2008), 7; Plantagenet, *A Description of the Province,* 25.

18. Smith, *Capt. John Smith*, cxii.
19. John Brickell, *The Natural History of North-Carolina* (Raleigh, 1737), 340.
20. Bradbury, *Bradbury's Travels*, 280.
21. Shakespeare, *Works of William Shakespeare*, vol. 6, 381, 414. "A *carbonado* is a piece of meat cut crossways for broiling."
22. *Notes and Queries*, 6th series, vol. 10, 327.
23. Andrew Burnaby, *Travels Through the Middle Settlements in North America in the Years 1759 and 1760*, 3rd edition (London, 1798), 29.
24. Quoted in Burnaby *Travels Through the Middle Settlements in North America in the Years 1759 and 1760*, 29. "Mons. De Willd, in his French translation of these travels, makes the following observation upon the word, Barbacue. 'Cet amusement barbare consiste a souetter les porcs jusqu' a la mort, pour en ymbol la chair delicate. Je ne sache pas que les ymbolss même le pratiquent.'"
25. Andrew Burnaby, *Travels Through the Middle Settlements in North America in the Years 1759 and 1760*, 3rd edition (London, 1798), 29.
26. "Sun-Tavern, Fish-Street Hill," *[London] General Advertiser*, December 5, 1750.
27. Foote, *The Patron*, 6.
28. James Grainger, *The Sugar-Cane: A Poem: In Four Books* (London, 1766), 105.
29. Michael Adams, Chapter XVII, The Society-Islands," in *The New Royal Geographical Magazine; Or, A Modern, Complete, Authentic, and Copious System of Universal Geography, Etc.* (London, 1794), 116.
30. Singleton, *General Description*, 15.
31. Lawson, *New Voyage*, 36.
32. Lawrence Butler, "Letters from Lawrence Butler, of Westmoreland County, Virginia, to Mrs. Anna F. Cradock, Cumley House, near Harborough, Leicestershire, England," in *Virginia Magazine of History and Biography*, vol. 40, no. 3, July 1932, 259–67.
33. Weld, *Travels through the States*, 187.
34. Smith, *Life and Labors*, 194.
35. Bradbury, *Travels into the Interior*, 280.
36. Duncan, *Travels through part of the United States*, vol. 1, 296–300.
37. "Cooked in a pit" is a reference to how pigs were cooked in earth ovens in Jamaica. See Chapter 2, "Herbert's Patta."
38. *Reynolds Newspaper*, "Snake Terror," February 21, 1858.
39. John Marchant, *A New, Complete and Universal English Dictionary* (London, 1764); James Barclay, *A Complete and Universal English Dictionary* (London, 1774).
40. Webster, *Noah Webster's First Edition*; *The Century Dictionary* (New York, 1906). Defines *barbecue* as: "1. To cure by smoking or drying on a barbecue. 2. To dress and roast whole, as an ox or a hog, by splitting it to the backbone, and roasting it on a gridiron."
41. Deane, *Licensed Traders' Dictionary*, 11.
42. Price, ed., *New Hazell Annual*, 39; emphasis added.
43. Murray, ed., *New English Dictionary*, vol. 1, part 2, 665.

44. "Hundred Auto Loads of Correspondents Guests at Barbecue," *Washington Times*, November 21, 1921.
45. "How American Papers do the Conference," *Manchester Guardian*, December 13, 1921.
46. Frank Colby, "Rambling Along Words," *Omaha World-Herald*, March 4, 1951; Colby, "Take My Word for It," *Omaha World-Herald*, October 12, 1947.
47. G. W. van der Meiden, "Barbecue en barbakot," in *Onze Taal, Maandblad van het Genootschap Onze Taal*, Jaargang 73, januari, 2004, 12–13, 81.
48. Valentin Anders, "BARBECUE," Etimologias.dechile.net, accessed June 14, 2020, http://etimologias.dechile.net/.
49. Trumbull, "Words derived from Indian Languages," 30.
50. James A.H. Murray, ed., *A New English Dictionary on Historical Principles: Founded Mainly on the Materials Collected by the Philological Society*, vol. 1, part 2 (Oxford, 1888), 1148.
51. Pierre Grenand and François Grenand, "Le Boucanage de la Viande et du Poisson," in *La viande: un aliment, des ymbols*, F. Aubaile, M. Bernard, P. Pasquet, eds. (Edisud, 2004), 69–83.
52. *Western Star and Roma [Queensland, Australia] Advertiser*, April 30, 1887.
53. April Lee Hatfield, *Atlantic Virginia: Intercolonial Relations in the Seventeenth Century* (Philadelphia: University of Pennsylvania Press, 2004), 1–3, 87, 137–39.
54. For an example of the Jamaican use, see "Jamaican Hominy Porridge," in *Jamaican Cooking Made Easy*, vol. 1 (New York: iUniverse, 2008), 44.
55. Richard Ligon, *A True and Exact History of the Island of Barbadoes* (London, 1657), 29.
56. William Strachey, *A Dictionary of Powhatan* (Bristol: Evolution Publishing, 2005), 64, 67.
57. Joseph R. Haynes, *Brunswick Stew: A Virginia Tradition* (Charleston, SC: The History Press, 2017), 41–46.
58. *[Philadelphia, PA] Independent Gazetteer*, March 4, 1783. "We hear from the Eastern Shore of Maryland, that several Refugee barges have lately taken a number of bay craft, and barbecued (a common term for stripping them of their all) the people on board."
59. "Perpetual Youth," [*Philadelphia, PA*] *Atkinson's Casket 8*, August 1, 1833.
60. Stuart Berg Flexner, *Listening to America: An Illustrated History of Words and Phrases from Our Lively and Splendid Past* (New York: Simon and Schuster, 1982), 491.
61. Cab Calloway, "The Hepster's Dictionary," dancesafari.com, n.d., page 1, accessed November 14, 2021, https://dancesafari.com/.
62. Conlin, *American Past*, vol. 2, 421.
63. *The [Linn County, Oregon] State Rights Democrat*, December 2, 1892.
64. "The Barbecue," *Buffalo [NY] Daily Republic*, October 29, 1856; "The 'Bar B Q' of Yesterday," *Buffalo [NY] Daily Republic*, October 30, 1856.
65. *The Garland* [Utah] *Globe*, "The North Pole – How to Get There," January 30, 1909.
66. *Marion* [Ohio] *Star*, March 28, 1916.
67. An internet search on various versions of the word *barbecue* in 2020 yielded the following results: "BBQ" 29,000,000, "Bar-B-Q" 9,530,000," and Bar-B-Que" 9,250,000. "Annual Free Barbecue," *Sedalia [MO] Democrat*, July 27, 1934.
68. "Old Dominion Institution," *[New Orleans, LA] Times-Picayune*, June 16, 1876.

69. *Chicago Daily Tribune*, November 3, 1892.
70. *The [Leesburg, VA] Genius of Liberty*, vol. IX, August 30, 1825.
71. Pickering, *A Vocabulary, or, Collection of Words*, 46.
72. Caldwell, *Tour through Part of Virginia*, 30.
73. Hooker, *Diary of Edward Hooker*, 890.
74. Lynde, *Diaries of Benjamin Lynde*, 33, 138. Lynde Sr.'s entry is listed as 1732, but according to Lynde's son, the event took place in 1733.

CHAPTER 6: GEORGE'S BARBICUE

1. "Around Capitol Square," *Rocky Mount [NC] Telegram*, November 2, 1951.
2. Tyler, *Men of Mark*, vol. 4, 142.
3. Washington, *Diaries of George Washington*, vol. 1, 326, 291; Washington, *Diaries of George Washington*, vol. 2, 124.
4. *[Charleston, SC] City Gazette*, November 9, 1793.
5. "The Old Fashioned Barbecue in Virginia," *The Richmond Whig*, April 27, 1858.
6. "Ancient Fredericksburg is Rich in Historic Lore and Traditions," *Richmond [VA] Times-Dispatch*, January 9, 1921.
7. Desmond, *George Washington's Mother*, 25; *Exclusively Yours*, vol. 26, July 27, 1973, 13.
8. Boteler, *My Ride to the Barbecue*, 18.
9. "Mr. Kincaid's Address," *Baltimore [MD] Patriot*, August 6, 1829.
10. Hetzel, *Building of a Monument*, 8–9. Claims 5,000 people enjoyed the barbecue.
11. "Fredericksburg, May-10," *[Richmond, Virginia] Enquirer*, May 14, 1833. Claims 500 people enjoyed the barbecue.
12. "Fact and Legend about Famous Washington Trees," *Washington [DC] Times*, March 22, 1903; Clark and Olmsted, *Annual Report*, 14; Moore, *Picturesque Washington*, 82–83.
13. State Street Trust Company, "Roast Ox and the French Revolution," in *State Street*, 18–19.
14. *Boston Evening*, August 17, 1767.
15. Holyoke Family, "Diary of Mrs. Mary (Vial) Holyoke of Salem, 1760-1800," in *The Holyoke diaries, 1709-1856* (Salem, 1911), 50, 73.
16. *New-York Daily Tribune*, Aug. 14, 1856.
17. *Burlington Weekly Hawk-eye*, "A Democratic Barbecue and Fight," July 4, 1860.
18. *The Mauston Star*, "News-Condensed," August 8, 1860.
19. *New York Times*, "The Kentucky Ox," Sep. 11, 1860.
20. *St. Johnsbury Caledonian*, "Editorial Jottings of News," Sept. 21, 1860.
21. *New York Times*, "The Kentucky Ox," Sep. 11, 1860.
22. *New York Times*, "The Republican Barbecue," Oct. 20, 1876.
23. William S. Walsh, *Curiosities of Popular Customs and of Rites, Ceremonies, Observances, and Miscellaneous Antiquities* (Philadelphia, 1898), 95–97.
24. *The Times*, "Cooking in the South," October 13, 1895. As late as 1902 it was said that a "barbecue . . . is not often to be seen above the Mason and Dixon line." "Steers to be Roasted for Fair Visitors," *Saint Paul [MN] Globe*, August 31, 1902.

25. "Humors from the Canvass," *New York Times*, September 14, 1860.
26. Michael Pollan, *Cooked: A Natural History of Transformation* (New York, 2013), 46. "The practice of grilling whole hogs over wood fires came to the American South with the slaves, many of whom passed through the Caribbean, where they observed Indians cooking whole animals split and sprayed out on top of green branches."; Ashli Quesinberry Stokes, Wendy Atkins-Sayre, *Consuming Identity: The Role of Food in Redefining the South* (University Mississippi Press, 2016), 106. "Historians note that slaves, who had watched Caribbean Indians cooking over fire, brought the barbecue tradition to the region [North Carolina] in the 1800s."
27. Blaut, *Colonizer's Model,* 11–20.
28. Steward, Julian H. "Diffusion and Independent Invention: A Critique of Logic." *American Anthropologist* 31, no. 3, 1929: 491–95. http://www.jstor.org/stable/661268.
29. Bob Holmes, "The real first farmers: How agriculture was a global invention," newscientist.com, October 28, 2015, accessed February 20, 2022, https://www.newscientist.com/.
30. Writing in the early twentieth century of how Europeans and Native Americans "fraternized" in the 1600s, John Clark Ridpath stated, "The Indian cooks taught the English women how to prepare corn meal, and to make therefrom corn bread and mush." "Mush" is known today as grits. Ridpath, *New Complete History,* 1071.
31. Haynes, *Brunswick Stew,* 41–47.
32. Ferguson, *Uncommon Ground,* 54.
33. Jacobs, "Colonial Williamsburg embarks on two-year study of African American pottery," pilotonline.com, November 8, 2019, accessed December 1, 2019, https://www.pilotonline.com/virginiagazette/; Christopher T. Espenshade, "Colonoware," in *World of a Slave*, vol. 2, Martha B. Katz-Hyman, Kym S. Rice, eds. (Santa Barbara: Greenwood, 2011), 135–40.
34. Rogers, "Bulldogs," *Beef and Liberty*, 110–122; *The Political State of Great Britain*, vol. 42 (London, 1731), 563; North, *England's Boy King,* 56. Men competed to be "the first to take away a goose's head which was hanged alive on two crossed posts."
35. Lodge, *Short History,* 85–86; "Description of a Gander Pulling," *[Philadelphia, PA] General Advertiser*, June 13, 1793; "A Virginia 'Gander Pulling' is an Insult," *New London [CT] Daily Chronicle*, August 9, 1850; "Wild Scenes and Sports," *Philadelphia Inquirer*, August 20, 1847; "Gander pulling in Virginia is 'not approved of,'" *Alexandria [VA] Gazette*, August 2, 1873; "Gander Pulling as an Amusement at a State Fair," *[Washington, DC] Evening Star*, October 17, 1873; "Fancy Balls—Fauquier Springs and Tournament—'Gander Pulling,'"
36. Haynes, *Virginia Barbecue,* 109–11. *Richmond [VA] Whig,* August 29, 1845; Lucia Stanton, "Dinner Etiquette," Thomas Jefferson's Monticello, https://www.monticello.org/; Sobel, *World They Made,* 52–53; Lodge, *Short History,* 85–86.
37. Ayto, "Barbecue," in *Word Origins*; Mencken, "Beginnings of American," in *The American Language: An Inquiry into the Development of English in the United States*, 45–73.
38. Campbell, *Account of the Spanish settlements,* 252.
39. Robertson, *History of America, Volume 2*, 430.; Cohen, "Creolization and Cultural Globalization," in *Globalizations*, 369–384.
40. Chernow, Alexander Hamilton, 511.

41. Leslie Ross, Medieval Art: A Topical Dictionary (Westport, 1996), 92–94; Floyd-Wilson, "English Epicures," 131–61.
42. *Creole Subjects in the Colonial Americas: Empires, Texts, Identities*, edited by Ralph Bauer and José Antonio Mazzotti, (Chapel Hill: University of North Carolina Press, 2009), 1.
43. Jean Bodin, *The Six Bookes of a Commonweale*, ed. Richard Knolles (London, 1606), 566.
44. Nathanael Carpenter, *Geography Delineated Forth in Two Bookes, etc.* (Oxford, 1635), 276–77.
45. Prynne, *The Vnlovelinesse, of Lovelockes.*
46. Canup, "Cotton Mather," 20–34; Hodgen, *Early Anthropology,* 260; Stewart, *Creolization History, x*; Marvin, *Life and Times*, x.
47. Turner, "Significance of the Frontier in American History," in *The Frontier in American History*, 3–4.
48. Chaplin, "Creoles in British America," in *Creolization: History, Ethnography, Theory*, Charles Stewart, ed., 47.
49. Robert Baron, "Amalgams and Mosaics, Syncretisms and Reinterpreations: Reading Herskovits and Contemproary Creolists for Metaphors of Creolization," in *Creolization as Cultural Creativity*, Robert Baron, Ana C. Cara, eds. (Jackson: University Press of Mississippi, 2011), 250; Stewart, "Creolization, Hybridity," 48–55.
50. Haring, "Techniques of Creolization," 19–35.
51. Ferguson, *Uncommon Ground,* xliii.
52. Delle, *Colonial Caribbean*, 28–35.
53. Hall, "Creolité and the Process of Creolization," in *Creolizing Europe: Legacies and Transformations*, Encarnación Gutiérrez Rodríguez and Shirley Anne Tate, eds., 12–25.
54. William Hugh Grove, "The Travel Journal of William Hugh Grove (1732)," *Encyclopedia Virginia*, accessed May 10, 2020, https://www.encyclopediavirginia.org/Grove.
55. Robertson, *America: in which is included the posthumous volume*, vol. 4, 32.
56. Carole Shammas, "English-Born and Creole Elites in Turn-of-the-Century Virginia," in *Local Government in European Overseas Empires*, 1450–1800, vol. 23, part 2, edited by A. J. R. Russell-Wood (New York, 2018).
57. Bernard W. Sheehan, "Dependence," in *Savagism and Civility: Indians and Englishmen in Colonial Virginia* (New York: Cambridge University Press, 1980), 113; Allan Kulikoff, "This Newfound Land," in *From British Peasants to Colonial American Farmers* (Chapel Hill: University of North Carolina Press, 2000), 93.
58. Clayton, "Letter to Nehemiah Grew, 1687," in *Philosophical Transactions*, vol. 8 (London, 1809), 328.
59. Great Britain Public Record Office, *Calendar of State Papers, Colonial Series, America and West Indies, 15 May, 1696–31 October 1697*, vol. 15, J. W. Fortescue, ed. (London, 1904), 655.
60. Henretta, et. al., *America: A Concise History*, 91.
61. America and West Indies: December 1718, 22–31, in *Calendar of State Papers Colonial, America and West Indies: Volume 30, 1717–1718*, ed. Cecil Headlam (London, 1930), 424–46. British History Online, accessed 14 October 2020, http://www.british-history.ac.uk/. Spotswood wrote a letter to the Earl of Orkney on Dec. 22, 1718, in which he referred to Virginians as "base disloyalists and ungrateful Creolians."

62. Barbara W. Tuchman, "'Asserting a Right You Know You Cannot Exert': 1765," in *The March of Folly: From Troy to Vietnam* (New York, 2014), 168.
63. Beverly, "Preface," in *History and Present,* para. 3.
64. Alexis de Tocqueville, *Democracy in America*, vol. 1 (New York: G. Adlard, 1839), 442; Sacvan Bercovitch, *The Puritan Origins of the American Self* (New Haven: Yale University Press, 2011), 143; Sir Richard Baker, *A Chronicle of the Kings of England, etc*, second ed. (London: J. Flesher & E. Cotes, 1653), 618. "The first plantation of the *English* in the *Indies*, was that which is now called *Virginia*."
65. Bauer and Mazzotti, eds., *Creole Subjects,* 31.
66. Feb. 17, 1740/41. Byrd Letterbook, VI, 240, Virginia Historical Society; A. G. Roeber, Faithful Magistrates and Republican Lawyers (UNC Press Books, 2017); *Creole Subjects in the Colonial Americas: Empires, Texts, Identities*, Ralph Bauer and José Antonio Mazzotti, eds., (Chapel Hill, 2009), 39; Charles Knight, *The English Cyclopædia: A New Dictionary of Universal Knowledge*, Part 4, vol. 6 (London, 1858), 463–64. Contains a biography of Sir Charles Wager.
67. Parish, "William Byrd II," 355–74; Byrd, *Dividing Line,* 88.
68. Dayan, *Haiti, History,* 162.
69. Chaplin, "Creoles in British America," in *Creolization: History, Ethnography, Theory*, Charles Stewart, ed., 45–65.
70. Bauer, *Cultural Geography,* 183.
71. Martin, *History of North Carolina*, vol. 2, 211–12; Lossing, *Our Country*, 659–60.
72. Thompson, "'Invectives . . . against the Americans,'" 25–36.
73. *Gazetteer and New Daily Advertiser,* December 23, 1765. Contains a letter from "Vindex Patriae" claiming American colonists can't do without tea because "Indian corn" is not easily digested. In the January 2, 1766, edition of the newspaper, an American colonist replied, "If Indian corn were as disagreeable and indigestible as the Stamp Act, does he imagine we can get nothing else for breakfast?"
74. Otis, *Collected Political Writings,* 198.
75. Gordon S. Wood, *The Americanization of Benjamin Franklin* (New York, 2005), 114.
76. Tuchman, *March of Folly*, 169.
77. Hannings, *Chronology of the American Revolution*, 435–36; Draper, *King's Mountain,* 236, 282–93.
78. *Formal Report of the Battle of King's Mountain*, October 1780.
79. John Littlejohn, "The Friend, no. III," *New Haven Gazette*, April 6, 1786.
80. Jefferson, *Notes on the State of Virginia*, 57–73.
81. Chaplin, "Creoles in British America," in *Creolization: History, Ethnography, Theory*, Charles Stewart, ed., 46, 60.
82. Anderson, *Imagined Communities,* 60; *Creole Subjects in the Colonial Americas: Empires, Texts, Identities*, Ralph Bauer and José Antonio Mazzotti, eds. (Chapel Hill, 2009), 31–32; Benedict Anderson, *Imagined Communities: Reflections on the Origin and Spread of Nationalism* (New York, 2006), 60
83. "The Preservation of Food," *Farmer's Magazine*, March 1865.

84. John Smith, *The General Historie of Virginia, New England and The Summer Isles*, vol. 1 (Glasgow, 1907), 60.
85. Historic Jamestown, Jamestown Rediscovery, "Nutting Stone," historicjamestown.org, accessed March 3, 2019, https://historicjamestowne.org/.
86. Ibid.
87. Knight, *Unveiled–The Twenty and Odd*, 5–12.
88. M'Quin, *Bill of Fare*, 51.
89. Warnes, *Savage Barbecue*, 21. Referring to the theory that *barbecue* is derived from *de la barbe à la queue*, Warnes observes: "It suggests that these authorities would want to insist on the simple truth of the matter: that the word barbecue bore no relation to barbarism."
90. "Roast Beef for the Multitude: How a Big Ox was Killed at a Barbecue," *American Kitchen Magazine*, vol. 6, no. 1, October 1896; North, Stella, "A Day by the Sea-side," *Bennington* [Vermont] *Banner*, January 7, 1859.
91. Webster, *Private Correspondence of Daniel Webster*, 365.
92. Mouer, "Chesapeake Creoles," in *Archeology of 17th-Century Virginia*, edited by Theodore R. Reinhart and Dennis J. Pogue, 105–66. Refers to "Chesapeake Creoles" in the Tidewater region of seventeenth-century Virginia.
93. Hess, *Carolina Rice Kitchen*, 5.
94. Alanson Skinner, "Little-wolf Joins the Medicine Lodge," in *American Indian Life*, Elsie Clews Parsons, ed. (Lincoln: University of Nebraska Press, 1967), 64.
95. Charles De Wolf Brownell, *The Indian Races of North and South America* (Boston, 1853), 477.
96. Bruce, *Travels to Discover*, vol. 6, 254; Association of Military Surgeons of the United States, *Journal of the Association of Military Surgeons of the United States*, vol. 18, 380.
97. J. B. Wight, *Tobacco: Its Use and Abuse* (Nashville, 1889), 30; Hendricks, *Backcountry Towns*, 19, 53, 69, 83. "At the end of the colonial period, less than 5 percent of Virginia's population was urban."
98. Trumbull, "Words Derived from Indian Languages," 30–31.
99. Charles S. Sydnor, *Gentlemen Freeholders: Political Practices in Washington's Virginia* (Chapel Hill: University of North Carolina Press, 1952), 51.
100. Robert Munford, *A Collection of Plays and Poems, by the Late Col. Robert Munford, of Mecklenburg County, in the State of Virginia. Now First Published Together* (Petersburg, 1798), 13–51.
101. Breck and Scudder, *Recollections of Samuel Breck*, 269.
102. *Nicholas Spencer to Secretary of State Henry Coventry*, July 9, 1680, in "Virginia in 1680 (Continued)." *The Virginia Magazine of History and Biography*, vol. 25, no. 2, Virginia Historical Society, 1917, 139–48.
103. Rainbolt, "Absence of Towns," 343–60.
104. Hening, *Statutes at Large*, xxiii, xxxii, 8, 127, 402.
105. George Crabb, Feast, Banquet, Carousal, Entertainment, Treat in *English Synonyms: With Copious Illustrations and Explanations, Drawn from the Best Writers* (London, 1826), 656.
106. Hening, *Statutes at Large*, 402.
107. Lodge, *Short History*, 85–86.

108. Jennings C. Wise, *Ye Kingdome of Accawmacke or, The Eastern Shore of Virginia in the Seventeenth Century* (Richmond, 1911), 320
109. Ibid.; Annie Lash Jester, *Domestic Life in Virginia in the Seventeenth Century* (Williamsburg, 1957), 75–79; Philip Alexander Bruce, *Institutional History of Virginia in the Seventeenth Century* (New York, 1910), 26.
110. Lanman, "Virginia Barbecue," 94–97.
111. *[New York] Weekly Messenger*, June 2, 1825.
112. Hooker, *Diary of Edward Hooker*, 890.
113. Lee Haring, "Techniques of Creolization," in *Creolization as Cultural Creativity*, Robert Baron, Ana C. Cara, eds. (Jackson: University Press of Mississippi, 2011), 178–79.
114. James D. Rice, "Rethinking the 'American Paradox': Bacon's Rebellion, Indians, and the U.S. History Survey," in *Why You Can't Teach United States History without American Indians*, Susan Smith, Juliana Barr, Jean M. O'Brien, Nancy Shoemaker and Scott Manning Stevens, eds. (Chapel Hill: University of North Carolina Press, 2015), 51.
115. Arnold Johnson Lien, *Privileges and Immunities of Citizens of the United States* (New York: Columbia University, 1913), 243; Jack P. Greene, *Selling a New World: Two Colonial South Carolina Promotional Pamphlets* (Columbia: University of South Carolina Press, 1989), 43, 87. Newspapers in New England are known to have printed advertisements for the sale of enslaved Native American cooks. Examples include an "Indian woman who is a very good cook," "Indian woman . . . fit for all manner of household work," "[a] lusty Carolina Indian woman . . . fit for any daily service" and an "Indian woman and her child . . . is a good cook." A pamphlet written to lure colonists to South Carolina recommended that new plantation owners purchase "three Indian Women as Cooks for the Slaves."
116. *American Turf Register and Sporting Magazine*, "A Virginia Fish Fry," August 1833.
117. Martha W. McCartney, *A Study of the Africans and African Americans on Jamestown Island and at Green Spring, 1619-1803* (Williamsburg: National Park Service, 2003), 8–9, 54; Christian Pinnen, "Chesapeake Colonies," in *Encyclopedia of African American History*, vol. 1, Leslie M. Alexander, Walter C. Rucker, eds. (Santa Barbara: ABC-CLIO, 2010), 32–33.
118. Frederick Douglass, *The Life and Times of Frederick Douglass*, John Lobb, ed. (London: Christian Age Office, 1882), 32, 120.
119. Beverly, *The History and Present State of Virginia*, book IV, part 1, 36.
120. Westbury, Susan. "Slaves of Colonial Virginia: Where They Came From." *The William and Mary Quarterly*, vol. 42, no. 2, 1985, 228–37; Martha W. McCartney, *A Study of the Africans and African Americans on Jamestown Island and at Green Spring, 1619-1803* (Williamsburg: National Park Service, 2003), 83, 91–92, 121.
121. Linda Fields, "Early Bajan: Creole or Non-Creole?" in *The Early Stages of Creolization*, Jacques Arends, ed. (Amsterdam: John Benjamins Publishing, 1996), 89–90.

CHAPTER 7: JUBA'S 'CUE

1. Louis Hughes, *Thirty Years a Slave, from Bondage to Freedom* (Milwaukee, 1897), 48–49.
2. "A Country Barbecue," *[Milledgeville, GA] Federal Union*, August 8, 1865.

3. Duke, *Recollections*, vol. 4, 3–4; *[Harrisonburg, VA] Daily News*, "A Southern Barbecue," June 9, 1905; Sweet, *On a Mexican Mustang*, 437; Astrop, "A Virginia Barbecue," 128–29.
4. Haynes, *Brunswick Stew*, 129–130; *Augusta [GA] Chronicle*, "The Barbecue," July 2, 1840.
5. Pierson, *In the Brush*, 95.
6. *Fredericksburg [VA] Herald*, July 9, 1855. The people of Fredericksburg, Virginia, and the surrounding counties held a July 4 barbecue. So much food was served that it was reported to have required 12 cooks working two days to prepare it and 150 waiters to serve it.
7. Boteler, *My Ride*, 79.
8. Avirett, *The Old Plantation*, 175.
9. "An Old Virginia Barbecue," *Alexandria [VA] Gazette*, September 14, 1849.
10. "Fourth of July," *Thomas Jefferson Encyclopedia*.
11. *The [Charlottesville, VA] Enquirer*, July 26, 1808.
12. Todd County History Book Committee, *Todd County Kentucky*, 184.
13. "A Virginia Barbecue," *The [Richmond, VA] Times*, September 17, 1901.
14. "B. Garth, Oracle, Receives Reward," *Washington Times*, November 20, 1906.
15. "Great Field Day in Greene County," *Richmond [VA] Times-Dispatch*, September 21, 1905.
16. Duke, *Recollections*, vol. 4, 3.
17. Ibid.
18. "Mile-Long Trench Dug for Inauguration Barbecue," *Morning Tulsa Daily World*, December 28, 1922.
19. Miller, *Black Smoke*, 168. Miller was surprised to learn of the high temperatures employed by some modern pitmasters.
20. Wilbur G. Kurtz, Interview with Will Hill, March 27, 1938, by Wilbur G. Kurtz. Courtesy Wilbur G. Kurtz III.
21. Meathead Goldwyn, "Barbecue History."
22. Martha McCulloch Williams, "Threads of Fate," in *Worthington's Magazine*, vol. 3, no. 2, February 1894.
23. Williams, *Dishes & Beverages*, 273–275.
24. "Fortunate Farmers," *The [Raleigh, NC] News and Observer*, December 12, 1911.
25. "A Virginia Barbecue," *Huron [Norwalk, OH] Reflector*, July 2, 1839.
26. *Richmond [VA] Times-Dispatch*, "Great Field Day in Greene County," September 21, 1905; Kurtz, Interview with Will Hill.
27. Duke, *Recollections*, vol. 4, v.
28. "A Virginia Barbecue," *Jackson [MI] Citizen Patriot*, December 12, 1884.
29. "To Please the Palate," *Chicago Daily Tribune*, January 23, 1888; "A Virginia Barbecue," *Daily Astorian*, August 20, 1882.
30. "Barbecued Pig and Barbecued Chicken Characteristic Dishes from North Carolina; Always Aid to Appetite," *Virginian-Pilot and the Norfolk Landmark*, July 3, 1931.
31. *Dipney* may have come from the Old English *dyppan*, which means "to immerse or dip." Dip, *Online Etymology Dictionary*, etymonline.com, accessed October 23, 2021, https://www.etymonline.com/word/dip.
32. Hess, *Carolina Rice Kitchen*, 109.

33. *[Norwalk, OH] Huron Reflector*, July 2, 1839; "A Country Barbecue," *[Milledgeville, GA] Federal Union*, August 8, 1865; Boteler, *My Ride to the Barbecue*, 58.
34. Federal Writers' Project: Slave Narrative Project, vol. 14, South Carolina, part 3, Jackson-Quattlebaum.
35. Herring, *Saturday Night Sketches*, 227.
36. Helen C. Rountree, "Cooking in Early Virginia Indian Society." *Encyclopedia Virginia*, May 30, 2014, accessed June 14, 2014, https://encyclopediavirginia.org/entries/.
37. Mary Randolph, *The Virginia Housewife: Or, Methodical Cook*, stereotype edition (University of South Carolina Press, 1984 [1838]), 63; Lettice Bryan, *The Kentucky Housewife* (Bedford, Applewood Books, 2001 [1839]), 91.
38. Baynard Rush Hall, *The New Purchase, or Early Years in the Far West*, (New York: Jno. R. Nunemacher, 1855), 459–65.
39. Perdue, *Weevils in the Wheat*, 153; Bernhard, *Travels through North America*, 63; "Slave Exodus," *Texas State Gazette*, February 12, 1859; Fischer and Kelly, *Bound Away*, 229–230.
40. T. Hall, *The Queen's Royal Cookery* (London, 1713), 84–85. Contains an example of a sauce to be served with broiled pork made with butter, vinegar, salt, pepper, mustard, and sugar.
41. Hannah Woolley, *The Accomplish'd Lady's Delight* (London, 1686), 179. Offers a sauce recipe for broiled pork made with butter, vinegar, sugar, and mustard.
42. Barton, *The Paternity of Abraham Lincoln*, 342; "A Member," *An Authentic Historical Memoir*, 92; Randolph, *Virginia Housewife*, 51.
43. "An Old Time Southern Festivity that is Passing Away," *Wichita Daily Eagle*, June 29, 1894.
44. Martha McCulloch Williams, "Barbecued Lamb," *Dishes & Beverages of the Old South* (New York: 1913), 274.
45. James Edmonds Saunders, *Early Settlers of Alabama* (New Orleans: Genealogical Publishing Co., Inc.), 223.
46. Boteler, *My Ride to the Barbecue*, 59–60; emphasis added.
47. "An 'Old Virginia' Barbecue," *Alexandria [VA] Gazette*, September 14, 1849.
48. "Pig and Pone. An Edgecombe County Barbecue," *Lenoir [NC] Topic*, June 19, 1889.
49. "A Virginia Barbecue," *[Norwalk, OH] Huron Reflector*, July 2, 1839.
50. Ibid.
51. Sweet, *On a Mexican Mustang*, 438.
52. Norris, "Virginia Barbecues," *Forest & Stream*, vol. 5, Issue 9, October 7, 1875.
53. Duncan, *Travels through Part of the United States*, 296–300.
54. Material in this paragraph and the two that follow from Norris, "Virginia Barbecues," *Forest & Stream*, vol. 5, Issue 9, October 7, 1875.
55. Haynes, *Brunswick Stew*, 138.
56. R. T. W. Duke Jr., *Recollections*, vol. 3 (Albemarle, 1924), 159.
57. "The Political Barbecue," *[Roanoke, VA] Evening News*, September 11, 1905.
58. Haynes, *Brunswick Stew*, 88–89.
59. George Wythe Munford, *The Two Parsons; Cupid's Sports; The Dream; and the Jewels of Virginia* (Richmond, 1884), 157.

60. Munford, *Two Parsons,* 331.
61. Day, *Down South*, 139–40.
62. Munford, *Two Parsons,* 326 –341; "The Richmond 'Barbacue (or Quoit) Club,'" *American Turf Register and Sporting Magazine*, September 1, 1829; Mordecai, *Richmond in By-Gone Days*, 188–91; Duke, *Recollections*, vol. 3, 155-64, vol. 4, 1-2; Albert and Shirley Small Special Collections Library, 1924; Day, *Down South,* 139–40.
63. R. T. W. Duke Jr., *Recollections*, vol. 3, Albemarle, 1924, 156, small.library.virginia.edu, Albert and Shirley Small Special Collections Library. "[O]ld fashioned Virginia Barbecues were held there from 'time whereof the memory of man runneth not to the contrary.'"
64. "Monroe Ward Barbecue Club," *Richmond [VA] Dispatch*, September 8, 1866.
65. "The Barbecue Club," *Hopkinsville Kentuckian*, August 10, 1912.
66. "Barbecue Club has a Feast at the Park," *El Paso [TX] Herald*, January 29, 1913.
67. "Prescription for Good Humor -- Barbecued Steak," *Corpus Christi [TX] Caller-Times*, June 22, 1941; *Oregonian*, May 31, 1940, 13.
68. Arinori, "Life among the Farmers," 182.
69. "An Old Dominion Institution," *[New Orleans, LA] Times-Picayune*, June 16, 1876.
70. "Changes in Campaign Methods," *Frank Leslie's Illustrated Newspaper*, August 27, 1887.
71. "Great Success of the Republican Barbecue at the Highland House," *Cincinnati [OH] Daily Gazette*, September 15, 1879.
72. "Indiana Barbecues," *Pittsburg [PA] Press*, October 16, 1892.
73. *Staunton [VA] Spectator and Vindicator*, "Day of Barbecues," January 18, 1910.
74. "Barbecues of Early Days," *Union County [ST] Courier*, April 21, 1893.
75. "Indiana Barbecues," *Pittsburg [PA] Press*, October 16, 1892.
76. Ibid.
77. Arnold Fleischmann, "Urbanization in the South," in the *Oxford Handbook of Southern Politics*, Charles S. Bullock III, Mark J. Rozell, eds. (New York: Oxford University Press, 2012), 80–102.
78. Raymond A. Sokolov, "Introduction," in *Fading Feast: A Compendium of Disappearing American Regional Foods* (New York: Farrar Straus Giroux, 1981), 7.
79. J. D. B. De Bow, *De Bow's Review*, 29 (November 1860): 613–14.
80. *Richmond Dispatch*, "The Day We Celebrate," July 4, 1891.
81. Rupert B. Vance, "The Urban Breakthrough in The South," in *Virginia Quarterly Review 31*, no. 2, 1955: 223–32; Blaine A. Brownell, "Urbanization in the South: A Unique Experience?" *Mississippi Quarterly* 26, no. 2, 1973: 105–20.
82. Donald J. Bogue, "Urbanism in the United States, 1950," in *American Journal of Sociology* 60, no. 5, 1955: 471–86.
83. For an example of an antebellum pitmaster who sold barbecue made from hogs he raised, see Haynes, "Thomas Griffin," in *Virginia Barbecue,* 168–71; *Daily Dispatch*, "A Fine Stock of Hogs, Raised by Tom Griffin, at Auction," September 15, 1864.
84. Reduced labor cost is a selling point for modern barbecue cookers. See "About Southern Pride," southernpride.com, accessed October 2, 2021, https://www.southernpride.com/.

"Better barbecue using less labor" and "their newly constructed barbecue smoker saved manpower."

85. "How Barbecues are Done," *Newark [NJ] Daily Advertiser*, September 4, 1856.
86. "Roasting an Ox for a Democratic Barbecue—A Scene at Midnight," *Frank Leslie's Illustrated Newspaper*, October 18, 1884.
87. Edward Ward, *A frolick to Horn-fair with a walk from Cuckold's-point thro' Deptford and Greenwich,* handle.net, 2003, accessed January 4, 2020, Oxford Text Archive, 13, http://hdl.handle.net/.
88. *Receipt Book of Elizabeth Coates Paschall*, 86.
89. Barton, *Paternity of Abraham Lincoln*, 342.
90. "An Old Dominion Institution," [New Orleans, LA] *Times-Picayune*, June 16, 1876.
91. Jessup Whitehead, *The Steward's Handbook* (Chicago: John Anderson & Co., 1889), 163–65.
92. John Dixon Long, *Pictures of Slavery in Church and State*, (Philadelphia: Published by the author, 1857), 89.
93. "A Kentucky Burgoo," *San Francisco Bulletin*, December 13, 1884.
94. "Rare Power in Politics," *The Sun*, October 29, 1899.

CHAPTER 8: NED'S BARBACUE

1. Alexander Abad-Santos, "North Carolina Revolts Against Perry's Taste in Barbecue," *The Atlantic*, December 30, 2013, accessed December 19, 2020, https://theatlantic.com/.
2. A Society of Gentlemen, *Critical Review,* 244.
3. Frank Colby, "Rambling Along Words," *Omaha [NE] World-Herald*, March 4, 1951; Frank Colby, "Take My Word for It," *Omaha [NE] World-Herald*, October 12, 1947.
4. L. F. Newman, "Weights and Measures," in *Folklore*, vol. 65, No. ¾, Dec. 1954: 129–48. "Live animals were weighed in stones of 14 lb; but, once slaughtered, their carcasses were weighed in stones of 8 lb." "Meat Prices," Parliamentary Debates (Hansard), United Kingdom: House of Lords, March 1, 1938, col. 901–2. "The price per stone of 8 lb. of the following classes of meat at Smithfield market on 21st February of this year and the corresponding Monday in 1935."
5. Carter, *Compleat City,* 194. In the 16th century, Malmsey was a strong, sweet white wine imported from Greece and the eastern Mediterranean islands. Nowadays it is associated by most people with Madeira, Portugal.
6. *[Washington, DC] Evening Star,* "Jamaican Roast," November 4, 1956.
7. Raffald, *Experienced English House-keeper*, 99; Bradley, *Country Housewife,* 165; Lady Charlotte Campbell Bury, *Lady's Own Cookery Book,* 133.
8. Anonymous, *Accomplish'd Housewife,* 169; Carter, *Compleat City,* 198; "A New Dunciad of Insects," *The [London, England] Daily Post*, October 8, 1729.
9. Mason, *Lady's Assistant,* 181.
10. Smith, *Compleat Housewife,* 34; Glasse, *Art of cookery,* 67–68.
11. Phillips, *Ladies Handmaid,* 124; *Lady Charlotte Campbell Bury, Lady's Own Cookery Book,* 133. The "catchup" is a reference to walnut or mushroom ketchup.
12. Phillips, *Ladies Handmaid,* 411.

13. Elizabeth Raffald, *The Experienced English House-keeper* (London, 1769), 99; Eliza Smith, *The Compleat Housewife, Or, Accomplished Gentlewoman's Companion* (London, 1773), 34; Charlotte Mason, *The Lady's Assistant for Regulating and Supplying Her Table* (London, 1777), 181; John Farley, *The London Art of Cookery* (London, 1792), 127; Maximilian Hazlemore, *Domestic Economy; or a complete system of English housekeeping* (London, 1794), 95; Mary Eaton, "Roast Pork," in *The Cook and Housekeeper's Complete and Universal Dictionary* (Bungay, 1823), 319–20.
14. John Townshend, "To barbicue a Pig," *The Universal Cook; Or, Lady's Complete Assistant*, (London, 1773), 88. "[L]ay your pig down a good distance from a large brisk fire." Lady Charlotte Campbell Bury, *Lady's Own Cookery Book*, 133. In the "Pig, to barbicue" recipe it states, "if an oven can be depended upon, it will be equally good baked." Richard Bradley, "An Hog barbecued, or broil'd whole. From Vaux-Hall, Surrey," in *The Country Housewife* (London, 1732), 165–66, The recipe for "An hog barbecued, or broil'd whole" calls for braising the carcass.
15. Smith, *Compleat Housewife*, 23.
16. Markham and Best, *English Housewife*, 93.
17. Colman, *Random Records*, vol. 1, 192.
18. Jones, *Present State of Virginia*, 42.
19. Richard Bradley, "An Hog barbecued, or broil'd whole. From Vaux-Hall, Surrey," in *The Country Housewife* (London, 1732), 165–66; Charles Carter, *The Compleat City and Country Cook* (London, 1736), 194.
20. Jones, *Present State of Virginia*, 42.
21. Moss and Hoffman, *Backcountry Housewife*, 108.
22. *Evening Star [Washington, DC]* "Jamaican Roast," November 4, 1956.
23. Howard William Troyer, *Ned Ward of Grubstreet; a Study of Sub-literary London in the Eighteenth Century* (Cambridge, 1946), 3–9.
24. Troyer, *Ned Ward of Grubstreet*, 95.
25. Mather, *Manuductio ad ministerium*, 46.
26. Southern Living, "The Southern History of Barbecue," youtube.com, December 7, 2016, accessed October 12, 2019, https://youtube/; Alexander Lee, "The History of the Barbecue," historytoday.com, August 8, 2019, accessed April 4, 2020, https://www.historytoday.com/archive/.
27. Kay Dian Kriz, "Curiosities, Commodities, and Transplanted Bodies in Hans Sloane's 'Natural History of Jamaica,'" *William and Mary Quarterly* 57, no. 1 (2000): 35–78. See note 1 on page 35.
28. Evan Haefeli, "Toleration and Empire: The Origins of American Religious Pluralism," in *British North America in the Seventeenth and Eighteenth Centuries*, Stephen Foster, ed. (Oxford: Oxford University Press, 2013), 107; Jack P. Greene, "Alterity and the Production of Identity in the Early Modern British American Empire and the Early United States," in *Creating the British Atlantic* (Charlottesville: University of Virginia Press, 2013), para. 10.
29. Ward, *Trip to Jamaica*, 14.
30. John Taylor, *Jamaica in 1687 the Taylor Manuscript at the National Library of Jamaica*, David Buisseret, ed. (Kingston, 2010), 240.

31. Paul Scanlon, Adrian Roscoe, *The Common Touch: Popular Literature from 1660 to the Mid-Eighteenth Century*, vol. 2 (Newcastle upon Tyne, 2017), 81–85.
32. Ward, *London-spy,* 207.
33. Ibid, 212, 210.
34. Ibid, 216.
35. Robert Appelbaum, *Aguecheek's Beef, Belch's Hiccup, and Other Gastronomic Interjections* (Chicago: University of Chicago Press, 2008), 1–8. Ward was expressing a common belief of his time. "Beef is a good meat for an Englishman." "And how well it doth agree with the nature of Englishmen."
36. Grose and Egan, *Grose's Classical Dictionary*, n.p.
37. Grose, *Dictionary in the Vulgar Tongue*, n.p.
38. Defoe, *Tour Thro the Whole Island,* 130–31.
39. Edward Ward, *A frolick to Horn-fair with a walk from Cuckold's-point thro' Deptford and Greenwich* (London, 1707), accessed July 20, 2019, https://quod.lib.umich.edu/.
40. Ibid.
41. Executors of Mr. Boyer, *The Political State of Great Britain*, vol. 42 (London, 1731), 563; Rogers, *Beef and Liberty*, 110–22.
42. Markham, *English Housewife*, 93.
43. Reed and Auchmutey claim the story took place in Jamaica. However, the pamphlet mentions "Rotherhithe," "Bermondsey," and "Deptford," which are districts of South London, not Jamaica. It also mentions "the Sign of the Red Cow in the Town of Peckham." The Red Cow, according to Robert Wissett's *Letters to John Bowles,* 26, was a public house in Peckham, England.
44. Ward, *Barbacue Feast*. According to Gordon Williams's *Dictionary of Sexual Language and Imagery in Shakespearean and Stuart Literature*, "Castor and Pollux" is a reference to testicles (63), "Higgle de Pigglede" refers to a public display of sex (1235), "Wapping Fire-Ship" was a term used to refer to prostitutes in the Wapping area near London that was frequented by sailors (489). Edward Ward, "Forward," in *The London-spy: The Vanities and Vices of the Town Exposed to View*, Arthur L. Haywood, ed. (New York, 1927), ix–x. "Ward wrote exclusively for men, and for men who did not suffer from squeamishness."
45. Ward, *Barbacue Feast,* 3.
46. Ibid, 5, 9.
47. Ibid, 4; Ward, *A frolick to Horn-fair*, 13.
48. Ward, *Barbacue Feast,* 5.
49. Ibid, 7.
50. Ibid, 6.
51. Ibid, 8.
52. Ibid, 12.
53. Ibid, 9.
54. Ibid, 8.
55. Ibid, 11.

56. Ibid, 14.
57. Ibid, 19.
58. Grose and Egan, *Grose's Classical Dictionary*, n.p.
59. Ward, *Barbacue Feast,* 9, 17, 12.
60. Ibid, 17, 7.
61. Ibid, 10, 13; Haim Schwarzbaum, *Studies in Jewish and World Folklore* (Walter De Gruyter & Co.: Berlin, 1968), 177–79. A reference to the parable about people who are forced to try to eat with long spoons. The spoons can reach the food, but they are too long reach the holder's mouth. Stingy people in Hell with the Devil starve. Generous people in Heaven use the long-handled spoons to feed their neighbors.
62. Ibid, 16.
63. Ibid, 27.
64. Ward, *Barbacue Feast,* 20.
65. "Heathenish Coquination," Ibid, 11; "True Englishmen," Ward, *London-spy,* 207; "Creolians," Ward, *A frolick to Horn-fair*, 13.
66. *The Cambridge Companion to Alexander Pope*, Pat Rogers, ed. (Cambridge: Cambridge University Press, 2007), i.
67. Samuel Johnson, "Pope," in *The Lives of the Most Eminent English Poets*, vol. 3 (London, 1821), 54–219; Jonathon Green, "The Sound of the City: No City. No Slang," in *The Vulgar Tongue: Green's History of Slang* (New York, Oxford University Press, 2015), 114–16.
68. Alexander Pope, *The Dunciad: An Heroic Poem. In Three Books*, vol. 2 (Dublin, printed, London, reprinted for A. Dodd, 1728), 37.
69. Alexander Pope, "The Second Satire of the Second Book of Horace," in *The Works of Alexander Pope*, vol. 3, William John Courthope, ed. (London: John Murry, 1881), 127.
70. James Boswell, *The Life of Samuel Johnson, LL.D: Including A Journal of His Tour to the Hebrides*, vol. 5 (Harper & Brothers, 1831), 438.
71. Johnson, "Preface," *Dictionary of the English Language* (1773), 6.
72. Alexander Pope, *The Works of Alexander Pope, Esq. with His Last Corrections, Additions, and Improvements; Together with All His Notes*, vol. 2 (London: Printed for W. Cavil, 1795), 127; Alexander Pope, *Imitations of Horace*, John Butt, ed. (London: Methuen & Co., 1939), 55.
73. Smith, *Slavery, Family and Gentry*, 203. "Frances March Jr managed Richard Oldfield's estate in Jamaica between 1736 and 1739." William Wing, "Bowles Pedigree," in *Notes and Queries, Fifth Series, Volume Seventh, January—June 1877* (London: Oxford University Press, 1877), 373. The May 12, 1877, edition states, "The tradition of the neighborhood [North Aston, England] is that two Oldfields became rich by enterprises in Jamaica."
74. Alexander Pope, *The Dunciad: An Heroic Poem. In Three Books*, vol. 2 (Dublin, printed, London, reprinted for A. Dodd, 1728), 11.
75. Timbs, *Clubs and Club Life,* 111–27; Wheatley, *London, Past and Present*, 149–52.
76. See Chapter 6, "George's Barbicue," for examples of British slurs against American colonials.
77. Gauci, *William Beckford,* 25, 54, 175; "Beckford, William (1709–1770)," in *Dictionary of National Biography*, Sidney Lee, ed., vol. 1 (New York, 1903), 80.

78. *Gentleman's Magazine,* vol. 32, 327.
79. "Dialog of the Living," *The North Briton,* November 13, 1762.
80. Gauci, *William Beckford,* 111.

CHAPTER 9: SAM'S BARBECUE

1. Stephen Smith, "A Southern Rite and Ritual," in *Cornbread Nation 2: The United States of Barbecue,* Lolis Eric Elie, ed. (Chapel Hill: University of North Carolina Press, 2004), 65; Kathleen Purvis, "Endangered Species: North Carolina Barbecue," gardenandgun.com, April 10, 2019, accessed April 14, 2019, https://gardenandgun.com/articles/. "The media has created this persona of a pit master, standing in a smoky haze with the sun at his back in the door of the cookhouse, with smut on his face and dirty pants. And if I'm that guy, I'm not running my business."
2. Egerton, *Southern Food,* 151; *Personal Correspondence,* there are reports of officials in Virginia's Shenandoah Valley who have vowed to put an end to open pit barbecuing in that region.
3. Jean Newton, "The Barbecue," *Flint [MI] Daily Journal,* August 12, 1922.
4. "Electric World," *Pittsburg Dispatch,* October 26, 1890.
5. *Times [Port Huron, MI] Herald,* August 7, 1915.
6. "Five Thousand Fed at Once at Electric Barbecue," *Bismarck [ND] Tribune,* February 9, 1924.
7. "Thousands Present to Participate in the Big Barbecue on Hudson," *The Ogden [UT] Standard,* September 9, 1916.
8. *Richmond Medical Journal,* March 1868, vol. 5, no. 1, 193–94.
9. "Armour & Co. Ship Barbecue Meat," *Retail Grocery Advocate,* vol. 24, no. 26, June 27, 1919.
10. *Bryan Daily Eagle and Pilot,* "Big Emancipation Celebration," June 19, 1909.
11. "Autoists Enjoy Run to Malibu," *Los Angeles Herald,* April 24, 1910; Morales, *Brick People,* 50; "Restoring El Rancho," *San Francisco Call,* August 8, 1909; "History of Pio Pico's 'El Ranchito,'" Pio Pico State Historic Park, 2012. 56. "Restoring El Rancho," *San Francisco Call,* August 8, 1909.
12. Charles Fellows, *Fellows' Menu Maker* (Chicago: The Hotel Monthly Press, 1910), 52. "Broiled Tenderloin Steak, Barbecue Gravy."
13. *Ada [OK] Evening News,* July 9, 1918.
14. Jane Eddington, "The Barbecue Gravies," *Seattle Daily Times,* May 16, 1927.
15. Mary Randolph, *The Virginia Housewife: Or, Methodical Cook,* stereotype edition (Baltimore: Plaskitt & Cugle, 1828), 51–52.
16. *New York Times,* October 24, 1915.
17. *The Rotarian,* vol. VII, no. 4, "What the Clubs are Doing," October, 1915; *Greensboro Daily News,* "Weeks Social Events in North Carolina," August 15, 1915.
18. *The Public Ledger,* "Movies of Barbecue," October 22, 1915.
19. *Richmond [VA] Times Dispatch,* "May Forbid Barbecues," March 6, 1917.
20. *El Paso [TX] Herald,* "Says Barbecues Wasteful," July 2, 1918.
21. *The Maui News,* "Goats Figure in Food Problem in Arizona," March 1, 1918.
22. *The Cornell Daily Sun,* "Production of Meat in U. S. Breaks Record," May 1, 1919.

23. R. T. W. Duke Jr., *Recollections*, Vol. 4, Albemarle, 1924, small.library.virginia.edu, Albert and Shirley Small Special Collections Library, accessed July 12, 2020, https://small.library.virginia.edu/collections/.
24. *The Indian Journal* [Eufaula, Oklahoma], "Making Ready for Walton Barbecue," January 4, 1923.
25. *Arizona Republic* [Phoenix], October 3, 1929.
26. *Times-Picayune* [New Orleans], October 1, 1927.
27. Speight, *Chemistry and Technology*, 531.
28. *Sunset's Barbecue Book*, George A. Sanderson and Virginia Rich, eds. (San Francisco: Lane Publishing Co., 1938). From the Foreword "*Sunset's Barbecue Book* is planned to help every barbecue enthusiast, whether he's a died-in-the-wool veteran or a neophyte."; For examples of 1930s barbecue sauce recipes, see *Boston [MA] Herald*, March 10, 1931, and Emma Speed Sampson, "Barbecue Sauce," *Richmond [VA] Times-Dispatch*, May 20, 1935; For stove-cooked barbecue, see *Boston [MA] Herald*, September 14, 1934, and Ann Kingsley, "Cookery News Notes," *Daily [Springfield] Illinois State Journal*, January 20, 1936; For the charcoal grill advertisement, see *Bradford [PA] Evening Star and The Bradford Daily Record*, July 8, 1935.
29. "Backyard Barbecue," *[San Diego, CA] Evening Tribune*, September 17, 1919; "Barbecue Sandwich Shops Spring Up like Mushrooms; Cooked Meats Serve Picnics," *[San Diego, CA] Evening Tribune*, July, 20, 1928; "Backyard Barbecue Solves War's Entertainment Problem," *The Odessa [TX] American*, June 16, 1942; "The Once Over," *The [Harrisburg, PA] Evening News*, June 20, 1942; "Charcoal Shortage to Hit Barbecues," *The San Bernardino County [CA]*, March 1, 1943; "Barbecue Aids Long on Color, variety and Uniquity," *The [Portland] Oregonian* July 20, 1945.
30. Spievak, *Barbecue Chef*, 1.
31. Robb Walsh, *Legends of Texas Barbecue Cookbook: Recipes and Recollections from the Pit Bosses* (San Francisco, 2002), 33–34, 96; Elizabeth S. D. Engelhardt, "Introduction," *Republic of Barbecue Stories beyond the Brisket* (Austin, 2009), xx; Derrick Riches, "Lift a Beer to the Inventors of Texas Barbecue," thespruceeats.com, January 6, 2020, accessed February 23, 2020, http://thespruceeats.com/.
32. Nick Zukin and Michael Zusman, *The Artisan Jewish Deli at Home* (Kansas City, 2013).
33. *The Oasis*, "Special Christmas Dinner," December 24, 1904.
34. Huntington Baker, *Popular Science Monthly*, "A Garden Barbecue," June 1918.
35. *Houston Post*, February 17, 1929.
36. *Houston Chronicle*, June 15, 1934, 19.
37. *Beaumont [TX] Journal*, "Here's One Robbery Where Loot is Lost," August 21, 1939.
38. *The Kansas City Times*, November 22, 1930, 2.
39. *Tulsa World*, August 30, 1941, 2.
40. "Backyard Barbecue," *Food: Fact or Fiction*, S04E26, Food Network, June 3, 2019.
41. "Il Barbecue: La Bellezza Del Gusto," dibaio.com, September 11, 2018, accessed December 30, 2020, http://www.dibaio.com/.
42. Daniel Vaughn, "Big City Barbecue," texasmonthly.com, December 6, 2016, accessed July 19, 2020, https://www.texasmonthly.com/bbq/.

43. Eliza Mackintosh, "The Brits Do Barbecue." roadsandkingdoms.com, June 4, 2018, accessed February 16, 2020, http://roadsandkingdoms.com/; "Barbecue, a U.S. Tradition with German Roots, Germanfoods.org, May 1, 2020, accessed June 8, 2020, https://germanfoods.org/; Barbara Woolsey, "The Next Big Hotspot for American Barbecue Isn't Even in America," tastingtable.com, August 10, 2017, accessed July 25, 2020, http://tastingtable.com/dine/national/.
44. Mauro F. Guillen, "Keeping Up with the Singhs and the Wangs," in *2030: How Today's Biggest Trends Will Collide and Reshape the Future of Everything* (New York: St. Martin's Press, 2020), para. 4–6; Shrabonti Bagchi and Anshul Dhamija, "License to Grill: India Takes to the Barbecue," indiatimes.com, November 19, 2011, accessed October 2, 2021, https://timesofindia.indiatimes.com/india/.
45. Robb Walsh, "7 Dirty Truths About BBQ (That Nobody Wants to Talk About)," *First We Feast*, June 1, 2018, accessed August 22, 2020, http://firstwefeast.com/eat/.
46. Daniel Gillespie, "Majority of Americans agree the best memories with family come from being around the grill," swnsdigital.com, August 26, 2021, accessed September 18, 2021, https://swnsdigital.com/2021/.
47. "The Barbecue," *The [Greenwood, SC] Index-Journal*, July 1, 1923.

SELECTED BIBLIOGRAPHY

Accomplished Housewife. *The Accomplish'd Housewife; Or, The Gentlewoman's Companion*. London: Printed for J. Newbery, 1745.

Albala, Ken. *Food: A Culinary History Course Guidebook.* Chantilly: The Great Courses, 2013.

Anderson, Benedict. *Imagined Communities: Reflections on the Origin and Spread of Nationalism.* New York: Verso, 2006.

Anderson, Charles Loftus Grant. *Life and Letters of Vasco Núñez de Balboa.* New York: Fleming H. Revell Company, 1941.

———. *Old Panama and Castilla Del Oro.* Boston: The Page Company, 1914.

Apicius. *Cooking and Dining in Imperial Rome.* Chicago: W.M. Hill, 1936.

Aubaile, F., M. Bernard, and P. Pasquet, eds. *La viande: un aliment, des énéral.* Aix-en-Provence: Edisud, 2005.

Auchmutey, Jim. *Smoke Lore: A Short History of Barbecue in America.* Athens: University of Georgia Press, 2019.

Ayto, John. *Word Origins: The Hidden Histories of English Words from A to Z.* London: A & C Black Publishers, 2005.

Bailey, Nathan. *Dictionarium Domesticum, Being a New and Compleat Household Dictionary.* London: C. Hitch, 1736.

Baker, Mona. *In Other Words: A Coursebook on Translation.* 3rd ed. London and New York: Routledge, 2018.

Banerjee-Dube, Ishita, ed. *Cooking Cultures: Convergent Histories of Food and Feeling.* Delhi: Cambridge University Press, 2016.

Baron, Robert, and Ana C. Cara, eds. *Creolization as Cultural Creativity.* Jackson: University Press of Mississippi, 2011.

Bauer, Ralph. *The Cultural Geography of Colonial American Literatures.* Cambridge: Cambridge University Press, 2003.

Bauer, Ralph, and José Antonio Mazzotti, eds. *Creole Subjects in the Colonial Americas: Empires, Texts, Identities.* Chapel Hill: University of North Carolina Press, 2009.

Beverley, Robert. *The History of Virginia: In Four Parts.* Richmond, VA: J. W. Randlolph, 1855.

Blaut, J. M. *The Colonizer's Model of the World: Geographical Diffusionism and Eurocentric History.* New York: Guilford Press, 1993.

Boteler, Alexander R. *My Ride to the Barbecue, or, Revolutionary Reminiscences of the Old Dominion.* New York: S. A. Rollo, 1860.

Bourne, Edward Gaylord. *Narratives of the career of Hernando de Soto in the conquest of Florida as told by a knight of Elvas, and in a relation by Luys Hernandez de Biedm.* New York: Allerton Book Co., 1904.

Bradley, Richard. *The Country Housewife and Lady's Director.* London: 1732.

Breckand, Samuel, and Elisha Horace Scudder. *Recollections of Samuel Breck with Passages from His Notebooks (1771–1862).* Philadelphia: Porter & Contes, 1877.

Bryan, Lettice. *The Kentucky Housewife.* Bedford, MA: Applewood Books, 2001 (1839).

Buel, James William. *Heroes of Unknown Seas and Savage Lands.* Philadelphia: Historical Publishing Co., 1891.

Burnaby, Andrew. *Travels Through the Middle Settlements in North America in the Years 1759 and 1760.* 3rd ed. London: Printed for T. Payne, 1798.

Burney, James. *History of the Buccaneers of America.* London: Printed by L. Hansard & Sons, for Payne and Foss, 1816.

Bury, Lady Charlotte Campbell. *The Lady's Own Cookery Book, and New Dinner-table Director.* London: Published for Henry Colburn, 1844.

Bustamante, Aaron Grageda, Zarina Estrada Fernández, and Andrés Acosta Félix, eds. *Artes, vocabularios, doctrinas y confesionarios en lenguas de México.* Hermosillio, Mexico: Universidad de Sonora, 2013.

Carey, Bev. *The Maroon Story.* St. Andrew: Agouti Press, 2012.

Carter, Charles. *The Compleat City and Country Cook.* London: Printed for A. Bettesworth & C. Hitch, 1736.

Cassidy, Federic G., and R. B. Le Page, eds. *Dictionary of Jamaican English.* Kingston, Jamaica: University of the West Indies Press, 2002.

Casteau, Lancelot de. *Ouverture de Cuisine.* Liege: 1604.

"Changes in Campaign Methods." *Frank Leslie's Illustrated Newspaper,* August 27, 1887.

Charlevoix, Pierre-François-Xavier de. *Histoire de l'Isle espagnole ou de S. Domingue.* Paris: Chez Jacques Guerin, Libraire-Imprimeur, Quay des Augultins, 1730.

Chernow, Ron. *Alexander Hamilton.* New York: Penguin, 2004.

Clinton, Catherine. *The Plantation Mistress: Woman's World in the Old South.* New York: Pantheon Books: 1982.

Cruxent, José María, and Kathleen A. Deagan. *Columbus's Outpost Among the Taínos.* New Haven: Yale University Press, 2002.

D'Abbeville, Claude. *Histoire De La Mission Des Peres Capucins en l'Isle de Maragnan et terres.* Paris: 1614.

Davis, Theodore R. *Harper's Weekly,* November 10, 1866.

Deagan, Kathleen. *Puerto Rico: The Archeology of a Sixteenth-Century Spanish Town in Hispaniola.* Gainesville: University Press of Florida, 1995.

Delle, James A. *The Colonial Caribbean: Landscapes of Power in Jamaica's Plantation System.* New York: Cambridge University Press, 2014.

DeWitt, Dave. *Hot & Spicy Caribbean.* Rocklin, CA: Prima Lifestyles, 1996.

Donnelly, Mark P., and Daniel Diehl. *Pirates of Virginia: Plunder and High Adventure on the Old Dominion Coastline.* Mechanicsburg, PA: Stackpole Books, 2012.

Doyle, Don Harrison. *Faulkner's County: The Historical Roots of Yoknapatawpha.* Chapel Hill: University of North Carolina Press, 2001.

Du Tertre, Jean Baptiste. *Histoire générale des isles de Christophe, de la Guadeloupe, et le Martinique et autre.* Paris: 1654.

Duke, R. T. W., Jr. *Recollections.* Albemarle, NC: 1924.

Duncan, John M. *Travels through Part of the United States and Canada in 1818 and 1819.* Vol. I. New York: W.B. Gilley, 1823.

Dworkin, Steven N. *A History of the Spanish Lexicon: A Linguistic Perspective.* Oxford: Oxford University Press, 2012.

Editorial Club de la Prensa. *Anglicismos en El Idioma Español de Madrid.* San Juan: Editorial Club de la Prensa, 1968.

Eells, Elsie Spicer. *South America's Story.* New York: Dodd, Mead & Company, 1935.

Egerton, John. *Southern Food: At Home, on the Road, in History.* Chapel Hill: University of North Carolina Press, 1993.

Elvas, Gentleman of. *The Discovery and Conquest of Terra Florida by Don Ferdinando De Soto and Six Hundred Spaniards His Followers.* Translated by Dr. Richard Hakluyt. Edited by William B. Rye. London: Hakluyt Society, 1851 (1611).

Engelhardt, Elizabeth S. D., *Republic of Barbecue: Stories beyond the Brisket.* Austin: University of Texas Press, 2009.

Esquemeling, John. *The Buccaneers of America.* London: George Allen & Company, LTD., 1684; 1911.

Exquemelin, Alexander Oliver. *Histoire des avanturiers qui se sont signalez dans les Indes.* Paris: 1686.

———. *De Americaensche Zee-Roovers.* Amsterdam: 1678.

Farley, John. *The London Art of Cookery.* London: Printed for J. Scatcherd and J. Whitaker, 1792.

Felix Jr., Emmanuel. *Understanding Haitian Voodoo.* Maitland, FL: Xulon Press, 2009.

Ferguson, Leland. *Uncommon Ground: Archaeology and Early African America, 1650–1800.* Washington, DC: Smithsonian Institution, 1992.

Fischer, David Hackett. *Historians Fallacies: Toward a Logic of Historical Thought.* New York: Harper & Row, 1970.

Fischer, David Hackett, and James C. Kelly. *Bound Away: Virginia and the Westward Movement.* Charlottesville: University of Virginia Press, 2000.

Fisher, M. F. K. *The Art of Eating.* Hoboken, NJ: Houghton Mifflin Harcourt, 2004.

Fitzpatrick, John C., ed. *The Writings of George Washington from the Original Manuscript Sources, 1745–1799.* Vol. II, 1757–69. Washington, DC: US Government Printing Office, 1944.

Gauci, Perry. *William Beckford: First Prime Minister of the London Empire.* New Haven, CT: Yale University Press, 2013.

Glasse, Hannah. *The art of cookery, made plain and easy, by a lady.* London: Printed for W. Strahan et al., 1784.

Goodrich, Charles A. *The Universal Traveller.* Hartford, CT: Robins & Smith, 1845.

Gordy, Wilbur Fisk. *Stories of American History.* New York: C. Scribner's Sons, 1917.

Görlach, Manfred, ed. *A Dictionary of European Anglicisms: A Usage Dictionary of Anglicisms in Sixteen European Languages.* Oxford: Oxford University Press, 2001.

Green, Jonathon. *The Vulgar Tongue: Green's History of Slang.* Oxford: Oxford University Press, 2014.

Hakluyt, Richard. *The Principal Navigations, Voyages, Traffiques & Discoveries of the English Nation.* Glasgow: J. MacLehose and Sons, 1904 (1589).

Hannings, Bud. *Chronology of the American Revolution.* Jefferson, NC: McFarland, 2014.

Harris, Dunstan A. *Island Barbecue: Spirited Recipes from the Caribbean.* San Francisco: Chronicle, 1995.

Harrison, Sarah. *The House-keeper's Pocket-book: And Compleat Family Cook.* London: Printed for R. Ware, 1739.

Hartley, L. P. *The Go-Between.* London: Hamish Hamilton, 1953.

Haynes, Joseph R. *Brunswick Stew: A Virginia Tradition.* Charleston, SC: History Press, 2017.

———. *Virginia Barbecue: A History.* Charleston, SC: History Press, 2016.

Hazlemore, Maximilian. *Domestic Economy; or a complete system of English housekeeping.* London: J. Creswick, and Company, 1794.

Henretta, James A., et al. *America: A Concise History.* Vol. I: To 1877. Boston: Bedford/St. Martin's, 2012.

Hess, Karen. *The Carolina Rice Kitchen: The African Connection.* Columbia: University of South Carolina Press, 1992.

High, Lake E. *A History of South Carolina Barbecue.* Charleston, SC: Arcadia Publishing, 2013.

Hilden, Patricia Penn. "Hunting North American Indians in Barbados." *Issues in Caribbean Amerindian Studies* VI, no. 2 (August 2004–August 2005).

Hill, A. P. *Mrs. Hill's Southern Practical Cookery and Receipt Book,* edited by Damon Lee Fowler. Columbia: University of South Carolina Press, 1995.

Hirbec, P., F. Hannequart, and J. Taillardat. *Histoire et Traditions Forestières.* No. 28. Paris: Les Dossiers Forestiers, l'Office national des forêts, 2015.

Hodgen, Margaret T. *Early Anthropology in the Sixteenth and Seventeenth Centuries.* Philadelphia: University of Pennsylvania Press, 1964.

Hughes, Louis. *Thirty Years a Slave, from Bondage to Freedom.* Milwaukee, WI: South Side Printing Co., 1897.

James, George Wharton. *The 1910 Trip of the H.M.M.B.A. to California and the Pacific Coast.* San Francisco: Press of Bolte & Braden Co., 1911.

Jester, Annie Lash. *Domestic Life in Virginia in the Seventeenth Century.* Williamsburg: Virginia 350th Anniversary Celebration Corporation, 1957.

Johnson, Samuel. *A Dictionary of the English Language.* London: W. Strahan, 1733; 1755.

Knight, K. I. *Unveiled–The Twenty and Odd: Documenting the First Africans in England's America, 1619–1625 and Beyond.* Clermont, FL: First Freedom Publishing, 2019.

Kulikoff, Alan. "The Origins of Afro-American Society in Tidewater Maryland and Virginia, 1700 to 1790." *The William and Mary Quarterly* 35, no. 2 (1978): 226–59.

La Varenne, François Pierre de. *The French Cook.* 3rd ed. Translated by J. D. G. London: 1673.

Labat, Jean Baptiste. *Nouveau voyage aux iles de l'Amerique.* Paris: 1742.

Labat, Père. *The Memoirs of Pere Labat, 1693–1705.* Translated by John Eaden. New York: Routledge, 2013.

Lanman, Charles. *Haw-ho-noo: Or, Records of a Tourist.* Philadelphia: 1850.

———, ed. *The Japanese in America.* Boston: University Publishing Company, 1872.

Laon, Jean de. *Relation du voyage des François fait av cap de Nord en Amériqve.* Paris: Pierre David, 1654.

Laudonnière, Réné Goulaine de. *History of the First Attempt of the French to Colonize the Newly Discovered Country of Florida.* Translated by Richard Hakluyt. Madison: Wisconsin Historical Society, 2003 (1869).

Lawson, John. *A New Voyage to Carolina.* London: 1709.

Léry, Jean de. *Histoire d'un voyage faict en la terre du Brésil.* Geneve: Antoine Chuppin, 1580.

———. *History of a Voyage to the Land of Brazil.* Translated by Janet Whatley. Berkeley: University of California Press, 1993.

Ligon, Richard. *A True and Exact History of the Island of Barbadoes.* London: Printed for Humphrey Moseley, 1657.

Littré, Emile. *Dictionnaire de la langue française.* Paris: Librairie De L. Hachette, 1863.

Lossing, Benson John. *Our Country: A Household History for All Readers.* New York: Johnson, Wilson & Co., 1877.

Maison Rustique Du Xix' Siècle. Encyclopedie d'Agriculture pratique. Paris: 1839.

Mancall, Peter C., ed. *The Atlantic World and Virginia, 1550–1624.* Chapel Hill: University of North Carolina Press, 2018.

Markham, Gervase. *The English Housewife.* Reprint ed. edited by Michael R. Best. Montreal: McGill-Queens University Press, 2003 (1615).

Mason, Charlotte. *The Lady's Assistant for Regulating and Supplying Her Table.* London: Printed for J. Walter, 1777.

Mather, Cotton. *Manuductio ad ministerium.* Boston: 1726.

May, Robert. *The Accomplisht Cook.* London: 1685.

McLaverty, James. *Pope, Print, and Meaning.* Oxford: Oxford University Press, 2001.

Mintz, Sidney W. *Tasting Food, Tasting Freedom: Excursions into Eating, Culture, and the Past.* Boston: Beacon Press, 1996.

Moss, Kay, and Kathryn Hoffman. *The Backcountry Housewife.* Gastonia, NC: Schiele Museum, 2001.

Moss, Robert F. *Barbecue: The History of an American Institution.* Tuscaloosa: University of Alabama Press, 2010.

M'Quin, Ange Denis. *Bill of Fare.* London: Sherwood, Neely, and Jones, 1820.

Munné, Juan Clemente Zamora. *Indigenismos en la Lengua de los Conquistadores.* Puerto Rico: Editorial Universitaria, Universidad de Puerto Rico, 1976.

Nelson, Scott Reynolds, Sheriff, Carol. *A People at War: Civilians and Soldiers in America's Civil War.* 1854–77. New York: Oxford University Press, 2007.

Nott, John. *The Cook's and Confectioner's Dictionary*. London: Printed for C. Rivington, 1723.

Otis, James. *Collected Political Writings of James Otis*, edited by Richard A. Samuelson. Indianapolis: Liberty Fund, 2015.

Penna, Ana Lucia Barretto, et al. *Fermented Foods of Latin America.* Boca Raton, FL: CRC Press, 2017.

Perdue, Charles. *Weevils in the Wheat: Interviews with Virginia Ex-slaves.* Charlottesville: University of Virginia Press, 1992.

Phillips (of Duke Street), Sarah. *The Ladies Handmaid: Or, a Compleat System of Cookery.* London: 1758.

Plantagenet, Beauchamp. *A Description of the Province of New Albion.* London: 1648.

Pope, Alexander. *The Complete Poetical Works*, edited by Henry W. Boynton. Boston and New York: Houghton, Mifflin & Co., 1903.

Price, Hannibal. *De la réhabilitation de la race noire par la République d'Haïti.* Port-au-Prince: J. Verrollot, 1900.

Quackenbos, George Payn. *Elementary History of the United States.* New York: D. Appleton and Company, 1870.

Raffald, Elizabeth. *The Experienced English House-keeper*. London: Printed for J. Harrop, 1769.

Raichlen, Steven. *BBQ USA: 425 Fiery Recipes from all Across America.* New York: Workman, 2003.

———. *Planet Barbecue!* New York: Workman, 2010.

Randolph, Mary. *The Virginia Housewife: Or, Methodical Cook*. Stereotype edition. Columbia: University of South Carolina Press, 1984 (1838).

Redon, Odile, et al. *The Medieval Kitchen: Recipes from France and Italy*. Chicago: University of Chicago Press, 1998.

Reed, John Shelton. *On Barbecue*. Knoxville: University of Tennessee Press, 2021.

Reed, John Shelton, and Dale Volberg Reed. *Holy Smoke: The Big Book of North Carolina Barbecue.* Chapel Hill: University of North Carolina Press, 2008.

Reinhart, Theodore R., and Dennis J. Pogue, eds. *The Archeology of 17th-Century Virginia.* Richmond: Archeological Society of Virginia, 1993.

Rogers, Pat, ed. *The Cambridge Companion to Alexander Pope.* Cambridge: Cambridge University Press, 2007.

Roorda, E. P., L. H. Derby, and R. González. *The Dominican Republic Reader: History, Culture, Politics.* Durham, NC: Duke University Press, 2014.

Rossi, Martino de. *The Art of Cooking: The First Modern Cookery Book*, edited by Luigi Ballerini. Los Angeles: University of California Press, 2005.

Rountree, Helen C. *The Powhatan Indians of Virginia: Their Traditional Culture.* Norman: University of Oklahoma Press, 1989.

Russell, William Clark. *William Dampier.* 1889.

Saint-Méry, Médéric Louis Elie Moreau de. *Description topographique, physique, civile, politique et historique de la partie française de l'île Saint-Domingue.* Paris: L. Guérin, 1876.

Scanlon, Paul, and Adrian Roscoe. *The Common Touch: Popular Literature from 1660 to the Mid-Eighteenth Century*. Newcastle upon Tyne: Cambridge Scholars Publishing, 2017.

Schmidel, Ulrich. *Vierte Schiffart: Warhafftige Historien einer wunderbare Schiffart, die Ulrich Schmidel von Straubing, von Anno 1534. biss Anno 1554 in Americam oder Newenwelt, bey Brasilia und Rio della Plata gethan*. 1612.

Scott, Sir James Sibbald David. *To Jamaica and Back*. London: Chapman and Hall, 1876.

Senior, Olive. *Encyclopedia of Jamaican Heritage*. St. Andrew, Jamaica: Twin Guinep Publishers, 2003.

Simmons, Amelia. *The First American Cookbook: A Facsimile of "American Cookery," 1796*. New York: Dover, 1984.

Sloane, Hans. *A Voyage to the Islands Madera, Barbados, Nieves, S. Christophers and Jamaica with the Natural History*. Vol. I. London: B. M., 1707.

Smith, Eliza. *The Compleat Housewife, Or, Accomplished Gentlewoman's Companion*. London: Printed for R. Ware, et al., 1750; 1773.

Smith, John. *The Generall Historie of Virginia, New England and the Summer Isles*. Glasgow: J. MacLehose and Sons, 1907.

Smith, S. D. *Slavery, Family and Gentry Capitalism in the British Atlantic*. New York: Cambridge University Press, 2006.

Smith, Susan, Juliana Barr, Jean M. O'Brien, Nancy Shoemaker, and Scott Manning Stevens, eds. *Why You Can't Teach United States History without American Indians*. Chapel Hill: University of North Carolina Press, 2015.

A Society of Gentlemen. *Critical Review: or Annals of Literature*. Vol. XXXI. London: A. Hamilton, 1771.

Spievak, Louis A. *Barbecue Chef*. Los Angeles: Spievak Corporation, 1950.

Staden, Hans. *Among the Wild Tribes of Eastern Brazil*. Translated by Albert Tootal. Annotated by Ricard F. Burton. London: Hakluyt Society, 1874.

———. *Warhaftige Historia und beschreibung eyner Landtschafft der Wilden Nacketen, Grimmigen Menschfresser-Leuthen in der Newenwelt America gelegen*. Marburg, Germany: 1557.

Stewart, Charles, ed. *Creolization History, Ethnography, Theory*. New York: Routledge, 2016.

Strother, David Hunter. *Virginia Illustrated: Containing a Visit to the Virginian Canaan, and the Adventures of Porte Crayon and His Cousins*. New York: Harper & Brothers, 1857.

Sydnor, Charles S. *Gentlemen Freeholders: Political Practices in Washington's Virginia*. Chapel Hill: University of North Carolina Press, 1952.

Taylor, John. *Jamaica in 1687: the Taylor Manuscript at the National Library of Jamaica*, edited by David Buisseret. Kingston, Jamaica: University of West Indies Press, 2010.

Thomas, Herbert T. *The Story of a West Indian Policeman*. Kingston, Jamaica: Gleaner Company, 1927.

Troyer, Howard William. *Ned Ward of Grubstreet; a Study of Sub-literary London in the Eighteenth Century*. Cambridge, MA: Harvard University Press, 1946.

Turner, Frederick Jackson. *The Frontier in American History*. New York: Henry Holt and Company, 1920.

Vega, Garcilaso de la. *La Florida del Inca*. Vol. I. Madrid: 1723.

Walsh, Robb. *Legends of Texas Barbecue Cookbook: Recipes and Recollections from the Pit Bosses*. San Francisco: Chronicle, 2002.

Ward, Edward. *The Barbacue Feast: or, The Three Pigs of Peckham, Broil'd Under an Apple-Tree*. London: 1707.

———. *A Frolick to Horn-fair with a Walk from Cuckold's-point thro' Deptford and Greenwich*. London: 1700.

———. *The London-spy: The Vanities and Vices of the Town Exposed to View*, edited by Arthur L. Haywood. New York: 1927.

———. *A Trip to Jamaica: with a True Character of the People and Island*. London: 1698.

———. *A Trip to New England. With a Character of the Country and People*. London: 1699.

Warnes, Andrew. *Savage Barbecue: Race, Culture, and the Invention of America's First Food*. Athens: University of Georgia Press, 2008.

Wheatley, Henry Benjamin. *London, Past and Present*. London: John Murray, 1891.

Whitehead, Jessup. *The Steward's Handbook*. Chicago: J. Anderson & Company, 1889.

Williams, Gordon. *A Dictionary of Sexual Language and Imagery in Shakespearean and Stuart Literature*. London: The Athlone Press, 2001.

Williams, Martha McCulloch. *Dishes & Beverages of the Old South*. New York: McBride, Nast & Company, 1913.

Wilmer, Lambert A. *The Life, Travels, Adventures of Ferdinand De Soto, Discoverer of the Mississippi*. Philadelphia: J.T. Lloyd, 1858.

Winship, George Parker. *The Coronado Expedition, 1540–1542*. Washington, DC: U.S. Government Printing Office, 1896.

Worgul, Doug. *The Grand Barbecue: A Celebration of the History, Places, Personalities and Technique of Kansas City Barbecue*. Kansas City, MO: Kansas City Star Books, 2001.

INDEX

Adams, John, 90, 142
ajoupa, 85
Allen, Charles W., 153
Anderson, Charles Loftus Grant, 17
Apicius, 88
Arawak, 28, 32, 77, 113
arepas, 139
aribelet, 37
Arinori, Mori, 195
asada, 37, 40
asado, 37, 39
Asador, 38, 40
Asbury, Francis, 120
Astrop, Robert Francis, 169
Auchmutey, Jim, 9
Australia, 43, 243
Avirett, James Battle, 170
Aztec, 18, 28, 34

baalbak-kaab, 42
backyard barbecue, 13–14, 65, 195, 236–37, 243; tainted, 236
Baker, Samuel W., 61
baking, 14
balbacoas, 31
Balboa, Vasco Núñez de, 34
Baldwin, Evelyn Briggs, 127
Ballentine, Lynton Yates, 130
banquets, 157
Bar B Q, hieroglyphics, 125
barbacans, 18
barbacoa, 25; definition, American, 31–32; anglicism, 39; bed, 32; burial, 31, 33; corncrib, 31; tap dancing, 34; 114; first appearance in English literature, 30; flat slabs, 55; grill or trivet, 29; loan word, 28; food preservation, 31, 35; definition, Spanish 32, 38; versatile structure, 31, 33; used to hide treasure, 34–35; wicker work, 42; World War II, 39, 123
barbacot, 96, 100, 113, 115; flat slabs, 116
barbacra. *See* typographical errors
barbacue, 117
Barbacue Feast, The, 214–20
barbacuing, 78
Barbadoes, 114. *See also* Barbados
Barbados, 114–15; enslaved people, 114, 124, 139, 219
Barbakude, 80
barbaque, 53
barbaro. *See* typographical errors
barbecado, 100–1, 110
barbecu, 80

barbecue, 121; astronauts, 227; the great barbecue, 125; bed, 80; California, 13, 195, 232, 239; Canada, 71; big city, 241; competition, 233; cousins, 113; Dominican Republic, 38; etymology, 112–15; social event, 12, 116, 121, 128, 166, 241; food preservation, 11, 28, 31, 60, 81, 94, 96, 99, 102–5, 205; gravy, 232–33; homogenization, 243; hurdle, 22, 29, 37, 53, 60, 62, 80, 100, 104, 108, 120, 151–52, 190; Indiana, 196; imitation, 201; first iron cooker, 198–99; intangibles, 243; Jamaica, 50, 57; Kansas City, burnt ends, 243; Latin American, 37–41; law, 140; Maroon fashion, 57; Native American, 99, 102–3, 151; New England, 126–27; New York, 126, 133–36; earth oven, 12, 50, 116; party of pleasure, 117; covered pits, 13–14, 176, 200; unified process, 102; sauce, 235, 240; scaffold, 37, 61, 124; flat slabs, 50; smoked, 13, 237–40, 239, 240; South Carolina origin theory, 45–46; central Texas, 14, 16, 237, 240, 243; vending machines, 7; Virginian word, 123–24; wicker work, 42, 57. *See also* Hubbard barbecuing method

Barbecue Bob, 235. *See also* Robert Hicks

barbecue hash, 187, 191

Barbecue History Body of Knowledge, 10

barbecue stews, 191–93

barbecue trees, 134–35

barbecued: dried pig, 105; elephant, 17; pike, 206; robbed, 124–25

barbecuriosity, 125–26

barbecute, 113

barbecuting, 62, 108

barbecutt, 113

barbequot, 112

barbicans. *See* barbacans

Barbicu, 45, 119

barbicue, 103, 118

barbicued, hog, 207–8; kid, 206; earth oven, 56; torture, 103

barbique, 120

bar-b-que, 125

barbracot, 112

barbucoa. *See* typographical errors

barbycu, 114, 124

barbygu'd, 19

barbykew, 125

barrabakoa, 32

BBQ, 125

beard to tail, 113. *See also* de la barbe à la queue

Beard, Caroline Maddocks, 232

Beckford of Somerley, William, 54, 144

Beckford, William, 224

berbeek, 122

berbekot, 78, 103, 113, 123

Beverly, Robert, 78, 103, 108, 116, 146, 163

BHBOK. *See* Barbecue History Body of Knowledge

Biedma, Luys Hernández de, 30

Black, Van, 122–23

bocans, 116

Bodin, Jean, 143

Borbecu's, 60, 80

Boston, 132–36

Boteler, Alexander R., 132, 187

boucan: definition, 20, 70–71; etymology, 72, 77; hut, 59; noise, 71; food preservation, 95, 97–98; food storage, 72, 97; wooden grill, 70

boucan de cochon, 84–85, 89

boucanage, 71; creole, 71, 150

boucané, 112

boucanées, 72

boucanent, 61

boucaner, 61, 112

boucanière, 72

Boucanniers, 72

boucquane, 97

boukannen, 20

boulan, 76

Bourne, Edward Gaylord, 27, 31

brabakoto, 123
braise, 87, 206, 209, 238
Brazil, 112, 114–15
bread hoe, 124
Brethren of the Coast, 73
Brickell, John, 116
Brinton, Daniel, 32
brisket, 105, 237–40
British barbecue, 42, 116, 119, 205–6; influence on American barbecue, 209; a barbecue, 117–18, 121, 206; beef gravy, 207, 209; chian [cayenne], 119; definition, 38, 121, 128, 225; English barbecue, 119, 234, 243; enslaved cooks, 160–63, 169–70; short lived, 13; Madeira wine, 118, 205, 207; earth oven, 57, 116–17; roasted, braised, or baked, 206; compared to Southern barbecue, 206; stuffed with spice, 221; Virginian shoats, 208; West Indies, 56, 121
Brunswick stew, 66, 169–70, 175, 178, 191–92; name of social events, 234
Bryan, George, 104
Bryan, Lettice, 105
bucaneros, 72
buccan, 42; buccaning process, 97; Native American, 97
buccaneer: used as a verb, 19
buccaneers, 50, 59, 77, 83, 113; creolization, 144; faded away, 74; how they were named, 18, 113
buckaneers, 73, 83
burgoo, 191
Burgoo King, 191
Burnaby, Andrew, 117, 120, 222
Burney, James, 18
Burton, Richard, 60
Butler, Lawrence, 120
Byrd, William, II, 146

caban, 51, 53
Caldwell, John Edwards, 128
Canada, 71–72, 91, 138
carbonado, 87, 101, 117
Caribbean Origins Theory, 7, 91; assumptions, 9, 49, 90, 204, 215; origin, 210, 220; summary, 8
Caribbe Indians, 18. *See also* Caribs; Charby Indians
Caribs, 19, 101. *See also* Caribbe Indians; Charby Indians
Carpenter, Nathanael, 143
Catlin, George, 104
Charby Indians, 102. *See also* Caribs; Caribbe Indians
Charlevoix, Pierre François Xavier de, 77
charquear, 35. *See also* charquini
charqui, 36; defined, 37; etymology, 35. *See also* jerky
charquini, 35, 99, 105. *See also* jerkin; jug beef
chasseurs, 83, 86. *See also* hog hunters
Chisapeek Bay, 81. *See also* Chesapeake Bay
Chesapeake Bay, 44, 81, 101, 116, 124
Chilton, Edward, 145
churrasco, 20, 40
cimarron, 49
citrus, 9, 59, 66, 86–89
Clayton, John, 62, 108, 145, 157
cochon boucanné, 54, 83–85
cold smoking, 15, 237; called barbecuing, 105
Coles, Elisha, 74
Colman the Younger, George, 207
colonoware, 139–40, 162
Columbus, Christopher, 7–8, 28
commercialization, 197, 231, 235
Cook, James, 42, 119
cookout, 9, 14, 16, 236
Coronado, Francisco Vázquez de, 31
Cortez, Hernando, 34
COT. *See* Caribbean Origins Theory
Cotton, John, 142
country feast, 85. *See also* festin champestre
cow killers, 59, 70, 72, 76–77, 83
Creole, 142, 145, 147, 148–51; barbecue, 138,

150; Cavaliers, 152–55; consciousness, 146; supposed degeneracy, 146 French, 124; language, 115; loaner cultures, 138, 176
Creolization, 138–39; 143–44; 155, 159–61, 163–64, 176, 227; in action, 159–64; Iberian colonies, 144; New England, 139; Virginia, 144–47
Cultural differences, 20, 24, 40; transatlantic, 118, 204

Dallas, Robert Charles, 54, 56
Dampier, William, 60, 78–79
de la barbe à la queue, 113, 152. *See also* beard to tail
Dictionaries, 17, 40, 220, 225
Diffusion, 138
dipney, 182
Dominican Republic, 8, 38. *See also* Santo Domingo
Drake, Francis, 36, 97
Duke, Richard Thomas Walker, Jr., 174, 234
Duncan, John M., 108, 120, 190
Dwight, Timothy, 149

Eaden, John, 85
earth oven: Africa, 43; Alaska, 44; Australia, 43; use of called barbecuing by Britons, 57, 117; Chile, 42; Fiji, 43; French Polynesia, 119; Hawaii, 42; Jamaica, 57; Mexico, 12, 41–45; New Zealand, 42; Peru, 42; Virginia, 44. *See also* moquém
Eddington, Jane, 232
electric cooker, 13, 201, 229
Elvas, Fidalgo de, 30
embellishments, 22–23
Emmons, George, 44
engagés, 72, 76
entertainments, 157
Esquemeling, 75. *See also* Exquemelin, Alexander
Exmelin, 77. *See also* Exquemelin, Alexander
Exquemelin, Alexander, 75
Exquemeling, 75. *See also* Exquemelin, Alexander

feasts, 158
Ferguson, Patrick, 151
festin champestre, 85. *See also* country feast
fireless cooker, 13, 231
Five Cs of Historical Analysis, 10–11; 17
flibustiers, 73
Ford, Henry, 236
freebooters, 73
Frontignières, Jean de, 77
fumer, 71

Gaffarel, Paul, 17
Garth, Billy, 171
Garth, Elijah, 170, 175
Garth, Juba, 170–76, 182–84
Garth, Mandy, 174, 182
gas cooker, 13
General language, 27; loan words, 28
Geohumoralism, 142–43
Germany, 95, 243
gluttony, 212, 217, 221–22
Goldsmith, J. B. M., 235
Goodrich, Charles Augustus, 21
Great Depression, 235–36
Grenand, Pierre, 113, 124
grilling, 15
Grove, William Hugh, 145
Guiana Amazonian Park, 102

Haiti, 8, 32, 36, 38–39, 67, 90. *See also* Saint-Domingue
Hakluyt, Richard, 30
Hall, Rush Baynard, 183
Hamilton, Alexander, 142
Harriot, Thomas, 99
healths, 140
Helps, Sir Arthur, 18

Hemings, James, 153
Hemings, Peter, 153
Hennepin, Louis, 80
Herring, John Lewis, 183
Hickeringill, Edmund, 73, 83, 101
Hicks, Robert, 235. See *also* Barbecue Bob
Hill, Will, 177, 188
hoecakes, 139
hog hunters, 49, 58, 62, 70, 72, 76, 83–84, 86–87. *See also* chasseurs
Holyoke, Mary, 133
Hooker, Edward, 128, 160
hot smoking, 15, 83, 202, 237; called barbecuing, 237
Hubbard barbecuing method, 187, 228
Hughes, Louis, 167
humors, 142–43, 147
Hurston, Zora Neale, 62

Ice Age, 61–62
illustration errors, 121–22
Incas, 28
Independent Invention, 46, 130, 138–40
Internet Barbecuing period, 14, 241, 243
Izard, Ralph, 45

Jackson, Andrew, 134
Jamaica: Abbot of, 50, 83, 99; American influence, 65–66; barbecued hog, 56–58; coffee dried on flat slabs called barbecues, 50; creolization, 46, 67; outdoor cooking, 65; earth ovens, 42; reputation among 17th- & 18th-century Britons, 74, 210; tourism, 65
Jaubert, Gustave 'Gus', 191
Jefferson, Anne Scott, 170
Jefferson, Thomas, 149, 153, 170
jerk'd, 80
jerked chicken, 63, 65–66
jerked pork: Jamaica, 50–58, 64; Anglicism, 67; compared to boucanage, 58–59; compared to southern barbecue, 66–67; embellishments, 55–56; modern, 65–66; Santo Domingo, 54; Venezuela, 59
jug beef, 254n43. *See also* charqui
jerkin, 99; etymology, 100. *See also* jerky
jerky, 13, 51, 58, 127; Africa, 61; North America, 103–9. *See also* charqui
Johnny cakes, 139
Johnson, Samuel, 17, 56, 220, 225
Jones, Hugh, 208
Jones, Wesley, 186
jus, 86, 182, 214, 233

Kurtz I, Wilbur G., 177

Labat, Jean-Baptiste, 70, 81–82; braising technique compared to the OSBT, 86–89; influence of European cooking, 87, 89; European recipe, 87
Lafayette, Marquis de, 128, 134
Lanman, Charles, 158, 223
Lawson, John, 119, 162
lechón, 26
Léry, Jean de, 21, 72, 96, 102
Lewis, Matthew 'Monk', 57
Ligon, Richard, 83, 114
Lincoln, Abraham, 136, 186, 200
Lincoln, Nancy, 200
Littlejohn, John, 149
Littré, Emile, 85
Livingstone, David, 60
Lodge, Henry Cabot, 159
Long, Edward, 57
Lynde, Benjamin, Sr., 128

Maclin, Edward M., 9
Madagascar, 71
Madison, James, 132
Maillard reaction, 187–88
Markham, Gervase, 186, 207
Maroons, 49, 50, 52–54, 56; 119, 144; African

influence, 59–62; etymology, 49; first Maroon war, 54
Marownaes, 72–73. *See also* Maroons
Mason-Dixon Line, 136, 138
Mather, Cotton, 142, 210
McNeill, Neill 'Red', 22
Mellor, Everett Watson, 105
Mistranslations, 18, 20, 40, 113
Mockaein, 95–96. *See also* moquém
Moody, Uncle Ben, 170
moquear, 100
moquém, 72, 96. *See also* earth oven
Moreton, J. B., 57
Moss, Robert F., 9
Munford, Robert, 156

New England: barbecue, 126–27; politics, 156
Nugent, Maria, 56–57

Oexmelin, 75. *See also* Exquemelin, Alexander
Oldfield, Richard, 221
Oliver, Tomás Buesa, 39
Original Southern Barbecuing Period, 12; end of, 196
Original Southern Barbecuing Technique, 12; origin, 162, 227
Ortiz, Juan, 31
OSBP, 12. *See also* Original Southern Barbecuing Period
OSBT, 12. *See also* Original Southern Barbecuing Technique
Otis, James, 149
Oviedo y Valdes, Gonzalo Fernandez de, 29; Oviedo et al., 29, 31–32, 46
ox feast, 212, 214, 223

pachamanca, 42
ṕada, 62. *See also* patta
Park, Mungo, 61
parrillada, 38, 40
patá, 62. *See also* patta
patta, 51, 53, 58, 116; etymology, 62
Pénicaut, Andre, 78
Penn, William, 49
Periodization, 11
Pickering, John, 126
pidgin, 114
Pierson, Hamilton, 169
Piraparati, 98
pirates, 50, 73–74
Plantagenet, Beauchamp, 100–1, 110; penname, 101
pone, 124
Pope, Alexander, 220; gluttony, 221–22; barbecue ignorance, 222–23
post-Southern Barbecuing period, 13
poulet boucané, 71
Powhatans, 100, 108–9, 124, 151–52, 155, 162; cooking pit, 155, 162; cuisine, 183; houses, 155; pots, 155; smokehouses, 145
Poyntz, John, 51
presentism, 10, 20, 31
pre-Southern Barbecuing period, 11
privateers, 74, 210
Progressive period, 196, 199, 201, 228–29, 231
Prohibition period, 158, 234–35
Prynne, William, 142

Quechua, 28, 35

racism, 164
Rafinesque, Constantine S., 32
Raichlen, Steven, 10
Raleigh, Sir Walter, 113
Randolph, Mary, 208
Ranjel, Rodrigo, 30
recipes: Antebellum-Style Barbecue Baste, 203; Apple-Vinegar BBQ Sauce, 226; Beef Jerky, 110; Jamaican-Style Jerked Pork, 68; Labat's braising liquid, 88; "Meat-Flavoring" BBQ Sauce, 165; original southern barbecue baste, 88; Poulet Boucané, 92; Sauce Chien,

93; Sauce for Barbecues, 129; Slow-Cooker Barbacoa, 47; Spotsy Dip, 245
Reconstruction period, 13, 175, 195–97, 200, 235; defined, 12, 132, 166, 196, 200
Reed, John Shelton, 10
Reid, Thomas Mayne, 55
Réunion Island, 71
Révoil, Georges, 60
roasting, 14, 21
Romero, Joe, 232–33
Rouen, 28
Rosetta Stone, 117–23

Sahagun, Bernardino de, 143
Saint-Domingue, 77, 89, 91. *See also* Haiti
Saint-Méry, Médéric Louis Élie Moreau de, 89, 147
Santa Elena, 45
Santo Domingo, 54, 59, 83, 86. *See also* Dominican Republic
Scott, Sibbald David, 55
Senior, Bernard Martin, 56
Shadrac, Uncle, 170
Sinclair, John, 228
slavery, 147, 159, 161, 164, 190–91
Smith, John, 83, 99, 108–9, 116, 151
soption, 182
Soto, Hernando de, 9, 25–27, 31; original southern barbecue myth, 9, 27; barbecue sauce myth, 9; pork, 25–26; treatment of indigenous people, 27
South America: bridges called barbacoas, 50; cannibals, 18; charqui, 36–37; creolization, 139; barbacoa houses in trees, 33; smokehouses, 72
Southern barbecue, 9; barbarous amusement, 117; community barbecue, 190–91; bark, 187–89; baste, 88, 168, 179, 189; baste, four flavors, 88; baste, inspired by European recipes, 186, 275n40; baste, salt water, 12, 180; baste, ubiquitous in antebellum times, 183; birth of, 151–52; clubs, 193–95; described, 12, 168; entertainments, 120, 157–58, 162, 164, 197, 224; feeder fire, 179, 214; games, 140, 157; gander pull, 140; gravy, 182; Kentucky, 201, 234; Independence Day, 170; compared to Latin America, 40–41; legacy, 201; origin, 9; paradox, 160; continuous performance, 177; pit, 176; politics, 131; red pepper, 183; sauce, 88, 186; tomato in sauce, 169, 183, 235–36; traditions, 9, 24
Spencer, Nicholas, 156
Spotswood, Alexander, 146
Staden, Hans, 95, 102
Stamp Act, 147
Storrow, James Jackson, II, 233

Taíno, 8, 16, 28; Arawak, 28; contrasted with southern barbecuing, 30
Taylor, John, 53, 210
Tertre, Jean Baptiste Du, 74
Thomas, Herbert Theodore, 50
Thornbury, George Walter, 77
Thornton, Richard Hopwood, 17
tortillas, 139
Trumbull, James Hammond, 123, 156
Tryon, William, 148
Tupinambá, 72, 96, 112
Turner, Frederick Jackson, 143
twentieth century, 13, 196, 202, 228, 230–33, 237, 241
Tylor, Edward, 32, 42, 113
typographical errors, 18–20; barbacra, 18; barbaro, 89–91; barbucoa, 19; boucauées, 72

urbanization, 197–98

Vaillant, François Le, 43
Vega, Garcilaso de la, 31
verbasco, 90
verjuice, 88
Veteto, James R., 9

viandes boucannées, 83
Virginia: barbecue, 120, 156, 159; creoles, 139, 144–47, 155, 163; drinking, 156–58; enslaved people, 9, 108, 147, 152–53, 160, 163, 167, 175; House of Burgesses, 130–31, 152, 158; indentured servants, 139, 145, 162; Indies, 146; indigenous people, 142; James River, 81, 194; Ladies barbecues, 189–91; barbecue law, 140; politics, 156–59; barbecue season, 132; barbecued sturgeon, 120; squirrel barbecue, 190; Tidewater, 116; bark called "uncle Brown," 188
Vodou, 90

Wafer, Lionel, 78, 80
Walton, Jack, 174, 235
Walton, William, 57
War of Independence, 116, 149
Ward, Edward, 210; Barbacue Society, 216, 223; Beefsteak Society, 223; Geohumoralism, 210; gluttony, 217; Grunter on a Grid-Iron, 213; barbecue ignorance, 213–15, 217, 219, 222–23; Jamaican fashion, 219; Magnificent Roast Ox, 212; Negroes Cookery, 213–14, 218; pillory, 210, 220; Savage Cookery, 213, 218; West India, 213, 218
Warnes, Andrew, 10, 247
Washington, George, 103, 105, 117, 131–34, 150, 165; laying the Capitol cornerstone barbecue, 131
Webster, Daniel, 153
Webster, Noah, 121
Weld, Isaac, 120, 222
West Indies, 22, 91, 128, 179, 205, 210, 213, 218, 225; supposed birthplace of barbecue, 91; British barbecue myth, 213–14, 218, 224; cannibalism, 12, 19, 77; jerkin beef, 77; lacks the tradition of holding barbecues, 91
White House, 134
White, John, 22, 100
Whitehead, Jessup, 199–200
Williams, Martha McCulloch, 180, 187
World War I, 65, 233–34; European food shortage, 234
World War II, 39, 65, 117, 123, 198, 236

Yankee Doodle, 140, 150
Yguatou, 97
Young, Caesar, 175–76

zee-roovers, 73